Creek Paths and Federal Roads

Creek Paths AND Federal Roads

INDIANS, SETTLERS, AND SLAVES AND THE MAKING OF THE AMERICAN SOUTH

Angela Pulley Hudson

The University of North Carolina Press
Chapel Hill

This book was published with the assistance of the Melbern G. Glasscock Center for Humanities Research at Texas A&M University.

© 2010 THE UNIVERSITY OF NORTH CAROLINA PRESS

ALL RIGHTS RESERVED

Designed by Michelle Coppedge

Set in Arno Pro and Snell Roundhand by Keystone Typesetting, Inc.

Manufactured in the United States of America

The paper in this book meets the guidelines for permanence and durability of the Committee on Production Guidelines for Book Longevity of the Council on Library Resources.

The University of North Carolina Press has been a member of the Green Press Initiative since 2003.

Library of Congress Cataloging-in-Publication Data

Hudson, Angela Pulley.

Creek paths and federal roads : Indians, settlers, and slaves and the making of the American South / Angela Pulley Hudson.—1st ed.

p. cm.

Includes bibliographical references and index.

ISBN 978-0-8078-3393-3 (cloth : alk. paper)—ISBN 978-0-8078-7121-8 (pbk. : alk. paper)

1. Creek Nation—History. 2. Creek Indians—Land tenure—Southern States—History. 3. Creek Indians—Government relations. 4. Creek Indians—Relocation. 5. Indian trails—Southern States—History. 6. Roads—Southern States—History. 7. Transportation—Southern States—History. 8. Creek War, 1813–1814. 9. Southern States—Boundaries—History. I. Title.

E99.C9H83 2010

975.004'97385—dc22

2009049093

cloth 14 13 12 11 10   5 4 3 2 1

paper 14 13 12 11 10   5 4 3 2 1

For my mother & father

Contents

Figures and Maps

Acknowledgments

I grew up on the road. Whether we were moving from one southern state to another or taking road trips to see family scattered from Louisiana to Virginia, Florida to Tennessee, I saw most of it from the window of my parents' car. I came to know the South as a migrant and still don't know exactly how to answer when people ask me where I'm from. So I have a peculiar appreciation for the familiarity of home and the strangeness of travel, for going and coming back, and going and not coming back, until travel feels familiar and home feels strange. And I have been privileged to spend most of my life in the woods, plains, forests, riversides, and wetlands that were home to the people described in this book. I share very little with them except the coincidental inhabitance of southern places and the experience of constant movement on the roads that bind them all together.

The process of researching this book also occasioned many journeys to places new and old, to libraries, collections, homes, and fields (both literal and academic), and I was fortunate to have the guidance and assistance of a number of institutions and individuals. I have benefited tremendously from funding provided by the American Antiquarian Society, the American Philosophical Society, the Beinecke Rare Book and Manuscript Library, the Melbern G. Glasscock Center for Humanities Research, the Howard R. Lamar Center for the Study of Frontiers and Borders at Yale University, the Newberry Library, the Southern Historical Collection at the University of North Carolina, the Office of the Vice President for Research at Texas A&M University, and the Yale Graduate School of Arts and Sciences. I am also deeply indebted to innumerable archivists, librarians, and scholars who enabled and enlivened my research at the following archives: the Alabama Department of Archives and History, the American Antiquarian Society, the Beinecke Rare Book and Manuscript Library, the Cushing Memorial Library and Archives at Texas A&M University, the Duke University Special Collections Library, the Georgia Department of Archives and History, the Hargrett Rare Book and Manuscript Library at the University of Georgia, the Hoskins Special

Collections Library at the University of Tennessee, the National Archives and Records Administration branches in Atlanta, Washington, D.C., and College Park, Maryland, the Newberry Library, the Southern Historical Collection at the University of North Carolina, and the Tennessee State Library and Archives. I must especially acknowledge and thank for their patience and expertise Philip J. Lampi at the American Antiquarian Society, Laura Clark Brown at the Southern Historical Collection, and Rickie Brunner at the Alabama Department of Archives and History.

Along the way, I also have relied on the advice and wisdom of many other individuals deserving of notice. I feel proud and humbled to have benefited from the mentorship of John Mack Faragher, Matthew Frye Jacobson, Seth Fein, Alicia Schmidt Camacho, Alyssa Mt. Pleasant, George Miles, Stephen Pitti, Timothy Powell, and Nancy Shoemaker. Each of these scholars has counseled me in their own inimitable ways as I have navigated this winding path and I am indebted to them for their directions. I have also been privileged to share my work, my frustrations, and my successes with a wide variety of friends and colleagues. Each of these individuals opened their minds, their hearts, and/or their homes to me during the process of researching and writing this book, nourishing me both physically and intellectually. For that I most heartily thank Lamont Brock, Katherine Charron, Chris Covert, Lisa Pinley Covert, Fiona Creed, Mark Dauber, Tasha Dubriwny, Laura and Josh Echols, Kate Carte Engel, Paul Grant-Costa, April Hatfield, Kate Reed Hauenstein, Michael Hauenstein, Tara Hottenstein, Michael Howard, Shannon Lewis, Clayton McGahee, Molly McGehee, Jennifer Meehan, Pat Oldfield, Jason and Pascale Parker, Theda Perdue, Jeff Pfefferkorn, Rebecca Hartkopf Schloss, Victorine Shepard, Ashley Riley Sousa, John Sousa, Melissa Stuckey, Roxanne Willis, Jeff and Marisa Winking, and Matt Woods. In addition, my editor, Mark Simpson-Vos, has ably shepherded me through a sometimes harrowing process, answering more questions than he may have bargained for and always doing so with grace and professionalism.

I reserve a special word of appreciation for two individuals who have read more drafts, critiqued more arguments, and suggested more possibilities than all others. For her friendship, her honesty, her encouragement, and her sparkling wit, Tammy Ingram deserves and has my unending gratitude. In her intellectual generosity and her unyielding support of my career, Robbie Ethridge has also proven to be an adviser of unmatched quality. She has pushed me to make this a better book and saved me from countless errors, both factual and methodological. Of course, none of these people deserves blame for any mistakes, missteps, or misinterpretations that may nevertheless remain. That I reserve especially for myself.

Starting and finishing this book, as well as everything in between, would have been impossible without the love and support of my family: my son, Hayden Hudson; my sisters, Tina Robinette and Kym Lawrence; my sister-in-law, Jody Hudson; my parents-in-law, Constance and William Hudson; and my aunt and uncle, Carolyn and Fritz Korte. I save my most personal thanks for my husband, Jonathan Hudson, who above all keeps me laughing. He has been utterly steadfast in his support of my work. He is an amazing partner, best friend, and father, and I couldn't begin to express the depth of my gratitude to him with mere words.

Finally, I have dedicated this book to my mother and father, Linda and Philip Pulley. They have never questioned my path even when it seemed strange and circuitous. They have been my copilots, my confidantes, and my home, wherever they are. This small token of my appreciation in no way compares to the profound gratefulness I feel for their love and support.

Creek Paths and Federal Roads

Introduction

OLD PATHS, NEW PATHS

*Just as there are no places without the bodies that sustain
and vivify them, so there are no lived bodies without the places
they inhabit and traverse.* —Edward S. Casey, 1996

In a 1774 talk to British Indian agent John Stuart, a party of Upper Creek leaders observed: "When a path is new made it does not at once become a great path."[1] The path in question was a new north-south trading route between Upper Creek towns on the Tallapoosa River and the port of Pensacola. They assured Stuart that this "new made" path would not supplant the "old path," an east-west route that had connected them to traders in Carolina for decades.[2] The Creeks had long pursued a policy of neutrality and openness that allowed them to maintain diplomatic and commercial relations with the British, the French, and the Spanish who competed for their attention from the east, west, and south, respectively.[3] By keeping old paths clear and periodically permitting new ones, the Creeks could remain in communication with traders and officials in each direction and pursue the most favorable terms of trade. After the Revolutionary War, however, Creek leaders sought new ways to maintain their autonomy in the absence of competing imperial interests. Defining their boundaries and controlling access to their lands was of paramount importance if peace and good trade were to prevail. While opening new paths was often a project begun by outsiders seeking access to the interior South, making them great—or not—was up to the Creeks.

Not surprisingly, territory and mobility were primary concerns for the Creeks in the early national period. Creek men and women routinely traveled to pursue game, to keep one another informed of local news, to perform important religious and ceremonial rites, to visit clan members, and to engage in trade with other groups. The physical network of paths through Creek country mirrored and supported the metaphysical network of kin and clan that held the diverse Creek towns together. While preserving the political autonomy and identity of individual tribal towns, by the 1790s Creek leaders began to articulate a sense of Creek nationhood based on the description of territorial boundaries.[4] When Americans began to press on the edges of their country and insist on the right to traverse it over land and by water, the Creeks drew on both longstanding traditions of mobility and emergent innovations of sovereignty to define their territory and attempt to control who would be able to enter it.

This book is a study of travel within and between the southeastern Indian nations and the states of the U.S. South from the founding of the new American nation through the forced removal of southeastern Indians in the 1830s. It focuses specifically on the delineation of boundaries between the Creek Nation and the states that grew up around it, particularly Georgia, Tennessee, and Alabama, and the opening of roads that crossed those boundaries. Such an emphasis engenders a wide variety of questions: How did the diverse inhabitants of the interior South make sense of their shared world and their freedom—or lack of freedom—to move through it? How did Indian, European, and African-descended peoples conceive of boundaries and what did it mean for them to cross those boundaries? What did travel, mobility, and roads symbolize to them? In what ways did these multicultural (and often mixed-heritage) peoples cooperate to forge a shared understanding of space? In what ways did they oppose one another? How did this contest and collaboration affect their daily lives? What impact did it have on the Creeks as a people, the South as a region, and the United States as a nation, economically, politically, and socially?

Instead of devising geographic metaphors for cross-cultural experiences, this work takes spatiality seriously as a central category of analysis.[5] Far more than simply setting a historical scene, understanding how people define place differentially helps us to understand how they generate a sense of cultural identity and how they narrate and situate their own histories.[6] This approach helps me to reconstruct some of the categories of meaning that Creek people used to make sense of their world while also discerning the divergent and convergent definitions of space and mobility devised by European-descended and African-descended peoples—all of whom inhabited and interpreted the places they shared in the lower South according to their own specific needs and desires. To accomplish this goal, I use ethnogeographical methods, seeking, as historian James T. Carson puts it, to provide "a sense of the subjective experience" of people "in the land."[7] Throughout the book, I argue that Creeks, settlers, and slaves each had their own philosophies regarding mobility and more often than not, those philosophies collided and converged on the roads that passed through Creek country.

Paths and trails of every size and description crossed Creek territory and kept their towns and settlements connected to one another and to the outside world. Some of these were ancient footpaths, originally used by large animals as they passed through the forests and fields to the waterways that sustained them, and were later adopted by Native peoples as useful travel routes from one river to another.[8] Over time, these narrow traces and the waterways they connected became vital linkages that held the Creek confederacy together. Creek hunters routinely traveled as far west as the Mississippi River Valley in search of game, and conducted trade, diplomacy, and warfare with westward groups in present-day Texas and Mexico, as far north as the upper Ohio Valley, and deep into the southern peninsula of Florida.[9] Far from a trackless wilderness, European explorers entering the Southeast found well-worn trails and a vast network of paths that they later used opportunistically in their quests for ancient kingdoms and abundant riches.[10]

The extent of Creek territory in this period is estimated to have exceeded 62,000 square miles. It included *talwas* (tribal towns) and *talofas* (daughter towns), their associated agricultural fields, ball grounds, hunting lands, and the trails that bound them all together.[11] A talwa might consist of one large town or several interdependent ones in relatively close proximity to one another.[12] Individual talwas tended to govern themselves independently in most affairs, including trade with neighbors, both indigenous and alien. The relationship between talwas was fluid but the tribal town remained the most potent political identifier in Creek life.[13]

Creek country in this era was divided into two primary sections. The Upper Creek towns were located on the Coosa, Tallapoosa, and Alabama rivers in what is now the state of Alabama. The roughly forty Upper Creek towns of the eighteenth century can be divided into four main provinces: Abihka, Tallapoosa, Okfuskee, and Alabama. Tuckabatchee was the head town of Tallapoosa while Abihka and Okfuskee each dominated provinces of the same name, respectively. Little Tallassee and Okchai were two other important towns among the Upper Creeks; along with Tuckabatchee, these were known as white towns and were frequently the site of diplomatic meetings.[14] The Abihka towns may have been related to the paramount chiefdom of Coosa, a powerful sixteenth-century polity that extended from the Coosawattee River in present-day Georgia to the Coosa River in present-day Alabama. Okfuskee was originally an Abihka town but grew in size and importance until it launched several daughter towns of its own.

One reason for Okfuskee's ascendance in the late seventeenth and early eighteenth centuries was that the primary road from Charleston, capital of the transatlantic Indian slave trade, passed directly through the town on its way to the Mississippi River Valley.[15] In addition, numbers of refugees and absorbed remnant groups, like Natchez and some Shawnee Indians, also inhabited the Abihka towns. The Alabama towns included speakers of the Muskogean-related Alabama and Koasati dialects and were located where the Coosa and Tallapoosa rivers join to form the Alabama.[16] Despite the roads connecting them to the British in Carolina, the Upper Creeks also maintained connections with both the French and the Spanish.[17]

The Lower towns were located primarily on the Ocmulgee, Flint, and Chattahoochee rivers in present-day Georgia. These twenty towns, which included Coweta, Cusseta, and Apalachicola, were largely remnants of the Apalachee chiefdom that may have consisted mostly of Hitchiti speakers but also encompassed Yuchi speaking towns and numerous Muskogean speakers from the west.[18] While their Upper Creek relatives maintained regular but distant relations with the English on the Atlantic coast, the Lower Creeks appear to have actively courted them. In the early 1700s, some of the towns from the Apalachicola province moved further east to the Ocmulgee River to secure their trade relations with the Carolinians. Because of their proximity to English settlements and trading posts, the Lower Creeks had more extensive communication with their Anglophone neighbors, but they too occasionally sought the support of the Spanish, primarily in St. Augustine as opposed to Pensacola or Mobile, the locales in which the Upper Towns placed most of their trust.[19] After the Yamassee War in 1715, however, the Lower Creeks moved back to the Chattahoochee and Flint river valleys and resettled the town sites there, having included in their numbers many refugees from the devastating war spawned by the ever-growing Indian slave trade.[20] During the period from the end of the Yamassee War through the founding of the Georgia colony in 1733, the Lower town of Coweta, in particular, began to rise to prominence.[21]

The operation, and indeed the expansion, of such a large and loosely organized Creek confederacy depended on the use and control of the routes that traversed their lands.[22] Taken in combination, the Upper and Lower divisions of the Creek confederacy were home to nearly 20,000 people in the late eighteenth century and were characterized by both ethnic and linguistic diversity.[23] One could expect to hear a wide variety of different tongues, from the various Muskogean and non-Muskogean dialects, to French, Spanish, and English, to Mobilian, the "lingua franca" of the Southeast used to conduct trade among the many peoples who lived there.[24] And, increasingly with the growth of the Indian trade, one might also expect to hear a variety of African languages and African-inflected dialects. Unity amidst such diversity required constant communication between the towns of the Creek confederacy and specially trained runners carried important messages across the region, sometimes even operating as a relay team.[25]

In addition to facilitating communication and cross-cultural exchange, the southern trails that crossed the region's borders were themselves significant sites of such exchange, whether in chance meetings of passersby, confrontations between hunters, or tense standoffs between travelers and bandits. A southern road may have been a link to the safety of white towns or a palisaded fort. But as a distinct space itself, it could also be a place of heady encounters and explosive danger. This was a daily possibility for the mobile inhabitants of the interior South and a cosmic reality for Creek people.[26]

Examining Creek stories is one way that we can learn how historic Creek people made sense of the land they inhabited and traversed—and how their lives *took place*. The majority of the diverse ethnic and linguistic groups that made up the Creek confederacy enshrined distinct ideas of both place and travel in their creation myths. The Alabamas and Muskogees each maintained that their origins could be traced to a discrete axis mundi—or center of the world—from which they emerged and then traveled to the east, finally arriving in their homelands.[27] Similarly, the Cussetas told of their migration from a western place of emergence to the east where they met the Chickasaws and Abihkas before finally settling on the Chattahoochee River.[28] A wide variety of Native North American societies similarly narrate their creation as a process of emergence and migration, and in Creek oral histories travel or, more broadly, mobility was nearly ubiquitous.[29] It not only helped them explain their arrival in a particular place on this earth but also their position in the universal order of existence.

Other myths originating from members of the Creek confederacy, particularly the Muskogees, Alabamas, and Yuchis, preserve the concept of travel in tales about death. Trader and traveler James Adair claimed that southern Indians believed that each person's death is destined to occur at a particular time and place and noted, "They frequently say, 'Such a one was weighed on the path, and made to be light.' "[30] Some accounts claimed that souls could leave the body and travel about only to return and report on their journeys to other worlds.[31] The most common stories, however, detailed the travels undertaken by souls after death. These spirits left the body and traveled to the west along a path known as the Spirits' Road or *poya fik-tcàlk innini*.[32] These paths led them on their journey to the Spirit World, where a variety of pleasures awaited, provided they could navigate their way past threatening animals and other obstacles that may impede them.[33] Some arrived in the Spirit World and some did not—all of them made the journey.

Chapter 1 begins by exploring the central role of spatial concepts in Creek cosmology, such as the "white path," and how those concepts emerged in Creek diplomatic language. I examine the importance of physical paths in Creek country and the centrality of territory and travel in Creek oral histories, emphasizing the fact that historic Creek people would probably not have recognized a division between the natural and supernatural worlds. A spirit path and a path through the woods could be one and the same and a journey that appears mundane at our historical remove could take on universal importance in the right circumstances. Drawing on recorded oral narratives, including migration stories and diplomatic references to them, this chapter establishes categories of territory and mobility with which Creek people narrated their world. It further explores how these concepts were transported and translated into interactions with outsiders, and how these interactions influenced U.S.-Indian affairs in the early years of the American republic.

Chapter 2 extends Creek understandings of space into the realm of surveying and cross-border travel. By focusing on debates regarding the delineation of boundaries between the Creeks and their neighbors, this section shows how treaties in the early nineteenth century produced not only marked papers describing the limits of Creek and American land, but also produced a coded landscape. The boundaries—and hatched trees—that emerged from surveying expeditions were exemplary specimens of land as contested space, as Creek and American representatives put their hands to paper and then to the land itself in an attempt to make borders legible for inhabitants on both sides. The old paths and new paths that increasingly crossed Creek boundaries were borderlands of a kind. Although we typically think of borders as dividing lines *between* people and places, this chapter shows that by the turn of the nineteenth century, Creek country roads were emerging as unique border spaces in their own right—places where cross-cultural encounters happened with frequency and intensity nearly unmatched on the literal boundaries separating Creek and American lands.[34]

Federal and state leaders hoped that increased access across these borders would enable them to transform the forests and fields of Creek country into the plantations and markets of American prosperity. Chapter 3 argues that the push for U.S. internal improvements (such as roads and canals) in the Early Republic cannot be adequately considered without an understanding of how these developments influenced Indian affairs and vice versa.[35] By focusing on travel writing, postal service records, and talks by Creek leaders, this section reveals that in the period between 1805 and 1811, American demands for greater and greater access to and through Creek country met with varying levels of resistance and acceptance from headmen and individual citizens. By the end of the first decade of the nineteenth century, U.S. officials were pressuring the Creeks to allow the expansion of a modest post path into a wagon road suitable for larger numbers of travelers, including soldiers.[36] In 1811, federal officials pushed hard for this road, later known as the Federal Road, at the very same Creek council meeting where Shawnee revolutionary Tecumseh exhorted the Creeks to join his Pan-Indian revolution—a call that many would answer as their nation descended into civil war.

In the period leading up to the Creek War (1813–1814), white and black travel into Creek lands had increased steadily but not without important checks put in place by U.S. Indian agent Benjamin Hawkins and the Creeks themselves. In the various treaty councils where roads were discussed, despite the apparent opposition of many Creek people, a handful of leaders ultimately agreed to allow the United States greater and greater access to Creek lands. While it is clear that many catalysts sparked the revolt, this chapter argues that the opening of the Federal Road and similar routes was a primary reason that "Red Stick" Creeks waged war on both the Americans and their allies in the Creek Nation. Chapter 4 takes up the role of such roads in the context of conflict in Creek country. They witnessed many of the bloodiest attacks as the Red Sticks tried to clean and straighten the path of their nation.[37]

The treaty that ended the war shrank the borders of the Creek Nation dramatically and encouraged an upsurge in migrants traveling through Indian lands. For an increasing number of American travelers, cotton was the enterprise of their dreams and they relied on the labor of African-descended peoples to make it a reality. Chapter 5 discusses American attempts to transform former Creek lands into cotton lands, largely through the forced migration of thousands of African Americans along the old and new roads of Creek country. By exposing the difficulties of bringing enslaved people southward along the roads, the alternating moments of opposition and cooperation by Creek leaders and ordinary citizens, and the dissident actions of enslaved peoples in the southern landscape, this chapter reveals the historical contingencies that characterized the uneven spread of plantation slavery into the interior South.[38]

Ultimately, this was a contest of visions. While the Creeks were defending their world, white Americans were busy reimagining it as vacant space. And by and large they believed that the labor of black bodies should fill this empty space. These issues—internal improvement, the expansion of slavery, and Indian dispossession—are not often discussed in combination with one another, but, as I make clear in Chapter 6, they were intimately connected and each also had an impact on the emergence of southern political separatism. We must recognize the operation of sectional politics not only in the contests over the extension of slavery in the 1820s, for example, but also in debates about Indian lands, federal roads, and state jurisdiction that characterized the same era.

Though it focuses on one of the most dismal periods of Creek history east of the Mississippi, this final chapter also emphasizes the creative adaptations of Creek people to the increased presence of white and black travelers in their lands. Some Creek men and women continued to resist, withholding produce from travelers, raiding stores of settlers' crops, mutilating livestock, and destroying fences in recently ceded lands. But other Creeks adopted divergent strategies for survival, developing commercial and entrepreneurial opportunities so that their families and communities might persist, even in the face of overwhelming pressure to remove.

Finally, I offer a word on terminology. Throughout this work, I use the term "Creek" or "Creeks" to describe the members of the southeastern Indian nation referred to elsewhere as Muskogee and Muscogulgee. Admittedly, "Creek" is a problematic term because it emerged as a misnomer originally devised by English colonists to refer to Native peoples settled around a tributary of the Ocmulgee River known as Ochese Creek. It was ultimately applied with abandon to all persons allied with the Muskogean-speaking peoples settled on the Coosa and Tallapoosa rivers, even when their linguistic and ethnic identities were distinct and separate. As Joel Martin states in defense of his own use of "Muskogee," the English use of the term "Creek" is a recourse to synecdoche, "a colonial signification that concealed and rendered invisible a tremendous diversity of peoples" and implied participation in a "nation." Martin claims that the imposition of nationhood *on* the Creeks enabled Georgians to rationalize violence against one group of Indians for the acts of another "on the basis of their common membership" in a fictitious Creek Nation.[39]

While I agree it is important to remain vigilant with regard to colonial systems of naming and to recognize the synecdochical tendency within the uneven relations of power, I am hesitant to accept Martin's explanation wholesale. This work pivots on the notion that by the 1790s, Creeks were increasingly *defining themselves* as a nation and defending their sovereign rights as such. Clearly, the concept of the nation-state was imported into Creek political thought, but with important distinctions and adaptations based on their epistemological traditions. Therefore, I do not agree that nationhood—or the use of the term Creeks—was entirely one-sided, imposed from the outside, and always interpreted the same way. While it remains problematic for the above reasons, the label "Creek" is ubiquitous in the documentary record for the period covered in this work and appears to have been used on many occasions both by Creeks and outsiders to describe the members of the Nation in general. Thus I have used it uniformly throughout. Whenever possible, however, I have designated individual people in terms of their specific geographic and civic identifiers in order to preserve local signification within the broader nomenclature. This is particularly true when speakers have referred to themselves as or were otherwise known to be members of a discrete province, town, or village.[40]

Furthermore, I use "African-descended" most frequently to describe African-diasporic peoples, whether enslaved or free, because it allows me to refer to both first-generation African individuals and members of subsequent American-born populations, some of whom mingled together on Creek country roads. By and large, I have not attempted to disaggregate African-born individuals from American-born individuals since such an effort would require ethnographic study beyond the scope of this work.

I use the term "American" to indicate European-descended peoples who settled in the original English colonies and migrated into the interior. Although this term is also problematic, in that it conflates the United States with America and homogenizes the ethnic, religious, and linguistic diversity of European-descended immigrants, I have chosen it because it is the most common recorded term that Creeks used to describe the inhabitants of the United States. Like their colonizing neighbors, the Creeks occasionally had recourse to synecdoche. For instance, they called all non-Spanish whites "Virginians" for a time. As far as the historical record conveys, they did not consistently distinguish, for example, between Scots and Irish or Presbyterians and Methodists. The term American, while occasionally vague, is a loose and flexible signifier and perhaps Creek people used it for these same reasons.

Chapter One

TERRITORIALITY AND MOBILITY IN EIGHTEENTH-CENTURY CREEK COUNTRY

On a bright sunny day in early November 1779, a Creek leader known to outsiders as the Tallassee King rose to speak to an assembly of Indians, traders, and American officials at the Savannah River plantation of trader and de facto Indian agent George Galphin. He took a white eagle feather in one hand and a string of white beads in the other and said these items signified "that the path may be kept perfect Clain and white from heare to the Nation."[1] In Creek cosmology, the color red is associated with action, aggression, and/or defense and often signifies affairs of war or retribution, while white signifies peace, negotiation, and calm reflection. Using white feathers and beads thus assured the Americans of the Creeks' determination to avoid hostilities.[2]

The Tallassee King, likely known to his own people as Tallassee Micco, had traveled eastward to the edge of Carolina to reaffirm Creek friendship with the Americans and show an earnest desire to continue to engage in trade along the east-west trading paths that led through the Upper and Lower Creek towns. He situated his talk within the terms of Creek metaphysics, invoking whiteness and cleanliness as a way of professing peace and friendly intentions and using the string of beads to symbolize both the literal path that passed from Charleston to the Upper Creek towns on the Coosa River and the Creek concept of right behavior known as "the sacred path."[3] Like the "bright chain of friendship" that connected the Iroquois and the British, the path that linked the Creeks and the Americans functioned on multiple levels and had to be carefully maintained.[4]

Among the Creeks, the practice of peaceful diplomacy was frequently referred to as keeping the paths "straight" and "clean" or "white," a responsibility with important cultural resonance.[5] In a similar talk a year earlier, the Tallassee King had asserted, "We have but one white path and that path I stand by."[6] By using the terms "white and clean," he thus indicated both a general disposition toward peaceful diplomatic relations and spiritual calm, but also an uninterrupted and pacific trade. The "straight"-ness of the path between Creeks and Americans similarly reflected the importance of order and clarity in Creek political and spiritual thought. Thus the word "straight" was often heard in diplomatic settings to indicate the propriety or acceptability of an agreement.[7] Crookedness, its opposite, signifies an association with snakes, whose dangerous reputation and sinuous shapes mirrored the invisible wave-like forces that sometimes shook the ground beneath the feet of Creek people.[8]

The overland trails that connected talwas and talofas to each other as well as to the outside world were vital links not only for the political well-being of the Creek Nation, but also for maintaining social and spiritual health of the confederacy. Such paths made it possible for Creek men and women to travel to visit clan members in distant communities and attend important annual gatherings, like the Green Corn ceremony (or *Busk/Boskita/Poskita*) typically held in early autumn, as well as frequent inter-town ball plays.[9] They also allowed townspeople to stay informed of the political goings-on in neighboring towns and to form coalitions to promote discrete agendas. When eighteenth-century Coweta headman Brims sought support for an uprising against abusive traders from Carolina, he sent runners bearing strands of deer hide seeking the pledges of each town to join the revolt. As each town promised allegiance, the strand was knotted, resulting in three six-foot-long cords.[10] Similarly, the towns of Tuckabatchee and Coweta maintained an important path between them for nearly a century, cementing both trade relations and kinship ties between the talwas that would continue to function for generations to come.[11]

Despite a growing consolidation of Creek political interests toward the end of the eighteenth century, individual talwas conducted trade and diplomatic negotiations independently according to both their external alliances and internal politics.[12] For instance, in 1778, the Tallassee King professed the friendship of his town to the Americans and also assured them of the peaceful intentions of the Apalachicolas, the Hitchitis, the Killigees, and the Tallushatchees. He cautioned, however, "I give no Towns but what I am sure of, there are many more Towns that their Talks, are not good, but by any Talk you will know who are your friends Towns."[13] Colonial (and later state) officials were not entirely ignorant of the town configuration, but they tended to acknowledge distinctions between talwas only when it was in their best interest to do so. They sometimes chose to deal with the Creeks as a nation, while other times entering agreements with a single town. When a boundary line was to be run or a peace talk held, headmen of specific talwas might be asked to attend. But if colonists sought repayment or retribution for real or imagined wrongs, one Creek town might be expected to pay the price for the misdeeds of another even if the two towns were largely unrelated.

In addition, towns might shift position as a result of changing political fortunes. Given the vast network of paths that connected the various talwas in both the Upper and Lower sections, it was unlikely that any given settlement would move completely out of contact with others in its province. On the contrary, townspeople sometimes removed themselves from one far-flung locale to a more centrally located place, where they might benefit more directly from the intersection of numerous paths. Similarly, townspeople from one talwa might launch a daughter town that enabled them to live closer to trade paths that brought much-desired goods. In 1775, for instance, Adair noted that since the 1760s, "the Muskoghe have settled several towns, seventy miles eastward from Okwhuske, on the Chatahooche river, near to the old trading path."[14] But such out-settled villages typically remained associated with and committed to their mother towns, a relationship enabled (if not required) not only by their kin and clan network but also by the network of trails that bound them together.[15]

The various paths that crisscrossed Creek country were not roads as we might picture them. By the eighteenth century, they were usually only wide enough for a single horse and rider, typically 18–24 inches in width, especially in close, hilly terrain.[16] The course of most paths was determined by the local topography. Some trails, particularly above the fall line, followed the course of rivers and streams when the ground was not too wet for travel.[17] Others passed along upland ridges. Of particular importance were places where paths crossed the region's many streams and rivers.[18] Precipitous bluffs or rocky descents often characterized the river banks of the interior Southeast, so finding fordable places on the rivers was essential, particularly for east-west travel.[19] Although Native peoples invested time in clearing paths (both literally and metaphorically), travelers sometimes had to choose between pausing to remove obstacles or finding a way around them.[20] But generations of use had made many of these routes unmistakable. Pathways were frequently defined by a series of notches and hatches in the bark of trees. The height of the hatch mark and the use of symbols indicated the age of the path and its destination.[21]

Surveyor and naturalist Bernard Romans, who traveled among the southeastern Indians in the 1770s, asserted that they always knew the "kind of people" that had made a certain path, "by the strokes of the hatchets in the trees and branches as they go along." He explained that each group marked the trees differently and thus left an identifiable reminder of their trail.[22] In addition, Creeks and other southern Indians sometimes inscribed messages or narratives on the timber alongside the trails they used. British traveler Philip Thicknesse observed a piece of cedar bark tied to a tree on which "in a very uncouth Manner several Figures were delineated." He interpreted this drawing to represent Upper Creek warriors who had been traveling the path and stopped to record the loss of two companions.[23] James Adair described a similar process used by war parties that would "strip the bark off several large trees in conspicuous places, and paint them with red and black hieroglyphics, thereby threatening the enemy with more blood and death."[24] For Native inhabitants who relied on oral rather than written traditions, landmarks such as these were part of a mental map that combined geography and history and coded the landscape according to their experiences within it.[25]

European explorers and surveyors imported their own techniques for making the landscape legible.[26] They cut marks—chops, blazes, or notches—on the trees that indicated the course of the trail; some enterprising explorers even carved their initials into trees or hurled bottles at them in unique ceremonies of possession.[27] To be a trailblazer denoted not only that one had passed along a certain route, but also had traced a decipherable remainder that would guide others along the way.

Hurricanes and tornadoes were often the culprits of the worst damage to these thoroughfares, generating impassable obstacles and obliterating notches and blazes that designated the trails. But because the ravage of such storms could sometimes be seen for decades, the shredded earth and mangled trees might also become nature's route markers.[28] The forces of weather and wear, combined with indigenous *and* imported techniques of land marking, produced a graphic landscape.

The land could also be read through Creek stories. In addition to creation myths such as those described in the Introduction, the larger body of Creek mythology also contains important references to travel and mobility. A series of stories concern the Tie Snake or Horned Serpent; although they vary in detail, each narrates a dangerous transformation that occurs when a person consumes a taboo food while traveling. As a result, the transgressor is transformed into a serpent and takes up residence in a nearby body of wa-ter.[29] Other stories concerning the Tie Snake or Strong Snake describe the creature's power and presence within rumbling or thundering waters, a sa-lient ecological feature of parts of Creek country.[30] While the core of these myths inscribes concepts of purity and reciprocity, we can distill another element that applies to our discussion of Creek territory and mobility.

In many of the Tie Snake stories, as well as other Creek myths, a person commits a taboo act or is otherwise endangered while traveling.[31] This may seem unremarkable since Creek hunting methods often required long peri-ods of time spent away from one's hometown. But taken together, these stories suggest that while travel was a necessity, it was also a time of in-creased risk—a time when a person might have to be especially on guard against danger and deception.

Water crossings represented a particular peril. A number of stories de-scribe situations in which travelers must cross over a precarious bridge or otherwise pass bodies of water.[32] These themes reflect the natural world of Creek country, where frequent river crossings were a dangerous fact of life. But they also incorporate southeastern Indian beliefs regarding the separa-tion of basic categories like earth and water, as well as a concern with bodies of water as portals to the chaotic underworld.[33] It is important here to recognize that bodies of water and the hidden realm they concealed were not always associated with evil. In fact, daily immersion or "going to water" was considered an important mode of assuring good health and spiritual purity.[34] In addition, at least one story, associated with Tuckabatchee, described the Tie Snake as a friendly being that accepts underwater visitors and renders aid to villages under attack.[35] Rivers, streams, and ponds could be frightening and awesome, not because they were innately malevolent, but because they represented a sort of threshold—a meeting place between this world and the world below. At such a place, cosmic power is concentrated and could be harnessed for good or ill purposes.

In addition to travel, paths themselves are of great importance in Creek stories. Consider, for example, the Cusseta migration legend told to Gover-nor James Oglethorpe by Tchikilli in 1735. An eastward-traveling party of Muskogeans, including a group known as the Cussetas, arrived at a white foot-path. According to Tchikilli, "the grass and everything around were white," and they understood this to mean that people had been there. They crossed the path and camped nearby, later turning back to try to determine what sort of people had made the white path. The traveling Muskogeans continued going eastward, searching for the people who made the white path. Over a series of years they followed the path, crossing numerous rivers and encountering many other groups of people. They finally arrived at the town of the Apalachicolas, where these peace-loving people convinced the "bloody-minded" Cussetas to abandon their aggression, telling them, "Our hearts are white, and yours must be white." Tchikilli, descended from the Apalachicolas, explained that the Cussetas joined with them but kept their "red hearts," although they "now know that the white path was the best for them."[36]

Part of the reason Tchikilli told this particular story to Oglethorpe (in the presence of other Creek headmen) was to establish himself and his town of origin as important and endowed with the diplomatic skill associated with the color white. In addition, this story both reiterated the tradition of Muskogee emergence and migration from a point in the west and also contained numerous other references to travel. Perhaps more significant here, however, is that the path, specifically the white path, figured as both a literal trail followed by the Muskogeans and a philosophical orientation or way of being. The concept of the white path existed in both realms simultaneously, both in the myths themselves and in political discourse invoking such concepts.[37]

The combined effect of these Creek stories is an understanding that travel was fundamentally necessary but frequently dangerous. A Creek person crossing a strong spring freshet would undoubtedly find fording the stream perilous, but he or she might also fear the Tie Snake that lived beneath the surface of the water. Creek men and women of the late eighteenth century inhabited a world that was simultaneously home to rivers, streams, grass, rocks, trees, horned serpents, giant eagles, wandering souls, red paths, and white paths. Humans were merely one of many kinds of living beings and not necessarily the most important or the smartest ones.[38] Thus, it would be a misrepresentation of Creek ethnogeography to assert that they maintained a strict intellectual distinction between a person and a tree, a path and a snake. All these concepts are relevant in a discussion of how Creek people made sense of their homelands and how these concepts emerged and functioned within their diplomacy.

These stories and the lessons they impart were not mere metaphors for the Creek world; they were foundational for understanding and experiencing it. But perhaps even more salient for our purposes is the fact that these myths and the worldview they emerge from demonstrate the multilayered nature of Creek concepts of place and travel. They understood the need to move across the land—to hunt, to trade, to visit, to survive—and they understand that it could be both dangerous and empowering. When European travelers and traders arrived in their lands, the Creeks were neither shocked by the presence of strangers nor were they averse to traveling in the direction whence they had come.

Increasingly after the mid-seventeenth century, outsiders did arrive regularly in the heart of Creek country. English traders moving west from their Atlantic outposts and French traders moving east from their positions on the Mississippi River frequented the overland trails that Native people had themselves appropriated from their animal neighbors. After the establishment of the Georgia colony in 1733 and the violent and divisive Seven Year's War (1756–1763), Crown officials tried to staunch the westward flow of people crossing the Appalachian barrier—compared to "the prodigious Wall that divides China and Tartary."[39] They declared an imaginary boundary that followed the mountain chain from its upper reaches in present-day Maine to its termination in what is now northern Alabama. The intention of this decree, known as the Proclamation of 1763, was to prevent unauthorized settlers and lawless vagabonds from wandering into Indian Country and igniting the same sorts of intrigues that had led to the French and Indian wars, but it was largely ignored. In the southern colonies, Crown officials were nearly powerless to stop the haphazard migration.[40] But the Indians were not powerless. Throughout the eighteenth century, they were the gatekeepers to the Trans-Appalachian West, and southeastern Indians, Creeks in particular, were universally noted for their willingness to defend the boundaries of their nations.

Over the course of the eighteenth century, Creek leaders from both the Upper and Lower towns began to refer to themselves as members and representatives of a singular, territorially bounded entity known as the Creek Nation.[41] In his talks to the Americans, the Tallassee headman quoted at the opening of this chapter used Creek-centric concepts of place and mobility to situate his community politically and spiritually. But he also used the political language of nascent nationalism. Referring to the trade path that left Charleston and passed through Augusta into Creek country, the Tallassee King hoped that the path would be "kept White through the Cussitas" and "from there through the Whole Nation."[42] As the turn of the century approached, Creek leaders from both the Upper and Lower divisions increasingly defined themselves as members of a sovereign polity with distinct geographical borders and the right to control who crossed those boundaries on the many paths that traversed their lands.

In 1785, a Creek man referred to as Cowerther Mayit, possibly known as Coweta Mate, sent a talk to the governor and Executive Council of Georgia in which he expressed his concern regarding American encroachment on the borders between the newly formed state and the Lower Creeks, including the town of Coweta, of which he was a headman. He explained that American trespasses on Creek hunting grounds jeopardized the Creeks' ability to procure deerskins with which to obtain trade goods. The situation threatened to worsen if the young Creek men could not be prevented from avenging themselves on interlopers and/or their livestock. As Cowerther Mayit put it, "We have Dun our Endavor to Keep our young people in good order and to Keep pece for the better Keeping our path White and Strait."[43]

Deploying the same rhetorical devices used by the Tallassee King a few years earlier, the Coweta headman made two points clear: peace depended on mutual respect of established boundaries, and the continuance of the Creek/American trade depended on peace. The Creeks had learned early in their relationship with the British that boundaries were necessary to control the expansionist tendencies of their neighbors in Georgia. As early as 1739, they had negotiated with Oglethorpe for a boundary to separate their lands from those of the colony.[44] Understanding that the Creeks valued boundaries as a potential prophylactic—a barrier between themselves and the unwanted trespassers who threatened to stream into their lands—is crucial to understanding their diplomacy in this era. Borders were not a foreign concept, nor were they simply imposed on the Creeks by outside forces. Creeks themselves saw the boundaries as one important way to maintain their autonomy and preserve their homelands.

After the Revolution, protecting Creek boundaries became both more important and more difficult since Americans saw southeastern Indians as defeated allies of the British, making their lands subject to forfeiture. Highlighting Creek participation in a transatlantic market in which they exchanged processed deerskins for trade goods from Europe and the West Indies, such as textiles, iron implements, and alcohol, Cowerther Mayit explicitly characterized trespasses over the Georgia/Creek boundary as a threat to Coweta's livelihood. But the problem of unwelcome settlers and their unfenced livestock was not an exclusively economic concern for the Creek Nation; the hunting grounds, and indeed all Creek lands, represented a multiplicity of meanings for Creek people and their potential loss was incalculably great in every respect. When Upper Creek leader Alexander McGillivray, or Hoboi-Hili-Miko, remarked that the loss of hunting grounds is "the greatest Injury an Indian can form an Idea of," he hardly overstated their importance in Creek life.[45]

Some hunting lands were shared spaces, communally used by Creeks from different towns and sometimes other Indians, as Cowerther Mayit noted: "We are not all the people that hunts thaer." While the Coweta head-man was probably referring to hunters from different Creek towns, hunters from various Indian nations also found themselves side by side during the winter hunts. Creeks and Cherokees had long contested certain hunting grounds along the upper portions of the Chattahoochee, and at various times Chickasaws and Creeks alternately shared and disputed lands north of the Tennessee River and west of the Black Warrior River.[46] The Creeks also battled the Choctaws over hunting lands along the Tombigbee, Alabama, and Escambia rivers.[47] Conflicts and misunderstandings about the exact extent of specific hunting lands figured prominently in numerous treaty discussions, particularly if one Indian nation believed that a neighbor had wrongfully ceded land that was not the property of any one nation but used, according to tradition or agreement, by many.

This is not to suggest that southeastern Indians did not have specific convictions about territory—quite the contrary. Creeks and their Indian neighbors defined territory in several distinct ways—including use rights, rights of way, and discrete types of lands, such as hunting lands and commu-nally cultivated fields. For instance, it is clear that Creek towns maintained the right to hunt in specific areas and vigorously defended those rights when threatened by intrusions or land cessions.[48] The loss of hunting grounds to treaties or squatters and the increasing inability of Creek leaders to prevent trespasses not only influenced inner tribal life but also had a particular politi-cal valence in the atmosphere of intertribal diplomacy.[49] But their definition of territoriality was grounded in a distinct cosmological and political milieu, not in English common law or abstract theories of right by conquest.[50]

Creek understandings of their world involved both seen and unseen forces often indivisible from one another. Indeed, indigenous people across the continent maintained robust definitions of territory, geography, bound-aries, and mobility that, not unlike those of their western counterparts, were grounded in their epistemologies. While it is true that most Indians did not conceive of property the same way as most Europeans of the same era, it would be inaccurate to assume that they did not understand the function of boundaries dividing lands and peoples.[51] When European colonizers im-ported their own definitions of these concepts, Native people were neither overwhelmed by the sophistication of their worldviews nor eager to shed their own beliefs in favor of those of the newcomers.

For example, one story that describes relations between two Creek towns hinges on a disputed landmark. The Cussetas discovered a "fish-killing place" alongside a river and, having found it, "broke off a pine limb and laid it upon a rock," thereby claiming the site. The Cowetas later found the same place, where they broke off a black weed called *ata'k la-lasti* and laid it down. The two groups argued over the rightful possession of the fish-killing place, each telling the other that they had marked it for themselves. Ultimately, they decided that there were two such places near one another and this agreement cemented their relationship as sister towns on opposite sides of the Chattahoochee River.[52] This story conveys a clear sense of territoriality —a belief that certain people belong to certain places, even if those places do not necessarily belong to those people.[53]

Another way in which Creek people defined their lands and who had access to them was along the axes of gender and kinship. Creek men typically hunted with men from their own clans on lands "traditionally tended" by those clans, and they returned to those grounds annually.[54] Naturalist William Bartram, who traveled among the Creeks in the eighteenth century, suggested that ethnic and linguistic divisions within the Creek confederacy also determined who hunted where.[55] Additionally, hunting parties were not exclusively male. Women possessed the skilled knowledge to prepare the deer hides for trade, a difficult process that involved removing the hair and remaining flesh and then smoking the hides to kill pests that infested them. They often accompanied their husbands on the long winter hunts—making them a very valuable component of the deerskin trade, being a sort of traveling factory.[56] Whether the deerskins were traded by Indian men for foreign goods or processed by women for food and clothing at home, the hunting grounds were vital to the sustenance of Creek communities both economically and culturally. In the social order of family, town, and clan, hunting lands specifically represented Creek men's ability to provide meat—a duty each Creek youth was expected to perform as a prerequisite to marriage. Thus, the hunting grounds were explicitly, if not narrowly, gendered spaces, assuming a potent symbolism as first the British and then the Americans tried to cut off these lands from the body of the Creek Nation.[57]

Hunting season typically lasted from November through February and left Creek towns largely deserted. During this time most everyone, except for the very young and the very old, would be "in the woods."[58] This phrase means what it literally says, but it also has another connotation. For Creek men and women, to be "in the woods" was to be engaged in a cosmic balancing act. Like traveling the region's paths, hunting was an activity of tense awareness, and hunting parties figure in a wide variety of Creek myths, including the Tie Snake or Horned Serpent stories. Each encroachment on the animal world was governed by a deep sense of reciprocity, which in turn maintained the equilibrium of the universe. Mistakes and transgressions might have long-ranging implications.[59] But it was also a time of potential confrontation between humans. Hunters sometimes helped themselves to settlers' livestock, especially if these animals were found grazing in the hunting grounds. And complaints of horse theft from both sides of the boundary tended to increase during the fall and winter months.[60]

Cowerther Mayit's talk during the summer of 1785 referenced such thefts, attributing them to "[mad] young people that has been Down that way a hunting." Although it is not clear when these particular thefts took place, the typical hunting season was during the winter months.[61] The possibility that Creek hunting parties would still be in the woods in late spring or summer suggests stress on the deer population and a subsequent decline in the deerskin trade that has been substantiated elsewhere.[62] The longer the hunts lasted, the more likely they were to provoke fierce competition and frustrated retaliations against ranchers and settlers. A young hunter unable to bring in a valuable haul of deerskins might reason that a few horses stolen from one settlement and sold in another would be equally lucrative and doubly retributive. As trader John Galphin observed, "You may be assured that it will be impossible to keep them [the Creeks] from stealing horses, when the White people will encroach upon their hunting grounds. They will not put up with it."[63] Creek autonomy depended on the viability of their established boundaries and their continued freedom to travel within and across those boundaries as their cultural and economic livelihood required.

The primary course by which Georgia and Carolina traders had for decades made their way in and out of the Lower Creek Nation was the Lower or Uchee Path, which passed from Augusta in Georgia to Coweta, on the Chattahoochee River, slightly southwesterly through Tuckabatchee, into present-day Mississippi, and then south toward New Orleans.[64] The Upper Path proceeded from just north of Augusta through the Upper Creek town of Okfuskee and on into the northern reaches of Mississippi (see map 1).[65] This route was connected to two important branches, leading northward to the Cherokees and westward to the Chickasaw and Choctaw Nations.[66] Indeed, there was a network of other roads by which one could move through the region, including the north-south "Great Warrior Path" that connected the southern Indian nations with their Iroquois and Shawnee neighbors in the Ohio River Valley and further northward.[67] In addition, archaeological evidence suggests that Creek country was cross cut with a series of smaller pathways that connected individual households.[68]

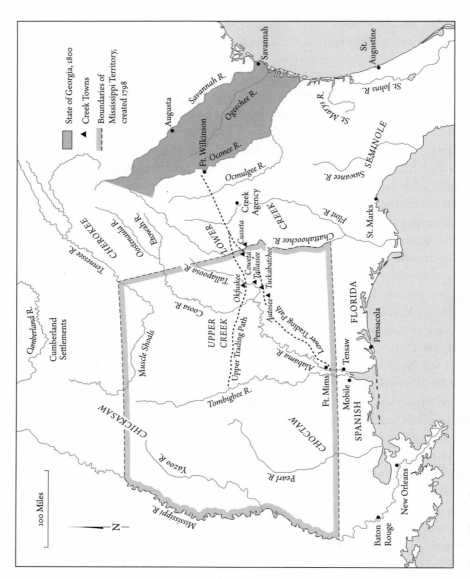

Map 1. The southern interior, ca. 1801

One of the oldest human-made roads in the region was the St. Augustine road or *Camino Real* that linked the oldest non-Indian town in the region to the Spanish missions along the Gulf coast.[69] The English around Charleston and Savannah also carved out new paths, specifically designed to link their settlements together, sometimes with defensive motives in mind.[70] English and French traders circulated back and forth from the Atlantic seacoast to the Mississippi River Valley and up and down from the Ohio River to the Gulf of Mexico, making use of long-established routes, creating a palimpsest in which rivers, roads, and trails assumed shifting importance depending on their purpose and the locales they connected. The Indian trade was the driving force behind most of the newly created pathways and it was the primary fiscal enterprise of both Carolina and Georgia for much of the eighteenth century. Similarly, although many maps of the eighteenth-century South underscored the defensive necessities of frontier life, noting forts and the roads that linked them and recommending areas for reinforcement, the next most frequently available type of maps were those that emphasized trade routes.[71] But there was a clear connection between military and commercial agendas. Establishing a stable trade route and trading relationship between a colony and an Indian nation meant that both partners potentially gained a military ally as well.

Creating new trade routes and controlling others was thus an important part of the imperial contest the English and French waged against one another on the southern frontier.[72] For the French in the Mississippi River Valley, the Tennessee River became an important thoroughfare, though it never supplanted the land routes to the north and south of it.[73] For the English at Charleston and Savannah, the Upper and Lower Trading paths were the most promising in terms of Indian commerce and imperial intrigue. Throughout the first half of the eighteenth century, British traders from the eastern seaboard tried to insinuate themselves among the French-allied Indian towns to the west.

Governor Francis Nicholson of Virginia was among the British officials determined to unseat the French and their hold on the Indian trade in the Mississippi River Valley. Nicholson, like other colonial leaders stationed in the east, received information about the westward Indian nations from travelers on both formal and informal reconnaissance missions. Most European travelers during this era derived the bulk of their topographical intelligence from Native people, and mapmakers often included textual commentaries as a supplement to the cartographic images.[74] One of Nicholson's informants was Lawrence Vanden Bosh, who wrote ominously of the dangers awaiting traders in the waters of the Mississippi River Valley. He reported that the rivers in the area were "so full of Crocodiles which devour men when they either swim or fall into the water" that the area Indians took great precautions to avoid arousing their attention. The navigability of rivers and potential for danger were fundamental pieces of information that colonial officials desired from far-flung emissaries. But such a report also makes clear that Indians were not the only ones who told stories of frightening creatures lurking at water's edge.[75]

Another segment of the population that was surprisingly familiar with many of the east-west Indian trails included enslaved people of African descent. For the increasing numbers of slaves introduced into the Southeast during the eighteenth century, however, the promise of these trails was uncertain. For the fugitive, the paths might lead to the putative protection of Spanish friars in Florida or the potential for adoption into an Indian family. But among those same populations, escaped slaves might find themselves once again placed in bondage.[76] Thus, slave mobility was inextricably bound up with the needs and desires of both their white owners and their Indian neighbors.

Some of these enslaved people may have had knowledge of particular Indian communities and paths that led to them as a result of first-hand experience in the Nation. At least in the beginning, traders did not often bring Africans or African Americans with them as burdeners; they typically hired Indian laborers or relied on packhorse men who accompanied them from the port cities.[77] But slaves employed as sawyers or boatmen were sometimes dispatched to assist with the construction of an interior fort or sent on long distance errands to drive cattle or carry messages.[78] In many ways, their freedom to move through the region was alternately enlarged or proscribed depending on the state of diplomatic affairs between outsiders and Indians and local rumors of slave revolts.

Whether they had traveled with traders, surveyors, or state officials or had simply learned from the reports of others who had, people of African descent in the east gleaned certain bits of information about Indian towns in the interior. And at least a few of them had also learned Muskogee or another language spoken in the Creek Nation. Indeed, outside observers occasionally noted the presence of African or African American interpreters within Creek country, indicating that at least some of them (whether fugitive or free) possessed a linguistic facility that permitted them greater mobility. Since the vast majority of Creek people did not speak English, slaves or former slaves who spoke both an Indian language and English (and perhaps Spanish too) were valuable allies. What's more, possessing such skills made escape more feasible since a fugitive who spoke an Indian language would find it easier to navigate within the Nation without arousing too much suspicion.[79]

In general, white traders and other non-Indian travelers who ventured into the Creek Nation were to do so only if they were licensed and had a passport or something similar that authorized their presence. As early as the first decade after the settlement of the Georgia colony, members of the Creek confederacy saw that British officials had little power to restrain the ranging populace.[80] Colonial leaders passed a variety of measures designed to limit the offenses committed against Indian people and Indian land. But southern Indians were themselves their own best representatives, and despite colonial settlements on nearly every side, they patrolled the vast interior territory. Controlling the number and character of travelers to Indian Country was a widely recognized strategy for preventing the sort of clashes that led to theft and subsequent confrontations over property.[81]

After the Revolutionary War, a state governor was most likely to be the source of such passports.[82] Southern Indians were likewise expected to have passes or certificates from a regional official to authorize travel beyond the boundaries of their own nations.[83] It was not just violent confrontations between travelers and Indian inhabitants that leaders on both sides feared. In the ungovernable backcountry, peddlers and smugglers of all kinds could ply their black-market trades largely without the oversight of headmen or governors.

Both legitimate and illegitimate Indian commerce in the eighteenth century depended on pack trains that trod the east-west trails into and out of Creek country.[84] While the earliest English traders had ventured into the Creek interior in the late seventeenth century in search of slaves, the deerskin trade soon supplanted the slave trade in importance to the colonies.[85] Each Creek town typically had its own trader or set of traders, who visited and ultimately came to reside among the townspeople.[86] Initially, these traders were welcomed and treated hospitably. They provided important services to Creek communities and were usually allowed to establish a household that included a small garden. The presence of a trader within each town assured the townspeople of a regular communication with the English colonies along the coast. They sometimes acted as de facto diplomats, carrying messages, talks, and sometimes treaty proposals along with their wares, back and forth between Creek country and the colonies.[87] Thus they were often seen as valuable residents in or near Creek communities. After all, traveling was something that Creek people both recognized and valued.

During the Revolutionary War, however, some traders fled Indian Country, leaving Creek towns bereft of their primary source of goods, including guns and ammunition. Others stood their ground, fighting alongside the British or the rebels, but they were unable to procure supplies because of blockades. Likewise, the perils of overland travel and transport were so great during the war that despite the common desire to continue the commerce, it was increasingly difficult to pack skins to the coast or return with duffels, guns, and rum.[88]

The diminution of the Indian trade was a significant blow to Creek welfare. While Creek people in the 1770s were largely self-sufficient—still making and preparing their own foodstuffs, clothing, and utensils—the exponential growth of the deerskin trade through the late seventeenth and early eighteenth centuries meant that Creek men and women, like many of their southeastern Indian neighbors, had become reliant on their participation in a transatlantic economy. Particularly with respect to the guns and ammunition that were now vital to their hunting practices as well as their national defense, Creek people were hard hit by the shortages spawned by the War for American Independence.[89]

After the Revolution, the increased presence of traders as capitalist vanguards opened the door for other Americans to begin to enter Creek country.[90] Some traders apparently went so far as to bring travelers into the Nation for a fee, adding guide to the list of avocations they could claim.[91] For Creek leaders, defending the boundaries of their nation included preventing undesirables from settling nearby. Besides squatting on Indian lands, backwoods banditti were also notorious for engaging in the black-market sale of property stolen from border settlements, thefts for which the Creeks were often blamed whether or not they were actually involved. Such alleged crimes often provided the rationale for compensatory demands of land by state officials, even when the identity of the thieves was dubious. There was an explicit connection between theft, debt, and Indian land cessions. Whether debts were incurred as a result of trade and credit practices or alleged thefts of property— the repayment plan was always the same and the currency of choice was land.

The Creeks' Indian neighbors gave voice to comparable concerns. In early 1786, Chickasaw leader and American ally Piomingo told U.S. treaty commissioners, "Such men as come properly to trade with us, will be very welcome . . . but the class of settlers we now have, are a pest."[92] The problematic relationship between trade and land claims was foremost in the minds of federal commissioners assigned to investigate irregularities in the Indian trade. They observed that "the Indians, in general, within the United States, want only to enjoy their lands without interruption, and to have their necessities regularly supplied by our traders."[93] With supply from the Americans unreliable, many Creeks continued to make the long trek to Pensacola to do business with British traders ensconced in Spanish Florida, proving that trade was intimately connected with both mobility and diplomacy.

Despite or perhaps because of these problems, early state officials began to push for more access to the Indian Country than had ever characterized the colonial era, even expanding the network of well-worn trade roads. The 1784 speech of Georgia governor John Houstoun to the Choctaws underscores the prevailing attitude: "Formerly when the people of Pensacola and Mobile were one and the same with Us, we did not carry on trade with you from this Country, and then there was no Occasion to ask a Path thro' the Creek Nation." He went on to explain that since the Spanish now controlled east and west Florida, it was necessary to have a new east-west path extending all the way to the Choctaws in the west. Thus, if the Choctaws wanted a regular trade with the Georgians, it was incumbent upon them to negotiate free and safe passage for the American traders through the Creek Nation.[94] By arguing for this right of way and impressing upon the Choctaws that their access to Georgia trade depended on preventing Creek warriors from blocking the trade paths, the Georgia officials hoped to enlarge their trade while simultaneously placing two Indian nations in competition. With prices for deerskins falling, the Creeks declined to grant the Choctaws access to the Georgia traders.[95] This move on the part of Creek leaders demonstrates their growing tendency to take active measures to protect their interests by limiting the number and character of travelers through their nation.

The increase in American interest in the Creek Nation was connected not only to trade but also to the shifting geopolitical climate that characterized the region following the Revolution. During the war, many southeastern Indians, including most Cherokees as well as the Upper Creeks under McGillivray, had joined with the British, an alliance for which they paid in lives and land. In triumphing over the Crown, the nascent United States granted itself "the right of conquest" and assumed title to all former British and allied lands, including portions of the Creek Nation.[96] In addition, generous if unrealistic military bounties promised westward land grants to Georgia patriots, many of whom were not content to wait for the necessary legislative acts and appropriations; they began to pour into the Trans-Appalachian region within a few months of the Treaty of Paris (1783). By the 1790s, Georgia was also embroiled in a massive land speculation scheme, known as the Yazoo controversy, which sent hordes of surveyors and speculators into the westward lands of the South. During this period, Creek warriors and hunters often greeted such trespassers with stern exhortations to move off, reserving their most aggressive policies for settlers who came along the old trade paths with their far-ranging livestock. The constant misunderstandings and confrontations of this era reveal the deep importance that Creek and American ways of looking at the world—and especially of comprehending territory and mobility—had in the lives of ordinary men and women along the frontier.

In the middle of the 1780s, Yntipaya Masla, a "principal warrior of the Lower Creek Indians," expressed the dilemma of advancing American interests in Creek country in a talk with St. Augustine's Spanish governor, Vizente Manuel de Zéspedes. He stated, "The Georgians, when they were English, had their frontier separated fifteen days' journey from our towns. Since then they have so encroached upon and usurped our land that at present they are distant from us only two days' march, not leaving us land enough for our hunting."[97] The general consensus across Indian Country during the years immediately following the outbreak of peace was that Americans, even more than their British, French, and Spanish predecessors, were a notoriously "rambling populace."[98] Despite the American ascendance, most Creek talwas intended to preserve relationships with the former imperial powers that had been insinuating themselves in the region for generations. The Tallassee King stated in 1778, for instance, that "formerly we were friends with three Mothers, the English, the French and Spaniards, and expect they will be so, and I will still hold them three fast by the hand." Yet, he informed the commissioners from the east, "I will always look to the sun rising for any sup[p]ly."[99]

McGillivray was explicit in his 1785 address to Spanish leaders charged with the responsibility of settling post-Revolutionary boundaries between His Catholic Majesty's holdings and those ceded by the British to the United States. He wrote, "As we were not partys [to the Treaty of Paris], so we are determined to pay no attention to the Manner in which the British Negotiatiors has drawn out the Lines of the Lands in question Ceded to the States of America—it being a notorious fact known to the Americans . . . that his Brittanick Majesty was never possessed either by session purchase or by right of Conquest of our Territorys and which the Said treaty gives away."[100] McGillivray recognized the need to establish tighter trade connections with Augusta, now under U.S. control, but he refused to accept encroachments on Creek lands, no matter what the repercussion regarding commerce. After all, he still had the support of the Spanish in Pensacola and the powerful expatriate British traders who also remained in Florida, such as Panton,

Leslie, & Co., with whom the Creek Nation did an increasing amount of its deerskin business.[101] McGillivray rigidly opposed détente with the Americans unless they categorically removed from disputed lands. In addition to the transfer of dubious land titles in agreements between empires, McGillivray was familiar with the mode of preemption that settlers used to claim lands beyond fixed boundaries. He would not support peaceful relations until squatters and trespassers respected Creek national boundaries, and as evidence of his intentions he courted both Spanish and British support long after the American ascendance.

Despite the stated intent of Creek leaders in the 1770s to keep their path to the Americans "white and straight," the 1780s were a period of constant confrontation. Creek warriors engaged in nearly continual raids on settlements in Cumberland and the frontiers of Georgia in retribution for encroachments by Americans that grew more and more common. Creek men were particularly incensed to find squatters and livestock violating the borders of their hunting lands, perhaps the most vigorously defended and hotly contested of their territorial claims. The pull of the Indian trade and the peace it required to be successful was simply not as compelling as the drive to seek retribution for such boundary trespasses. Individual acts of vengeance conflicted with a consolidation of Creek leadership under figures like McGillivray who increasingly articulated a Creek national identity. Furthermore, by the middle of the decade, the nascent American nation had begun to debate its own proper structure and organization.

During the colonial period, many of the colonies conducted relations with neighboring Indian nations largely independent of one another. While this protocol often led to confusion and mistrust, it afforded Native inhabitants the opportunity to outmaneuver colonial officials by pitting one polity against another in much the same way that they played European imperial powers off one another to gain favorable trade terms.[102] The Cherokees, for instance, consistently used the proximity and pliability of Virginia to threaten South Carolina's hold on its share of the deerskin trade. In the era of the New Republic, however, the Indian nations of the Southeast confronted a new amorphous creature, the confederated states of America. While each state, like the colonies that preceded them, continued to proceed largely independent of one another, there was an increased unity of Indian policy on the federal level. Native people were to be traded with and treated according to federal, not local mandates. But convincing Indians and local officials of the wisdom or authority of this new approach was difficult at best, and enforcing it was next to impossible. Indeed, the divisive conflict between the southern states and the federal government over states' rights has its origins in these early and ongoing debates over Indian policy.[103]

Although the Articles of Confederation and later the Constitution stipulated that only the United States could conduct treaties with and wage war on Indian nations, enforcing the federal will in the southern backcountry was no easy task.[104] Additionally, a number of agreements that were suspended during the Revolution were infinitely complicated by the new national government that emerged from it.[105] The right of the states to determine their own Indian policies was a salient political point in this period and formed the basis for the growth of a rabid form of southern and western republicanism that eschewed the heavy-handed interference of a federal body thousands of miles from the heat of frontier battles. By the mid-1780s, the State of Georgia had engaged in various Indian conferences designed to put a stop to hostilities between Creeks and westward wandering squatters and to acquire, once and for all, the desirable lands around the Oconee and Ocmulgee rivers, believing that natural boundaries were the most conducive to preventing trespass in either direction.

At Galphinton in 1785 and Shoulderbone Creek in 1786, Georgia officials wrestled two highly controversial treaties from the Creeks. Despite clear stipulations that Indian affairs were the exclusive province of the federal polity, Georgian citizens pushed for these negotiations to end the recent wave of violence. Rumors and complaints about the frequent depredations committed by Creek and Cherokee warriors against settlers in Tennessee and Georgia filled the local newspapers and the respective governors' incoming mail.[106] One inflammatory report of clashes between the Tennessee militia and the Creeks provided a "List of prisoners, citizens of the United States, in the Creek nation who are treated as slaves, and sold from master to master, at as high a price and in the same manner as negroes are sold."[107] Another informed Georgia governor Edward Telfair that the Creeks had driven border settlers off their farms and referred to the Indians as "very sassy."[108] A follow-up report resolved, "It is now time you take your Gun up. [T]he field is now open for execution."[109]

The problem with the Galphinton and Shoulderbone treaties was that only a minority of Creeks showed up at the treaty convention, and it was clear that they did not act on behalf of the Creek Nation, despite state claims to the contrary. Nevertheless, Georgia settlers who had been steadily advancing beyond established territorial limits were eager to secure the valuable lands between the branches of the Oconee River, just south of present-day Athens and the lands from the fork of Oconee and Ocmulgee rivers to the southeast toward the St. Mary's River.[110] At both conventions, U.S. representatives eschewed the contemplated treaty proceedings since only a tiny fraction of Creek leaders deigned to show up. The U.S. commissioners rightly observed that this was a calculated effort, engineered mainly by McGillivray, to resist further treaties and land cessions and that pursuing a treaty with such a small minority of chiefs would simply lead to more misunderstandings and bloodshed, since the majority of the Nation would not observe its stipulations anyway. The Georgia commissioners, however, had no such cautious foresight and signed two illegitimate treaties with the handful of Creeks who were present, in one case, literally at bayonet point.[111]

These two treaties purported to authorize cessions of lands that to a large degree were already being settled by American squatters.[112] Such conferences, however, were contrary to the Articles of Confederation and created a serious rift between federal and state powers. Noting the importance of boundaries to the southeastern Indians, a Continental Congress committee in the late 1780s observed that a number of illegal American settlements had raised the ire of the Creeks. Particularly in the area around the forks of the Oconee River, they noted, "various pretences seem to be set up by the white people for making those settlements, which the Indians, tenacious of their rights, appear to be determined to oppose."[113] While the Georgia treaty commissioners at Galphinton and Shoulderbone had made much of the alleged murders of American citizens, what they really pushed for was the immediate surveying of the newly established boundaries between the Creek Nation and the state—boundaries that gave to the state large tracts of additional land.[114] If they proceeded to mark the lines quickly enough, Creek complaints to the U.S. government would not have time to take hold before Georgia settlers would be firmly ensconced in the new lands.

A note appended to Cowerther Mayit's 1785 talk seems to indicate that the strategy occasionally worked, at least as a stalling technique. The headman noted that a white man had arrived at Coweta days earlier and told the headman that some Creeks had come to squatter settlements and ordered the Americans to move off. The stranger wanted to know whether these orders emanated from "the Nation." Cowerther Mayit reported that he told the people "to Stay on [their] [places] until the Line was run and then Sutch as was over the Line we [hoped] [would] obay ther Governor and move from all Sutch placeses over the Line."[115] It was rapidly becoming clear to both Creeks and Americans that borders of ink were easily crossed. Marking the lines on paper and on land would dominate not just the local conversations of this turbulent decade but the national ones as well.

The trend of state treaties with Indian nations came to a close with the Treaty of New York in 1790. This agreement represents a significant turning point in Georgia, Creek, and U.S. affairs because it unequivocally established the federal government as the only source of treaty-making and, by extension, border-making authority. For many in the southern and western territories, it marked a new era in which the rights of states would be subordinated to the responsibilities of the federal government in treaties with Indian nations.[116] In essence, it abrogated the state treaties of Galphinton (1785) and Shoulderbone (1786), but partially affirmed the long-debated Treaty of Augusta (1783), in an effort to secure some of the lands Georgia had sought while also appeasing Creek interests. In a letter accompanying the treaty, President Washington acknowledged that the overall purpose of the treaty was to restore peace to the "southern frontier," but he further expressed his hope that it would also "be the means of firmly attaching the Creeks and the neighboring tribes to the interests of the United States."[117]

Washington and Secretary of War Henry Knox observed that the Creeks had positively refused to part with the land adjacent to the Ocmulgee River. Since that tract was "sunken and barren" and only marginally valuable to the United States but of supreme importance to the Creeks, "constituting some of their most valuable winter hunting ground," it was unwise to press them further for it. Accordingly, the commissioners of the Treaty of New York appear to have taken seriously Creek claims regarding the importance of their hunting grounds, as well as their broader right to make such territorial claims. The Creeks staunchly refused to part with anything but a portion of the Oconee lands that the Georgians had squawked about for over a decade.[118]

Despite the preservation of the Ocmulgee lands, many Lower Creeks were dissatisfied with the treaty, feeling that McGillivray had betrayed their interests by agreeing to cede their hunting grounds while preserving the Upper towns' land. Perhaps as distressing was the realization that the diplomatic machinery was greased with money. In addition to establishing an annuity of $1,500 a year for the Creeks in exchange for the ceded lands, McGillivray himself received a commission in the U.S. military and $1,200 a year for the rest of his life.[119] While this "secret article" would not come to light for many years, suspicions abounded within Creek country about the personal benefits McGillivray stood to gain by accommodating the Americans.

Dissatisfaction with the New York treaty was, in fact, widespread. Traveler John Bradshaw found himself an unwelcome trespasser in the Creek Nation in November of 1790, despite his official passport from the Georgia governor, cosigned by McGillivray. After ignoring the advice of Indian countrymen to leave the Nation, Bradshaw's men were fired upon and had their horses stolen during the night. Obliged to proceed on foot, he later reported that the Creeks were "very much disatisfied with the Treaty held at New York and also with McGillivray, paying very little respect to his authority, and declaring that Congress might do what they pleased with the Treaty, for that they intended to do as they pleased with it—this they uttered in great contempt."[120] McGillivray's acquiescence to the Americans in New York represented both a personal about-face with regard to his previously anti-American policies and a new era of self-interested leadership that would continue to fracture Creek politics in the decades to come. It also signaled a new style of treaty making, wherein Indian leaders might travel far from home and enter into backroom deals with federal officials thousands of miles from the actual lands under discussion. While the state-led treaties were clearly problematic, they at least took place along the very boundaries in question. If allowed to become a trend, this new style of making treaties threatened to undermine local authority by shifting power to a small group of national spokesmen and away from the leaders of individual talwas.

Nor were Georgians satisfied with the Treaty of New York. Among other complaints, the treaty "solemnly guaranteed" to the Creeks all of their lands not explicitly ceded to Georgia in the agreement. In a published tirade following the ratification of the treaty, author "Manlius" described the frontier state of Georgia as the "foremost of the states to adopt [the Constitution]; at that time her citizens were harassed by the savages—she had for a long time witnessed the murders, the robberies, the devastations and cruelties of those barbarians." The state, he maintained, had to put the majority of its resources toward the defense of its frontiers. Rather than send aid, the federal government had actually negotiated a "Knoxonian" treaty that restored some lands to the Creeks while reauthorizing those ceded in the Augusta treaty, namely the lands between the Oconee and Ogeechee rivers. He mourned the loss of faith in the federal government and in defending the treaties of Galphinton and Shoulderbone, said state citizens were incensed to find that lands "bought by the state some years since" had been inexplicably restored to the Creeks. He finally concluded that the Georgians must surely be "like Issachar: 'a strong ass couching down between two burdens;' if we servilely submit to bear them, richly do we deserve them."[121]

Despite its importance, the Treaty of New York was not the only catalyst of change along the borders of Creek country in the 1790s. Due to simultaneously falling skin prices and declining deer populations, the deerskin trade had dwindled considerably by the turn of the nineteenth century. Prospects for southern commerce were beginning to shift decisively away from white-tailed deer and toward white-tipped cotton plants, especially after the invention of the labor-saving cotton gin in 1793.[122] Additionally, despite widespread disdain for the Treaty of New York, over the next decade a tenuous peace would be established along the borders of the Creek Nation, due in large part to the presence of U.S. agent Benjamin Hawkins, who was appointed to oversee the southeastern Indian department and sent to live among the Creeks in 1796.[123] In addition, the U.S. Constitution (ratified in 1789) and the Trade and Intercourse Act (passed in 1790), along with the Treaty of New York, established that Indian affairs, including land cessions, were the province of the federal government, ending speculation-driven state treaties such as those of Galphinton and Shoulderbone.[124]

The "Plan of Civilization" for the southern Indians was also launched in this era. In fact, it was included in the language of the Treaty of New York itself. Article 12 read: "That the Creek nation may be led to a greater degree of civilization, and to become herdsmen and cultivators, instead of remaining in a state of hunters, the United States will, from time to time, furnish gratuitously the said nation with useful domestic animals, and implements of husbandry."[125] The plan to transform the southern Indians from hunters to farmers, which conveniently ignored their long history of crop cultivation, would come to dominate the relationship between Hawkins and the Creeks. The plan was to introduce the implements of farming and domestic production to the southern Indians—in part by establishing government trading houses or factories on their land where they could trade the fruits of their labor for various goods and utensils. Hawkins encouraged the Creeks, in Jefferson's words, to become "sensible of the superiority" of the "practice of husbandry, and of the household arts."[126] In exchange for cessions of territory (and later concessions regarding roads and travel), the Creeks were promised not only cash in the form of an annuity but also "implements of husbandry," as well as access to workmen like blacksmiths and strikers.[127] These skilled individuals were not imported for the repair of guns, as many Creek men may have wished, but for the production and repair of agricultural implements and items used for domestic manufacture of textiles.

Since planting and domestic production had traditionally been the province of Creek women, many of these provisions appear to have had a strengthening effect on the status of women in the talwas.[128] The civilization program urged Creek men to abandon the large-scale hunting efforts that had historically characterized the division of labor and begin to concentrate on raising livestock, fencing their lands, and assisting the women with planting. Stock-raising, though still not widely heralded, appeared to hold the most promise, as Hawkins observed early on: "Raising of Stock . . . is more relished by the Creeks, than any other part of the plan devised for civilization. . . . Cattle, till lately, were not held in much estimation; but since the failure of supplies from hunting, they are resorted to."[129] Over the next decade, these changes in Creek domestic economy—the circumscription of hunting lands, the shift among some men to agriculture and stock-raising, and the emergence of Creek women as a distinct economic force—would likewise be woven into the fabric of Creek social relations. But perhaps the most definitive result of these transformations was that Creek land and American access to it was becoming a commodity: traded not for peace or a straight white path, but for money.[130]

Chapter Two

SETTLING BOUNDARIES

AND NEGOTIATING ACCESS

As a result of competing claims by state, federal, and indigenous interests, a shifting maze of boundary lines made figuring out whose side one was on a tricky proposition. Once boundaries were agreed upon in treaty conventions and the various documents delivered to each party, there still remained the problem of how to make the newly determined lines legible to the people who lived on the southern frontiers. "Marking the land" was not just an expression describing the process of surveying tracts; it literally meant marking the posts, trees, and rocks that lined the boundaries and paths between the Americans and the Creeks. The hope was that a tree with the letters "CN" on one side and "US" on the other would be unmistakable to anyone who might encounter it. The Creeks also used their own symbols, like red-painted sticks and mutilated livestock, to warn squatters of their trespass and travelers of their peril. These informal markers and competing land claims augmented confusion and misunderstanding between the inhabitants of the southern borderlands.

In an effort to prevent future doubts about the boundaries that separated them, most treaties of this era included a clause providing for a certain number of state *and* Indian leaders to attend the running of lines. Samuel Elbert, Georgia governor over 1785–1786, assured the "Kings, Head Men and Warriors of the Creek Nation" that he and his citizens wanted to "keep the path open and straight between our two Countries." He promised that the Augusta traders would "send as many goods to your Nation as you stand in need of," but insisted that the new boundaries be delineated, and not just on paper. His speech is worth quoting at length:

> When our Men were considering your talk, they found that paper alone, was not sufficient to mark the Line on, between us to prevent bad people from going over it, and therefore to convince you of their sincerity and good intentions, they directed me to chuse three beloved men on our part and to request that you will chuse beloved Men on your part, to meet on the very ground and these hold a talk together and set up posts and mark trees and stones and drink out of the waters that lay on the Line which you shall agree upon to be the boundary between you and us, and when this is done, no Land on your side of that Line shall be touched by our people on any pretence whatever, and if any should have been marked or the trees blazed, it shall go for nothing and those that did it, if we can find them out shall be made examples of.[1]

Elbert insisted that the mutual respect of borders between the Creeks and Americans depended upon a collaborative experience of the land itself, to "meet on the very ground," "mark trees and stones," "drink out of the waters," emphasizing the need for Creek delegates to travel *with* surveyors and authorize the lines to be run according to agreement. This experiential approach to mapping and surveying was characteristic of Creek conceptualizations of space, in which knowing the land was paramount to representing it pictorially or politically, although it is unclear whether Elbert intended to honor Creek practice or accidentally converged with it.[2]

With the creation of the Mississippi Territory (1798) and the massive addition of the Louisiana Purchase (1803), the drive to establish the exact boundaries of the new American states and connect their capitals in a network of roads, rivers, and ports became an engine for marking the land in accordance with the marked papers and maps that purported to represent it. The difficulty of such efforts was exemplified in the Lewis and Clark expedition and came into sharp relief in other parts of the United States as well.[3] Like Lewis and Clark, southern surveyors were heavily reliant on local Native knowledge of landscape, watercourses, and indigenous affiliations. In fact, most treaties signed in this era contained a specific provision ensuring that Indian leaders would supply a certain number of authorized individuals to assist in the expeditions to "run the lines."[4] For decades, Creek leaders had alternately accepted and refused treaty stipulations that required them to furnish guides, guards, and supplies to surveying parties charged with demarcating the shifting borders of the region.[5] Despite a general sense that boundaries between the Creeks and their American neighbors might prevent trespasses, government representatives often found it necessary to reassure Creek leaders of the benign intent of such boundary lines and constantly described them as borders of "mutual good."

Many Creeks were rightly skeptical of these pronouncements, since surveying was often a mechanism of colonial control, an effort on the part of settlers and speculators to know, name, and ultimately possess the land.[6] It was also not uncommon for southern statesmen to oppose the running of certain boundaries, such as the Treaty of New York (1790) lines, which were seen as injurious to the rights of southern states.[7] In the end, marking boundary lines required a mutual understanding of the meaning of the borders and a shared, though not always serene, experience of their inscription.

In 1796, the Creeks signed the Treaty of Coleraine, which reaffirmed the Treaty of New York, changed the location of the factory (or government trading house), and made provisions for running a temporary boundary between Georgia and the Creeks. When the line was finally run in 1798, the assembled commissioners had an overabundance of ideas on how the line should be literally marked. With two Georgia commissioners, one U.S. commissioner, and five Creek commissioners, the party inexplicably decided to use *all* of their initials as well as a variety of chops to mark the trees along the line. They also recorded "the Number of Miles from the starting point marked on trees in Roman Characters and figures also U:S: on the right side and C on the left."[8] The resulting boundaries—and mutilated trees—were exemplary specimens of contested and yet collaborative survey expeditions.

For both Creeks and Americans, the establishment of national boundaries was paramount to protecting their rights as sovereign polities. And maintaining travel routes was important to building and preserving unity. For the Americans, opening roads was not only central for securing their nation but also for expanding it. U.S. officials ultimately deemed roads across Indian land essential and began a protracted series of negotiations to secure the right to traverse Creek country.

In 1795 the United States entered into a treaty with Spain that secured a significant portion of what are now the states of Mississippi and Louisiana. The compact required that commissioners from both sides meet and demarcate a boundary line between the new U.S. possession, known as the Mississippi Territory, and the remaining Spanish holdings at Mobile and in West Florida. The running of the line, later known as Ellicott's Line after the chief U.S. surveyor, was the cause of great concern among the Lower Creeks and their brethren to the southeast, the Seminoles.[9] In a talk delivered to U.S.

agent James Seagrove, a headman named Methlogee complained of surveyors traipsing through Lower Creek and Seminole lands, marking the trees
and producing considerable unease in the towns through which the boundary would eventually pass.[10] Methlogee indicated that the line, which began
at the Mississippi River and was proceeding eastward roughly along the 31st
parallel, was the source of great alarm to his townspeople. He recounted that
in a conference at Pensacola with Benjamin Hawkins and several other U.S.
and Spanish representatives, he and other chiefs had refused the call to
attend the survey as guides, saying that they were "pointedly opposed to the
lines running any further for the present." Hawkins replied that the United
States would run the line whatever the cost, even if it meant losing 1,000 men
in the process.[11]

Methlogee, similarly overstating his influence, warned that he spoke not
just for the Lower Creeks or Seminoles but for the majority of the Creeks,
who had become outraged after concluding that they were to "be robbed of
their lands which is their only support."[12] While it might be understood that
a boundary between the Indians and their American neighbors could be
mutually beneficial, not all borders were created equal. Methlogee made it
clear that survey lines through the heart of their territory would invariably be
equated with imminent land loss.[13] Why else would the Americans insist on
drawing lines through their land if not to mark out their desired stake? He
cautioned, "I am confident that there will be a war unless prevented by the
news I may carry home."[14] Marking the line was only as effective as the ways
in which the symbols on the trees would be actually interpreted by individual Creeks, most of whom had not been privy to distant treaty proceedings.

Seagrove tried to assuage Methlogee's fears by reminding him that the
Treaty of Coleraine had provided a clause for marking this line at some
future time when it was agreed upon by the United States and Spain. Since
the accord had finally been reached, the U.S. commissioners were simply
carrying out the treaty stipulation. He assured the impassioned headman
that the line would have no material effect on the lives of Seminoles and
Lower Creeks, telling Methlogee that he considered the boundary "quite
harmless to your interests" and pledging that the United States would never
take land from the Indians without their consent. What harm could the line
do, he asked, when the Indians "will enjoy their lands on either side of it as
they have done when there was no such line." In a distillation of the general
philosophy behind the frenzy of surveying that characterized the 1790s, Seagrove concluded,

When your old Friends the English people lived in America and the Spaniards in Florida; this same boundary line was agreed upon between them, and was marked in all their Treaty's, and tho' it was not actually marked on the trees, still it was marked on the papers of both Nations, and by them well understood. . . . The line that is now about to be marked by the Spanish and American Governments is merely to prevent at a future day, any misunderstanding, in not knowing, how far the Government of either extend, without having any view to land. Lines of a similar kind are established between all white nations, whereby wars and much injury is prevented.[15]

Several things make this brief speech especially notable. First, Seagrove's insistence on the line as one separating "white nations" implies that the Creeks and Seminoles whose towns were bisected by the border were merely temporary tenants living within Spanish or American limits. This was an entirely different sort of boundary than the 1739 line separating the Creeks from the Georgia colony, for this one passed through, not around, the Indian nation and carried the implicit assumption that Indians on either side were subject to the government of the Americans or the Spanish. Second, Seagrove's attempt to dissolve Methlogee's concerns was directly connected to the immediate need for Lower Creek and Seminole representatives to attend the running of the line. Without their cooperation, the surveyors would be unable to procure provisions from the towns through which the line must pass and the security and success of their mission would be jeopardized.[16]

Pressing the question of the boundary line was equally important to southern slaveholders, since knowing the actual extent of U.S. versus Spanish territory was instrumental to the recovery of fugitives. Enslaved Africans and African Americans in Georgia had often found refuge in lands to the south, both those held by the Seminoles and those held by Spain. Whether they sought the protection of Spanish friars, the ostensibly more relaxed slave system exercised by Spanish subjects, or integration into Seminole towns, African and African American people traveled southward in droves.[17] And increasingly after the Revolutionary War, renegade Creeks, often with British or U.S. accomplices, stole slaves, horses, and stock and drove them south for black market sale in Pensacola.[18] The rise in such contraband commerce is intimately connected to changing economic conditions in the Creek Nation and the South at large.

Large-scale planting and ranching both contributed to the degradation of deer populations and the circumscription of Creek hunting grounds, since the former enabled vast quantities of land to be cultivated and the latter required vast areas of forage that impinged on deer habitats. Thus, these thefts and the subsequent monies received were one way in which Creek young men could replace revenues lost to the declining deerskin trade, while also exacting personal revenge on the encroachments of Americans and their property. In many ways, this behavior can be seen as an adaptive extension of male youth culture among the Creeks—a society in which young men were expected to prove their manhood in the hunt and in battle but faced diminishing opportunities to do both.[19] Spanish officials in Florida, always eager to find ways to secure their foothold in the region, often encouraged such actions. U.S. commissioners insisted that a decrease in such ungovernable commerce, and perhaps the ultimate end of the Spanish presence in the Gulf, hinged on the clear delineation and mutual recognition of national borders.

U.S. officials also trumpeted the effect such boundary lines would have on the permanent establishment of good relations between the red and white nations of the region. They insisted to Indian leaders that surveying and marking borders was indispensable to maintaining peace. While many American settlers could not understand and would not respect the sovereignty of Indian nations, a line of marked trees would be seen and understood by all. The Creeks seemed to accept this argument, hoping at the very least that, once established, these borders could be policed and their lands would be protected from the incursions of American squatters. A few years after the Treaty of New York, Ellicott had told the headman at Cusseta that he had come to mark the line between "you and our beloved people in the State of Georgia, and . . . to make it straight that the white people might see how far they had aright to hunt and settle upon."[20] Others expressed an optimistic faith in the power of boundary lines, perhaps concurring with John Carr, who sighed, "I wish to god that the Line was Ronn Between us and the indins and that would pot a stope to any further debts and quarrels."[21] All these pronouncements rested on the belief that "paper alone, was not sufficient to mark the Line on" and that limits must be etched on the physical landscape in order to be effective.[22] But hatched trees and marked posts could also prove duplicitous.

In contrast to claims that running the lines would have no material impact on Indian land holdings, surveyors like Ellicott performed a sort of resource reconnaissance as they passed through Indian lands. They noted patches of arable farmland, the type and quality of timber, the nature and frequency of waterways and mineral deposits, and the general desirability of particular sites. For example, in running the "temporary boundary line between" Georgia and the Creek Indians in 1798, the commissioners observed, "There is a Large proportion of fine Land" along the Oconee River.[23] Georgians coveted the Oconee lands and had sought them since at least the 1760s, when colonial governor James Wright suggested that permission to settle on the southwest side of the river would allow the province to "encrease and flourish very considerably."[24]

Regional maps likewise tended to include some indication as to the quality of the lands represented, particularly if they were Indian lands or were believed to be vacant—both of which translated as available. For example, "A New and Accurate Map of the Province of Georgia in North America," published in the *Universal Magazine* in London in 1779, includes the comments "Very Good Land" and "Exceeding Good Land" over the area widely known to be inhabited by the Creeks. Meanwhile, the label "The Country of the Creek Indians Inhabited by the Muskohge Nation" appears in the far left of the frame, effectively relocating them at least on paper if not in reality. Similarly, in Ellicott's survey, which he repeatedly referred to as "not a line of property, but of jurisdiction," he nevertheless recorded this observation of the Lower Creek lands: "These are remarkably rich, and extremely fertile."[25]

As noted in Methlogee's testimony, the relationship between running even temporary or so-called experimental lines and the subsequent pressure for more land cessions did not go unnoticed by Creek people. Upper Creek leader Alexander McGillivray observed that despite federal pronouncements regarding the necessity of lines for preventing encroachment, "the state of Georgia in greediness for lands has always disregarded the orders of Congress."[26] In other words, there was considerable distance between word and deed. The Creeks generally agreed to the idea of boundary lines to prevent American squatters from coming onto their hunting lands. Indeed, as we have seen, they maintained mental maps of their hunting grounds as bounded territory, separated from the grounds of other nations, even subdividing some areas as the particular hunting lands of a certain talwa or clan. But in practice, boundaries between the Creeks and the Americans were simply not as effective. As a result, they became increasingly disenchanted with federal claims about the need for such dividing lines and began to see these requests in a less and less favorable light.

Creeks opposed to the running of a particular line used whatever means necessary to impede the expedition's progress, whether that meant simply dissimulating when asked to attend as guides and guards, or actively intervening to prevent the survey.[27] The most common strategy for preventing such surveys was simply not to show up. While certainly a more passive form of resistance than stealing horses or attacking the chainmen, it was nevertheless maddening for the surveying parties to have to wait out in the field, exhausting their provisions and wasting time until guides and Indian commissioners deigned to appear. James Wilkinson showed his frustration in a talk to Efau Haujo, or Mad Dog, and Tustunnuggee Thlucco, or Big Warrior, telling them, "It is now twelve days since the period has passed by, which we appointed for meeting here to Run the line; this has given me some concern, because it is not usual for the Father to Wait for the Child."[28] Years later, the same strategy was still in use, as surveyor William Green communicated to Georgia governor William Rabun: "I have not yet received any intelligence of the Indian Escort—Wearied & provoked, thus waiting in suspence on those trifling people."[29] One party of Cherokees pursued an opposite course, sending nearly 300 men to the running of a line pursuant to the Treaty of Holston (1794) when only a handful of the principal chiefs were supposed to attend. Hawkins was flabbergasted and realized immediately that provisioning so many Cherokee representatives would create an enormous if not prohibitive expense for the expedition.[30]

In other cases, the methods of interruption were more aggressive. Murdock McLeod informed Georgia governor James Jackson that "a party of Indians from the Tallasee [towns] together with those of the Seminoles came down to the line stole twenty odd Horses twenty two rifle guns and robed a little Sloop which the commissioners had chartered around from Pensacola . . . and entirely stopt the line from going on."[31] Young Creek men in particular used the presence of surveying parties as an opportunity to steal or run off the parties' horses and perhaps even threaten them physically. Such resistance occurred despite repeated claims by Americans that many boundaries were "between white people, and not intended in any way to affect the Indians in either their property, manners, customs, or religion."[32] One party of Creeks who intervened to stop a survey boldly declared their intention to plunder the campsite and drive the party away.[33] In some cases, debates between individual talwas regarding the appropriateness of a particular land cession and boundary location found one Creek polity pitted against another in the effort to finally run the lines. Moreover, long-standing territorial disputes between southern Indian nations also conspired to prevent or delay many surveys during this period.[34]

When surveyors and speculators—sometimes one and the same, called by the Creeks *ecunnaunuxulgee*, "those greedily grasping after our lands"—appeared in Indian territory, the prospect of conflict, both internal and external, was nearly inevitable.[35] Some surveyors had become notorious not only among the Indians but also among their fellow citizens for their self-interested schemes. For example, in 1784 John Habersham reported to Georgia governor John Houstoun that surveyors along Georgia borders are "generally complained of for inattention to the Law, and a most flagrant partiality to themselves, several of them having purchased large numbers of Certificates."[36] Such problems were further exacerbated by the infamous Yazoo land frauds that exploded onto the national scene during this period, as the speculation bubble burst with far-reaching financial and political consequences.

Speculating in land exemplified the vast conceptual distance between the actual territory inhabited by the southern Indians and the imagined territory bought and sold in state capitals and federal land offices.[37] In 1795, Georgia state representatives, palms greased by speculators, decided to settle state revenue problems by parceling off millions of acres of its western lands. These sales relied on the shaky authority of the original colonial charter, a loose interpretation of the Constitution, and a recent relinquishment of Spanish claims to secure Georgia's "ownership" of the land extending from the Atlantic coast to the Mississippi River. The state subsequently sold title to these "vacant" lands to four primary groups of investors (the Georgia Company, the Georgia Mississippi Company, the Upper Mississippi Company, and the Tennessee Company) who were then allowed to begin surveying and reselling the land titles to individual investors.

The problem was that these lands were hardly vacant and scarcely available since aboriginal title to them had never been relinquished. In fact, in an affirmation of Indian territorial rights, the Treaty of New York had guaranteed to the Creeks all their lands west of Oconee River *in perpetuity*. Not coincidentally, many of the most interested parties in this scheme, including John Sevier, William Blount, Andrew Jackson, and James Wilkinson, were also deeply involved in Indian affairs. They stood to gain the most, personally and politically, if the southern states could execute their will over and above the protests of the Indians whose lands they sought to confiscate for sale.[38] The prominence of the speculators and the relationship between private gain and public office ensured that the repeal of the act would divide southern political interests for decades to come.[39] The ultimate resolution of the Yazoo scandal—described by one politician as "a system of fraud and swindling, more complicated in its machinery and varied in its operations, than any which has disgraced the character of man"—would not be reached until well into the nineteenth century, but one important result is worth mentioning here.[40]

The Land Ordinance, passed by the Continental Congress in 1785, had institutionalized a new system of measuring lands and boundaries for the division and distribution of western lands ostensibly acquired in the Treaty of Paris. These western lands included those ceded in the 1780s by New York, Connecticut, and Massachusetts, later known as the Northwest Territory, and those ceded between 1790 and 1802 by Virginia, North Carolina, and eventually Georgia, part of which became known as the Southwest Territory.[41] After the state of Georgia declared the Yazoo sales void in 1796 (by burning the act on the capitol steps), the state and the federal governments agreed to the Georgia Cession of 1802, widely known as the Georgia Compact. According to the 1802 cession, the state of Georgia yielded to the United States "all the right, title, and claim" to lands lying "south of the State of Tennessee, and west of a line, beginning on the western bank of the Chattahoochee river, where the same crosses the boundary line between the United States and Spain."[42] In exchange, the state was to be given $1,250,000 and the federal government agreed to extinguish Indian title to lands within the new boundaries of the state "as early as the same can be peaceably obtained on reasonable terms."[43]

Like the Treaty of New York and the Trade and Intercourse Acts, the Georgia Compact consolidated the issue of indigenous land claims in the hands of the federal government. Indeed, this agreement would become the linchpin of efforts to remove Indian people from the South as the nineteenth century progressed and would provide endless difficulties for the establishment of distinct boundaries between the southern states themselves for at least twenty-five years.

In the same year that the Georgia Compact was signed, U.S. commissioners led by notorious speculator James Wilkinson approached the Creeks to negotiate the Treaty of Fort Wilkinson. The agreement was primarily concerned with the cession of land between the Oconee and Ocmulgee rivers that Georgians had sought for decades. This valuable area, lying to the west of the main branch of the Oconee River as far as the Ocmulgee River and a mere thirty miles from the fledgling university in Athens, had been "solemnly guarantee[d]" to the Creeks by the U.S. government in the Treaty of New York. The Cusseta King, Little Prince, and Little Warrior, all Lower Creek leaders, noted as much in a talk to the Upper Creek headmen, warning them "wee are to be called to a meeting at Oconee." The Georgia commissioners, they cautioned, intended to "demand the land as far as the Ock-mulgee," but "at our last talk we ware told never any more demand for land should be asked of us from the white people of America."[44] So fervent was the desire for this "fine Land" that state leaders continued to press both the Creeks and the federal government to open them to legal white settlement.

By 1802, eager settlers had already been making steady incursions onto Oconee's western shores for at least a decade. The most infamous of these trespasses was Georgia state representative Elijah Clarke's attempt to estab-lish the "Trans-Oconee Republic," an independently governed and patently illegal settlement on the southwest bank of the Oconee River.[45] While Clarke claimed that he and his followers were unaware of the location of the bound-ary dictated in the Treaty of New York, the agreement had required that a line of trees "at least twenty feet wide" be felled for the entire distance of the line, "in order that the said boundary shall be rendered distinct."[46] Clarke's actions exposed the willingness of prominent southerners—not just back-woods banditti—to defy federal mandates against encroaching on Indian lands. The controversy eventually raised the ire of George Washington and his attorney general and set the stage for the Treaty of Fort Wilkinson.

Creek leaders opened the Fort Wilkinson meeting with an important display of symbols and actions that established the tone for the discussions to follow and emphasized the inviolability of their territorial rights. After the performance of a sacred eagletail dance, a red-painted bow and arrow were broken and buried as evidence of the abandonment of aggression. White-painted deerskins were placed on the ground atop the buried items and the Creek commissioners seated themselves thereon, inviting the U.S. commis-sioners to place their feet on the edge of the skins. Efau Haujo, acting as the Creek national speaker, began the proceedings by emphatically demarcating the meeting place as Creek space. He declared, "I am happy we meet in our own land under the shades of our own trees fanned with our own air with straight hearts. Some time since our father Washington left us and is buried the advice he gave us was food for us, we see it and know it. . . . When the old President Washington sent Commrs. to the Chiefs of the Creeks he said when that line was run it should be fixed and permanent. His successor following him gave us the same assurances and we shall take their advice."[47]

Efau Haujo not only stressed Creek ownership of the lands under discus-sion, but also invoked the traditional importance of "straightness" and "fix-ity" with respect to the diplomatic relationship between Creeks and Ameri-cans. In drawing on their common history and summoning the collective memory of George Washington, himself a surveyor, Efau Haujo reminded his guests that the Creeks had been repeatedly assured that once a line was run it was permanent and inviolable. Why, then, were the Americans again clamoring for more land beyond the "solemnly guaranteed" bounds?

Despite their skillful appropriation of U.S. political rhetoric and their repeated efforts to remind the Americans that these lands were guaranteed in perpetuity, the problems of massive Creek debts to the trading house at Fort Wilkinson, alleged thefts of slaves, horses, and livestock from American citizens, and the promise of an additional annuity ultimately convinced Creek leaders to cede a small swath of land along the western bank of the Oconee. But they steadfastly refused to relinquish lands all the way to the Ocmulgee, thus necessitating another artificial boundary of marked trees and posts between the two rivers and the two nations. And although the Creek delegates capitulated in this instance, Efau Haujo's statements are significant in that they demonstrate that southern Indians had distinct notions of bounded territory, despite still popular beliefs to the contrary. This was not a simple assimilation of imported definitions of property and territory.[48] For decades Creek peoples and their Indian neighbors had worked to define and maintain their territorial claims, even enlarging their limits from time to time by conquering and absorbing smaller societies. Their stories help us to understand one set of Creek ideas about territory. Their tendency to reference mental maps in diplomatic efforts explains another.[49]

In the early years of the Georgia colony, Yamacraw leader Tomo Chi Chi, along with Hylispilli, "his chief War Captain," expressed their "disgust" at Carolina settlers who had cleared and planted lands across the Ebenezer and Savannah rivers, contrary to both Georgia's and the Yamacraws' directives, demonstrating their understanding of not only their own territorial rights and limits, but those of the two competing colonies as well.[50] The tendency to describe and defend the territorial limits of Creek lands is an articulation of a nascent national identity and represents a significant political strategy for the Creeks. As their relationship with outsiders grew more intimate and also more threatening, Creek leaders began with increasing frequency to delimit their lands and their influence by referring to a bounded space and political body called the Creek Nation.

Tomo Chi Chi's successor, Malatchi, may have been the first leader to consistently represent the Creeks as a territorially defined entity known as the Creek Nation.[51] In part, this trend reflected the language of the newcomers who had begun to refer to something called the Creek Nation several years before Creeks themselves used the term. But by 1802, a level of national consciousness was sufficiently established to permit the language of the

Treaty of Fort Wilkinson to refer specifically to the claims of "the Creek Nation" and its "national" representatives, to which at least a part of the Creek leadership put their hand. Creek headmen most assiduously asserted their nationhood when attempting to defend their land, whereas American officials tended to overtly acknowledge the national character of the Creeks when acquiring land from them. And while most Creek individuals would probably not have referred to themselves as citizens of the Creek Nation, choosing instead to use family, clan, and town identifiers, when they reached a tree marked "CN" on one side and "US" on the other, their national identity mattered.

Southern Indians, in general, were also extraordinarily cognizant of the relationship of their boundaries with one another, although these were often reconsidered and adjusted under pressure from acquisitive neighbors. It is clear that they maintained independent knowledge of these boundaries and, at least for a time, enforced them according to their own usages. An example can be found in the talk of Tussekiah Micco to Hawkins in 1797, reporting his conference with their "younger brothers," the Chickasaws, with whom the Creeks had long fought.[52] Tussekiah Micco reported that he reached an agreement with Chickasaw leaders to respect the boundaries of their hunting grounds but not to exact revenge on errant hunters who may be found on the wrong side. Similarly, Yaholo Micco attended a meeting of the four nations held among the Cherokees in which they agreed to "hunt the game" and "be friendly to each other," rather than pursue vengeful tactics for encroachments on one another's hunting grounds. Such intertribal pacts, often sealed with white beads and repeated at all the sacred fires, underscore southern Indians' distinct notions of their own bounds and show how they attempted to maintain peace between themselves across such borders by emphasizing their relatedness and shared destinies. It was just such a belief in the importance of the boundaries that sparked a remark by a Chickasaw leader that "when the American people come you may go to them, and show your lines, they are a just people . . . they will respect them."[53] But knowing these intertribal boundaries and making them clear to outsiders were two different things.

Secretary of War Henry Dearborn recognized the opacity of intertribal territorial understandings. He observed to the Senate, "In cases of controversies between the Indians, respecting the divisional lines of their countries, it must always be difficult for us to interfere."[54] For his part, Hawkins believed that the Creeks were reluctant to delineate their boundaries with neighboring Indian nations because if they agreed to distinct borders, it would facilitate the cession of previously shared or ambiguously defined lands.[55] Creek leaders may have considered their Indian neighbors more willing than themselves to part with their lands and feared that disputed borderlands might end up in the hands of the Americans. Whether or not this perception was borne out in terms of actual acreage ceded by the different nations, the Creeks continued to maintain that they were the "elder brothers," or *lawa*, of the four nations and tried to influence the transactions they felt their "younger" siblings might enter.[56] What's more, as the putative head of the four nations, Creek leaders may have wished to preserve their ability to cede their neighbors' lands while protecting their own. Handing over a swath of Choctaw or Cherokee borderland would complicate relations within the four nations but it would be better than losing a parcel of Creek land to the Americans.

Despite beliefs in the importance of intertribal and interterritorial boundaries, this period is marked by continuous inconsistencies on the part of U.S. officials as to the reliability and legibility of lines marked on paper and lines marked on trees. Such contradictions are embodied in Hawkins's ritual insistence that Creek representatives attend the running of boundary lines and his simultaneous belief that "a line of marked trees cannot be a line of peace."[57] Hawkins was not alone in his equivocations. Secretary of War Dearborn was equally contradictory, telling the Creeks publicly that they must observe the survey lines separating them from the Americans but admitting to Hawkins privately that "a mere mathematical line in the woods between them [Creeks] and the white people can never prevent the cattle of both parties from ranging where they please."[58] Hawkins concurred and concluded that the problem of livestock crossing the lines would inevitably cause problems since Creek warriors would seize or kill the animals, inciting the reprisal of American stockowners.[59]

Perhaps the most revealing episode in these debates on the efficacy of natural and artificial borders came at the negotiation of the Treaty of Washington. In November 1805, a delegation of Creeks led by Tustunnuggee Hutkee, or William McIntosh, a Lower Creek leader who would later rise to controversial prominence, arrived in Washington to meet with President Jefferson and negotiate a new treaty. Jefferson initially addressed the party by reaffirming the Treaty of New York and paying special attention to his pet project, the civilization plan. But the lecture quickly turned to the matter of establishing a natural boundary between the state of Georgia and the Creek Nation. The U.S. president intoned, "When we treated at Fort Wilkinson, for the lands in the Fork of Oconee & Ocmulgee, we pushed to have obtained the whole lands from River to river; because neither your cattle nor ours regard a marked line—They trespass on both sides & this produces trespasses by men."[60]

Jefferson reasserted the need to agree on the Ocmulgee River as the "plain Boundary, a water path that our people could not trespass through ignorance." Of course, it was not ignorance that led Americans to encroach on Indian lands; it was the intentional search for livestock forage, escaped or stolen slaves, valuable timber, and farmlands. But Jefferson's logic suggests that the marks on the southern trees were somehow invisible or at least illegible to Georgia citizens, who, though many were illiterate, were by no means blind. In fact, despite their knowledge of Jefferson's duplicitous rhetoric, not all the Creeks were completely averse to a sale of this land—as long as they received a fair price for it. But according to the president, the price demanded was far too high. Jefferson complained, "Nothing like that price was ever before asked or given in any of the purchases we have ever made from your neighbours."[61]

On the following day, McIntosh replied to Jefferson regarding the Oconee Lands. He described the character of the Ocmulgee River which, like the Oconee, is shallow and shoally at places so that animals and their owners may fairly easily cross it. "Now," he asked, "how are stocks to be kept from going across the River, more than a marked line?" In addition, he demanded to know how the U.S. government intended to handle the constant confusion that might result from Indian and American livestock mixing back and forth along the ostensibly more permanent natural boundary. Years before, he reminded the delegation, when they had agreed to a river boundary, it did not prevent the "bad white people" from crossing it to forage their stock or to hunt.

The real sticking point, McIntosh made clear, was that the Creeks "now begin to know the value of land." He insisted that the Creeks would suffer financially from the loss of game on the land and that accepting such a low price would only worsen their situation.[62] The exchange made clear how flimsy Jefferson's argument was. The idea that the Creeks should cede valuable lands between the Oconee and Ocmulgee rivers—lands that Georgians had been clamoring over for nearly fifty years—simply to prevent trespasses over a supposedly more indelible natural barrier was absurd. It was an argument designed to coax the Creeks into accepting a smaller than reasonable payment for the cession. Nevertheless, the small Creek delegation under McIntosh, seduced by lucrative personal payments and promises of American patronage, ultimately agreed to the Ocmulgee as the boundary between

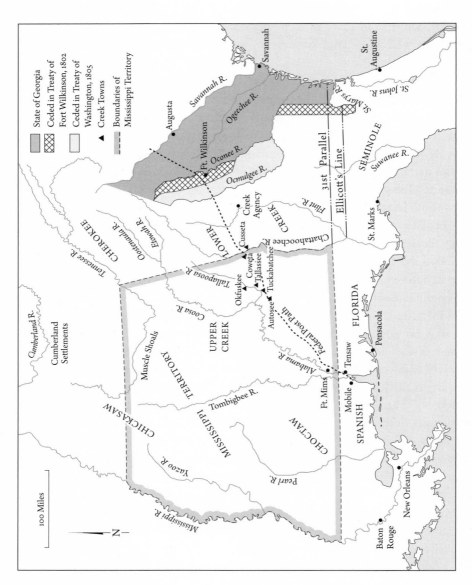

Map 2. The southern interior, 1805

the Creek Nation and the state of Georgia (see map 2). The Creek Nation would receive approximately $206,000, from which their debts to the U.S. factory and claims of Georgia citizens would be deducted.[63]

The impending resolution of claims against the Creeks did nothing to ameliorate the strife caused by American trespassers and their misdeeds in Creek country, however. Hawkins complained to Governor John Milledge that Georgians had been seen stealing cattle and gathering up strays from both sides of the line to sell.[64] Creeks living along the border knew that neither a line of marked trees *nor* an ancient waterway was likely to be a line of peace, despite agreements that claimed the contrary.[65]

Treaties in this era sought not only to establish the proper limits of U.S. and Indian territory, but also to recover any property that had made its way over the lines.[66] It was not just livestock that crossed the national boundaries at will. Since the mid-1780s, the numbers of African-descended slaves who ran away or were taken into the Creek Nation had increased dramatically, and it was fairly common for governors to grant passports to those individuals who wanted to enter Creek lands in search of fugitives.[67] In addition, some slave owners tried to employ one tribe to recover slaves from another.[68] Often, in desperation, owners published advertisements in local newspapers, indicating their suspicions that their slaves may have run away or been "taken off" into Creek country. These ads are significant for what they reveal about slave mobility, both physical and social, across the borders between the Creeks and Americans.

One runaway ad sought the return of Charlie, age twenty, Isaac, sixteen or seventeen, and Adam, fourteen, the last two having been "lately brought from the Creek Nation, and can speak their tongue; to which place it was expected they would attempt to get."[69] Efforts to recover fugitives often relied on descriptions of their bodies as evidence of their identities, and, by association, their owners' identities. In his complaint about an entire family of slaves that had run away to "the Nation," Georgia state representative Andrew Walthour noted that the family head, named Jack, has "his Country marks on his body . . . [and] marks of the whip."[70] In this way, the marked bodies of the slaves worked in tandem with the marked boundaries. The hatched trees were a sort of threshold at which property, including marked slaves and unmarked cattle, went from being legitimately owned to being contraband, even if that property had stolen itself.

Despite the frequent pronouncements about the power of boundaries in this period, it quickly became apparent that the new borders achieved their true significance primarily when they were breached. Like the mutual recognition of national limits, the establishment of the overland travel routes that crossed them was a mounting concern around 1800. And despite contentious political debates, in the early nineteenth century the federal government began to turn its attention to improving commerce and communication between the various states by providing important arteries along which the information vital to the nation's existence (and growth) would flow. Such thoroughfares were of paramount importance to Americans in the Early Republic, but concerns about "communication by land" were at least as old as the settlement of the southern colonies.

As early as 1735, Georgia founder James Oglethorpe had insisted that an expedition be launched to determine the best location for a proposed road between Savannah and the new town of Frederica.[71] The difference between early ad hoc endeavors to improve communication between settlements and the efforts of the federal government to secure stable routes after 1783 was that they had become national projects. It was imperative for the success of the fragile union that the disparate states be bound together in a vast communication network.[72] The northern and mid-Atlantic states were fairly well connected already. Both roads and maps depicting them were generally accessible, although neither was of very high quality. By contrast, much of the interior South remained unknown to literate Americans on the east coast, although by 1789 one could obtain a survey of the roads as far south as the Carolinas, complete with maps and landmarks, including bridges, churches, mills, taverns, blacksmith shops, and "negro pens."[73] Within a few years it was possible for travelers to find information about routes in Tennessee and toward New Orleans, though these were primarily water routes rather than established roadways.[74]

With the creation of the Mississippi Territory and the Yazoo disputes beginning to fade, a surge of American migrants began heading through Indian Country. They sought their fortunes in the area known to many as the "Southwest" or "Bigbee," a reference to the lands around the lower Tombigbee River.[75] A significant number of these travelers had originally moved from Virginia, the Carolinas, and Georgia to find, as one amateur poet put it, "All you tha want to purchase wit / here you may buy a plenty / & Let your purse be er'e so full / you soon may have it Emty."[76]

An assistant to Creek agent Benjamin Hawkins reported that at least 800 people passed through Creek lands during the winter of 1801–1802, "some with papers but generally they passed without any . . . [and] that the Indians were greatly displeased at and opposed to the traveling of families thro' their country."[77] Indeed, the number of applications for passports through the

Creek territory that appear in the papers of the Georgia governors from 1799 to 1803 are disproportionately small given these estimates of the actual number of travelers.[78] This may be owing to the fact that a greater and greater number of travelers sought passports from Hawkins himself instead of the governors. Hawkins reportedly issued upward of one hundred passports per month in 1802, compared to about six per month during 1798 and 1799.[79] In any case, more settlers and prospective settlers began to ply the Indian trails, with or without papers authorizing them to do so. Creek people seem to have been most distressed by the presence of families, especially those with slaves. This was not a manifestation of abstract racial prejudice nor was it a moral objection to slavery. Rather it was a clear recognition that these migrants were not mere travelers passing through; they meant to stay.

Efau Haujo told Hawkins that many families from Georgia had passed through the Creek Nation during the winter. Some had traveled what he called the "usual path," probably a reference to the old Lower Trading path, but more often they were being conducted along the less frequented trails, typically "under the guidance of half breeds, traders or Indians of bad or doubtful character."[80] Hawkins's assistant repeatedly observed that the Creeks were made uneasy by such large numbers of families traveling their trails.[81] While the Creeks understood the importance of mobility and were consummate travelers themselves, increased American travel through Creek land tended to preface renewed pressure for land cessions. Settlers seeking fresh lands often preempted both treaty cessions and surveys and settled themselves in opposition to both Creek territorial rights and federal mandates. As Efau Haujo put it, "The white people were . . . so impatient and eager in pursuit of it as to set down any where without obtaining the right of the Indians or that of their own government." Backcountry families, often seeking open range for their livestock, were especially likely to "set down" wherever they chose. Efau Haujo concluded, "I do not know what to think of such conduct."[82]

The headmen were also concerned with the increased presence of unauthorized travelers in the Nation because it increased the danger of crime for which the Creeks—as a nation—would undoubtedly be chastised. As discussed earlier, Indian debts and alleged thefts were the two most oft-raised issues in most of the treaty conventions that took place in the late eighteenth century, and though pressure for outright land cessions gradually eclipsed these issues, remuneration was still key. Creek leaders worried that when travelers crossed their lands, unruly young men, often suffering from severe debts to traders and increasingly unwilling to heed the warnings of their elders, were more and more inclined to steal horses, livestock, and slaves from the passersby.

Having only agreed to open certain paths to regular American travel, Creek headmen were openly distressed that families were being led along unauthorized routes where disastrous confrontations were more likely to occur. Efau Haujo articulated this very concern to Hawkins: "It was to be apprehended that the adherents to the mischiefmakers would robb and distress [the travelers]."[83] Such an episode took place in 1798 when Creeks robbed three families traveling from South Carolina to Mobile along the Lower Trading Path, taking their horses, clothing, and provisions, without otherwise harming them. The Chattahoochee town headmen agreed that the harassment was committed under the belief that the families' passports were irregular, if not fake, and reflected the widespread sentiment that they should "put a stop to white people traveling through their land."[84]

Stragglers heading through Creek country also increased the likelihood that Creek horses and other property would be similarly pilfered and carried into the Mississippi Territory, where recovery was more difficult. Secretary of War Dearborn acknowledged as much: "It is suggested, that the Indians will oppose our request for opening roads, for the two following reasons: that their cattle and horses will travel too far from home in such roads, and be driven away, and stolen by the white people, who may travel on said roads."[85] The difference, of course, was that thefts of American property were considered the collective action of the Creek Nation and would be met with punitive treaty measures designed to pay back the losses with cessions of Creek land. Conversely, thefts of Creek property by Americans were considered petty crimes committed by rogue actors, not representing the collective will of the United States.

The proposed solution to these problems was to establish a primary national route through the individual Indian nations. It would be a sort of neutral zone where authorized American citizens would be allowed to travel with the assurance of protection from molestation and the Indians could, presumably, seek redress for any depredations committed by Americans by appealing to their U.S. agent. Additionally, it was argued, those Indians living near the road could become legitimate entrepreneurs; men could earn income from the operation of ferries and taverns, while women could profit from providing foodstuffs and baskets to travelers. Opening these roads was deemed crucial to the secure conveyance of the U.S. mail from state to state and into the new territories. It was considered especially important to strengthen commercial links to the great southern port of New Orleans, much of which relied on control of the region's mails. But federal planners could not control the many uses that southerners—free and unfree, Indian and emigrant—would find for the roads.

After the Louisiana Purchase in 1803, Jefferson lobbied for the opening of a post path that would bisect the Creek Nation and connect the extant road from Washington, D.C., to Athens with a new section to be extended from Athens to New Orleans.[86] Jefferson's postmaster general, Gideon Granger, summarized the significance of the project: "As New Orleans will unquestionably be the place of deposit for the products of the Western World, its connection with the Atlantic Capitals must be incalculably great and important. The road to and from thence will become the great thoroughfare of the United States."[87] The acquisition of New Orleans was considered key to the growth of southern commerce, especially the burgeoning cotton trade; it was to be "the greatest entrepot for merchandize in the world."[88]

While planters were certainly interested in obtaining Indian lands in the lower South for their various agricultural endeavors, it was equally important to open reliable routes upon which the produce of these plantations could be taken to market.[89] As Jefferson explained to the Creeks in 1805, the former Spanish lands had passed to French hands and had now come into American possession. It was thus "indispensable" to have roads connecting the eastern and western American states and territories.[90] The trails across the Lower South that had long served as the arteries of the deerskin trade were now recast as highways of agrarian prosperity bringing Creek territory into the path of American mobility.

Since communication between the original states and the newly acquired territories was considered crucial, the establishment of regular postal routes through former French and Spanish holdings was especially important. One anonymous writer opined in the *Orleans Gazette for the Country*, "Certain it is, that in a country like ours, next to the blessings of the press, the advantages arising from the diffusion of information through the channel of the post-office, are to be most highly appreciated."[91] Citizens from every corner began to petition the local and federal officials to consider carefully the location of new post roads and a frontrunner quickly emerged.[92] Similar sentiments echoed throughout the pages of southern newspapers, which, like all newspapers of the era, depended on the regular delivery of the mail to obtain news to publish. Newspaper editors typically exchanged copies of their papers with editors in other states and most of them received publications like the *National Intelligencer*. They thus depended on being able to reprint national news and stories from other regions as well as the local news to fill their pages.[93] Reciprocally, readers of southern newspapers depended on them for information about the opening of post offices and the times and rates for mail pickup and delivery.

Mails were typically carried in leather portmanteaux on horseback and, in the more frequently traveled northern routes, in stagecoaches. Postmaster Granger noted that the postal service was the "channel of remittance for the commercial interest" of the United States and used this to impress upon his hirelings the care with which they should treat the contents of the mail.[94] Though post routes were relatively well established in New England and the Chesapeake regions, southern mails were in constant disarray.[95]

Post riders were expected to cover a certain number of miles per day, depending on the "nature of the ground," and were to protect the mail from theft and damage at all costs. Given what we know about the hazards of travel in the early South, protecting oneself from tumbling into a river or falling prey to bandits on the road was difficult enough. But protecting a heavy mailbag, which often contained cash and important documents, was particularly tricky. This was especially true in the late winter and spring months when high waters made river and stream crossings more treacherous. Post riders crossed on fallen trees (called "raccoon bridges") carrying the mail on their backs while swimming their horse(s) alongside.[96] Or, in the event that the waterway was too wide or too deep to ford, riders were expected to hire or otherwise procure a canoe or other craft with which to cross.[97] They were easily waylaid on the road by Indian criminals, Spanish and British spies, and petty thieves of every stripe.[98] In addition, whether attributable to the long lonely hours or the availability of alcohol along the way or both, a propensity for drunkenness was rife among southern post riders.[99]

As a result, the southern mail was notoriously unreliable. After three consecutive deliveries were delayed, one Georgia editor groaned, "The frequent disappointments, of this kind, and the length of time before we receive intelligence from the northward by the mail, very much lessens to the inhabitants of this state, the value, and advantages of this excellent establishment [the Post Office department]."[100] A few years later, the mails were still not much improved, leading Granger to observe that the frequent interruptions in the post service between Washington and New Orleans were not the result of the department's negligence, but a consequence of "the length of the way & the state of the Country."[101]

Another reason for establishing safe national routes through southern Indian lands arose from the continued intervention of Spanish officials at

Mobile and Pensacola.[102] Ephraim Kirby, a Superior Court judge assigned to the Mississippi Territory, reported to Postmaster Granger in 1804 that Spanish officials at Mobile had recently imposed duties as high as twelve and a half percent on American produce descending the Mobile River. He warned that such practices would have a detrimental effect on American settlement in the area.[103] While Kirby's ultimate desire was U.S. possession of Mobile and eventually Pensacola, the problem of locating alternate, if temporary, routes quickly came into view. In the absence of an open port at Mobile, planters in surrounding areas would necessarily have to transport their produce by land to New Orleans. To do so required stable, accessible land routes that passed through Creek country and on to New Orleans, with branches connecting to other regional routes. Not all farmers could be expected to live close enough to a navigable river to make it their only means of transporting their commodities to market. Thus, the emphasis on acquiring unfettered access to navigable waterways went hand in hand with the establishment of reliable land routes.

The commercial success of the region likewise depended in part on the success of the postal service. The mail was the means by which planters could be informed of market prices, receive communications from federal officials and distant family members, acquire seeds and instructions on agricultural techniques, and collect monies that might be put toward land titles or local merchandise necessary for the operation of their enterprises. Kirby grumbled about the lack of communication after his arduous journey to Fort Stoddert in the Mississippi Territory, telling Jefferson that the people of the lower Mississippi Territory were essentially cut off from all forms of communication with other sections of the country. In either direction (east or west) they had to travel through several hundred miles of "wilderness, possessed by Savages," to reach a commercial center.[104] He similarly complained to Granger that no mail from Washington had reached him and that as a result of its isolated location, cash money was virtually unknown in the Territory. This last was particularly problematic because the settlers would have difficulty finding enough money to pay for surveys and titles necessary to legally settle in the area.[105] Naturally, not all the newcomers were concerned with obtaining legal title to the lands, but Kirby, Granger, and Jefferson all knew the social and financial value of attracting law-abiding settlers.

Granger apparently concurred with Kirby's estimate of the situation and shortly after wrote, "It must hence become of the greatest importance to the Government and all the commercial towns of the U.S. that there be a road opened so as to render communication as speedy as possible."[106] He suggested that the contemplated road to New Orleans would best meet this need and that mail could very likely be conveyed at the rate of ninety miles per day.

The lack of communication across the Southwest Territory had always been an issue of national security as well, as Jefferson reminded the Congress in 1805. Because of Spanish aggression around the Gulf ports and in the recently transferred territories, he found it necessary to ready troops in those areas.[107] Naturally, troop readiness depended in part on their ability to move swiftly to the seat of the hostile activity. And with Spain controlling the ports of Mobile and Pensacola, water routes were practically out of the question.

Given the importance of accessible roads to and through the southern states and new territories, federal officials pushed for immediate conventions with the southern Indian nations in order to secure their permission and assistance for opening such routes. The primary route to be opened from the Tennessee settlements, often referred to as the Mero District, would come to be known as the Natchez Trace, and largely followed existing Indian trails that led across the Tennessee River, through Chickasaw and Choctaw land, and on to Natchez in present-day Mississippi. The path from Georgia to the Tombigbee River region would connect with an extant road from Washington, D.C., and follow a portion of the Lower Trading Path to the southwest through Creek country. When Secretary of War Dearborn sent James Wilkinson southward in 1801 to open roads through the Indian nations, he equipped him with a copy of his instructions and a map. In addition, Dearborn told him that if the commission was successful in obtaining the Indians' consent, he should waste no time putting troops to work opening the road.[108]

The Chickasaws were the first to acquiesce to the commissioners' requests to open a road to the Mississippi Territory with an 1801 treaty described as one of "reciprocal advantages and mutual convenience."[109] On the surface, the rhetoric of reciprocal advantage appears to have proved true. In exchange for permission to open the road and assistance in determining its proper course, the Chickasaws would receive exclusive ferriage rights at all water crossings, as well as $700 for the Chickasaw Mingo, or headman, and his deputies who attended the laying out of the road. Perhaps the Chickasaw leaders were more willing than their Indian neighbors to agree to the opening of the road because the request was not accompanied with a demand for cessions of land. In addition, they were permitted to defer the question of establishing "houses of entertainment," or places where travelers could bed and board, preferring to take the matter "home for further deliberation."[110]

But it is important to remember that the "advantages" promised to the Chickasaws were not equally enjoyed. Few but the most elite leaders, men like George Colbert and his brother Levi, reaped any of the publicized benefits.[111] In his assessment of the agreement, Dearborn confessed, "The Chickasaws . . . made no objection to our opening a road through their Country for a trifling consideration."[112]

In convening with the Cherokees, the commissioners were directed to obtain land between the Tennessee River and Duck River near the Cumberland settlements, as well as to secure the right to open a road from the Tennessee River to Natchez. Tennessee officials had long sought particular slips of land that separated their settlements from one another and prevented their unencumbered use of the Tennessee River. In 1798, for instance, Governor John Sevier instructed one of several failed treaty commissions to focus their attention on acquiring land where the Holston and Clinch rivers join with the Tennessee. A swath of Cherokee hunting ground nearly eighty miles wide separated the districts of Mero and Hamilton and was of particular concern to Sevier since it hampered commerce between the settlements. He summarized the significance of these proceedings in his concluding instructions, describing roads within and across Tennessee as important, convenient, and useful to "facilitate, and make easy as possible the importation and exportation of all the articles necessary for the commercial intercourse of the State."[113]

Nevertheless, obtaining Cherokee permission to open a road from the boundary line to the Tennessee River and to establish "two or three white families on said road" was so important that commissioners were advised to press the road question even if the desired land cessions were not granted. And if all of the proposed provisions should fail, the commissioners should still pressure them to cede all land lying northward of the road from Knoxville to Nashville or at least the land immediately adjacent to this road along its entire length.[114]

If the Cherokees agreed to the land cessions and/or the road provisions, they were to be paid $1,000 in "goods suitable for their use" in addition to their annuity. Secretary of War Dearborn was sensitive to the potential Cherokee reaction to these proposals and ultimately added an addendum to the instructions, desperately cautioning the commissioners, "You should not *press* [emphasis in original] on them any other subjects than those which relate to roads, and settlers thereon. You will impress upon them the belief the United States have no desire to purchase any of their land, unless they are quite willing to sell; that we are not in want of lands, but only wish to be accommodated with such roads as are necessary to keep up a communication with all parts of the United States, without trespassing on the lands of the red people."[115] Using equally revealing language, he told Cherokee agent Return J. Meigs that "we shall not consider the Cherokees good neighbours unless they will allow their best friends who are taking every means in their power to make them happy, to make a road at their own expense to pass through their Country from one settlement to another."[116] To all of these demands and entreaties, the Cherokees flatly refused.

The Choctaws initially rejected a road treaty until they could settle their boundaries with the Natchez district to the west and the Creeks to the east (a goal that would not be fully met until several years after the Creek War of 1813–1814).[117] The Choctaws had apparently made their boundary concerns clear to U.S. representatives in the past, since the instructions given to commissioners appointed to negotiate with them specifically cautioned them not to require the Choctaws to directly acknowledge an older cession of land that separated them from Natchez. Instead, they should endeavor to indirectly "draw from them an acknowledgement of its authenticity." Obtaining this oblique acknowledgment of the boundary between the Choctaws and the Natchez district was crucial to securing their consent to open a road through their lands to Natchez, along with permission to settle a handful of American families on the road to refresh and accommodate travelers and post riders.[118] After some deliberation, the Choctaw leadership signed the Treaty of Fort Adams in 1801 and agreed to a new road that would follow the far older Chickasaw Trace. The new path eventually formed the southern section of the Natchez Trace, a trail that became an important interregional travel route in the nineteenth century.[119]

The importance of intertribal diplomacy to the establishment of both boundaries and roads cannot be overestimated. For example, both the Cherokees and the Chickasaws claimed lands on either side of the Tennessee River for some distance. In their deliberations with the American commissioners, Chickasaw leaders insisted on their exclusive right to grant permission to pass through the lands sought from the Cherokees. The U.S. commissioners remarked to Dearborn, "It seems fortunate the Cherokees did not consent to open a road from Nashville to the Tennessee, because we find the proposed route embraced by the limits of the Chickasaws, which have been clearly defined in that quarter, and explicitly recognized in a declaration of President Washington."[120] Similarly, in advance of their journey to the national capital to negotiate the Treaty of Washington (1805), Creek headmen received a Cherokee delegation who reported on the Chickasaw claims north of the Tennessee River and warned the Creek National Council of the Chickasaws' intent to sell these disputed lands to the United States—an announcement that "produced serious agitation on the whole assembly."[121] Furthermore, before the 1805 road negotiations with the Creeks began, Hawkins read aloud a talk of the Choctaws in which they reiterated their specific land claims and told them to "take this claim into consideration, to make their minds up on it and to return a friendly answer."[122]

Despite concerns for the future of the four nations, in 1805 Creek and Cherokee leadership officially agreed to allow travelers to pass through their territories. The Cherokees ultimately agreed to American travel on two established roads. The first, known later as the Cherokee Federal Road, passed from the head of Stone's River toward the southern boundary of the Cherokee nation and connected with the road to the Creeks. The second passed from the neighborhood of Franklin, near the Tennessee–North Carolina border, to the west and crossed the Tennessee River at the Muscle Shoals. A few years earlier, they had reluctantly agreed to give up lands around the road that went from Knoxville to Savannah, arguably as important to interstate commerce as the two abovementioned roads.

A key issue at hand in both cases was the promise of the Cherokee headmen that their people would not molest travelers on the roads. The pledge was nearly impossible to uphold in a largely noncoercive society and seemed doomed to fail. The inevitable confrontations between Native peoples and American travelers in their midst would likely result in more pressure from neighboring states for land cessions as payment for alleged thefts or, worse, in bloody reprisals by local militias. But as with the other nations, the entrepreneurial interests of Cherokee leaders who hoped to establish taverns and ferries trumped most other concerns.[123]

For the Creeks, agreeing to the horse path that would later be known as the Creek Federal Road, or simply the Federal Road, was no less fraught. In the talks that preceded the Treaty of Washington (1805), McIntosh spoke at length on the prospect of opening a road through the Creek Nation, echoing the concern heard elsewhere that "it would be attended with bad consequences to our Nation, owing to the hostile acts that might be committed." Again linking the Creeks with their Indian neighbors, he pointed out that the four nations had already granted the Americans the right to navigate the Tennessee River, and the Chickasaw and Choctaw Nations had agreed to have roads built through territories. Thus the Creeks, who were approached last, argued that since their little brothers had agreed to such routes of access, there was not a pressing need for them to concede. Still, they were willing to allow their "friends and Brothers, the White people" to "pass daily through our land, on the little blind paths we have in our land," and agreed to provide them such goods and services as they might need on their journeys.[124]

Like the cession of the Ocmulgee Fork, however, the Creek delegation under McIntosh's leadership ultimately caved with the promise of considerable personal gain. Their concession came in Article Two, which stipulated that the United States would have the right to a "horse path" through Creek country from the Ocmulgee River to the Mobile River. The treaty provided for clearing the path and laying logs for bridges, as well as establishing of ferries and "houses of entertainment." The last two types of facility were to be the special property of Creek headmen. The exact course of the road was not specified, but regardless of its ultimate location, the treaty dictated that U.S. citizens should have the right to pass peaceably upon it "at all times."[125]

The Treaty of Washington purported to provide the Creeks with some of the same entrepreneurial opportunities that were held out to the Chickasaws in their 1801 road convention—the exclusive operation of ferries and the right to establish taverns and stands, for example. But Creeks were not allowed to set the prices for ferriage and "entertainment of men and horses." These were to be determined by their agent Hawkins alone. And as with the Chickasaws, the advertised commercial opportunities were not universally available to everyone in the Creek Nation. In fact, the concessions made by the Creek delegation, including both the Ocmulgee boundary *and* the opening of the Federal Road, mark a serious fracture in Creek national politics.

William McIntosh had gone to Washington because the Creek national speaker refused to go. Speaker Hopoie Micco, already in trouble for his part in the Treaty of Fort Wilkinson, declined to attend, telling Hawkins that he would be blamed by the warriors for any concessions that might be made.[126] Despite his speech to the contrary, McIntosh and his supporters saw the opening of the road as a prospect for financial success and individual prosperity. Indeed, as Hawkins noted, "The possession of the stages was a principal inducement on the part of the Chiefs to permit the free use of a path thro' their country."[127] McIntosh's filibuster may have been a strategy to secure such advantages for himself and his supporters before finally signing the document.[128] But the average Creek person probably looked on the development with skepticism, if not fear.

Just as the presence of surveyors was often a harbinger of smaller hunting grounds, the increased presence of American travelers—fed and ferried by their own headmen—was a sign of bad things to come. In fact, McIntosh and the Long Lieutenant, another signer of the Treaty of Washington, were removed from office or "broken" by the Creek National Council in late 1807 as a result of their acquiescence to the road.[129] American leaders may not have realized the deleterious effects the road would have on internal Creek politics, but they optimistically connected the new roads to the demise of the southeastern Indian presence nonetheless. When Jefferson mentioned the contemplated Federal Road to New Orleans in a letter to Georgia governor John Milledge in 1802, he continued immediately by claiming, "The acquisition of Louisiana will it is agreed must put in our power the means of inducing all the Indians on this side to transplant themselves to the other side of the Mississippi before many years get about."[130]

Like the boundary lines that had been scored on the timber in the preceding years, the route of the new path would also be blazed on the trees alongside it. The increasing presence of Americans traveling and settling along the road would likewise signal the permanence of the project. Granger reported on his efforts to put the mail from Athens to Coweta in order and specifically on his desire to obtain Creek consent for allowing some "good steady persons to move into Indian Country & make establishments, at the more important Streams, where flats will be kept."[131] This move signaled a shift away from the original intent of the Treaty of Washington, which stipulated that the handful of Creek headmen who signed the treaty would be the ones to operate stands on the road. The presence of these American establishments along the road would serve as a sign of the official nature of this route. Though it was carved into the landscape of Creek country, it would in fact be an American path.

Whereas in the eighteenth century, Creeks had sought to keep the path between themselves and the Americans "white and straight," it is clear that they never intended it to be a path for white Americans straight into the heart of their country. The confusion and strife wrought by the Treaty of Washington meant that the Creek majority now had to manage new boundaries *and* a new road. Negotiating American access and contesting the meanings of both territory and mobility would become the exemplary concerns of a changing Creek country over the next decade.

Chapter Three

OPENING ROADS THROUGH

CREEK COUNTRY

In the opening months of 1806, the Creek delegation returned from Washington to the fields and forests of their homelands during the height of the deer-hunting season. In their absence, many Creek men and women had proceeded with their winter tasks, largely unacquainted with the profound changes proposed in the Treaty of Washington. Ranging farther to find enough game, Creek hunters were more and more likely to encounter Americans in their territory. Over the preceding decade, travel into and through the Creek Nation had increased at a relatively stable pace as Americans made their way across traces and paths, much as they were doing in Tennessee and Kentucky where the roads were reportedly "full of families."[1] Some traveled along predetermined routes, while others simply "found trale followed it."[2]

The Mississippi Territory, which lay to the west of Creek country, was a particular draw for settlers from Georgia, Tennessee, and the Carolinas as cotton fever trumped fears of yellow fever and the widely bemoaned "insalubrity of the climes."[3] Hawkins noted of his Georgia environs, "Our neighbours in this quarter are turning their eyes westward, Louisiana seems to be in the estimation of some the New Jerusalem."[4] Such travel was not uniformly American—nor was it entirely unchecked. The difficulties of travel on overland routes and the conflicts between travelers and the Creek people whose land they traversed had provided some of the impetus for the Treaty of Washington. But the decisions codified in that document would take many years to implement, if they were implemented at all. In the meantime, the reality on the ground was far messier than the tidy treaty agreement conveyed.

Although they had ceded parcels of land on their eastern boundary to the United States in the Treaties of Fort Wilkinson (1802) and Washington (1805), Creek country was still comparatively large, comprising several thousand square miles. And travel within and across the Creek Nation was still vital for Creek people. The web of paths and trails that crisscrossed Creek homelands provided crucial links between talwas and talofas and connected families and clans in a vast network of kinship and commerce. While some Creek men and women had converted to a system of staple crop cultivation and domestic production of cloth and other products, many still pursued the dwindling game through the winter months and relied on older food-gathering techniques. Hunting, in particular, required the Creeks to routinely traverse large parcels of land on an annual basis.

It is not coincidental that Jefferson's civilization plan, endorsed so vigorously by Hawkins in Creek country, encouraged the Creeks to be more sedentary and less mobile—consequently needing less land to support themselves. In fact, Jefferson expressed as much in an 1805 talk, telling the Creeks, "A little land cultivated in corn & cotton will go further in providing sustenance and clothing for your people, than the most extensive range of Country can furnish by hunting."[5] Of course, Creeks and their southeastern Indian neighbors had been raising corn and other crops for generations. But the civilization plan also required a commitment to individually owned fields, rather than communal ones, and the adoption of iron farming implements that Jefferson urged them to buy using funds from the sale of "waste and useless lands."[6]

Some of these transformations had already begun in Creek country. But many Creek men and women still followed the seasonal schedule of travel in search of deer, bear, turkeys, and other game, leaving their towns nearly empty for much of the winter. These hunting parties primarily followed the trails that had been carved into the landscape over many generations and had only recently become thoroughfares for interstate or interterritorial travel. As the scarcity of game became more acute in the later years of the eighteenth century, however, Creek hunters had to travel further and further from their traditional hunting lands in order to procure enough meat and skins to both pay their debts to the trading houses and survive the winter. And the scarcity of game meant that many would not survive.[7] The further they traveled, the greater the likelihood that they would run into Americans who had crossed state borders in their own quest for prosperity. As the Creek Nation's land was circumscribed by the surrounding states, Creek people likewise experienced a constriction of their individual mobility.

Concurrently, in the years leading up to the Treaty of Washington, American mobility in Creek country increased, though not without distinct challenges. It is certain that most of the hardships these travelers endured were a consequence of their unfamiliarity with the terrain and the appropriate season in which to travel, rather than violent encounters with Native people. But in either case, few if any of these early travelers remembered their paths as easy or pleasant. They characterized the journey as "tedious" and filled with "perils . . . sufferings . . . [and] escapes."[8] One emigrant lamented, "The traveller must be a considerable time in the woods and compelled to swim unfordable streams."[9] Isaac Briggs, a U.S. surveyor charged with scouting a portion of the new federal post path, admitted that he had severely underestimated the difficulties and dangers he would face in his travels across the region. He complained of scaling bluffs, wandering in swamps, and losing nearly all his provisions.[10] Some emigrants were reported to have returned to their homes, "almost naked and perfectly Indianised" after their travails in the wilderness.[11] Despite the fact that most travelers had more to fear from the terrain and the weather, passport applications from this period tend to emphasize the concern for Indian attack on the overland journey, seeking official authority to "pass and repass unmolested."[12] It was beyond the governor's power to command the land and weather to behave, but perhaps a proper pass would protect travelers from harassment.

Like many unfortunate travelers to come, Matthew Phelps took an overland route to the Mississippi Territory and lost his wife and two children, the latter drowning during a hazardous river crossing. But not all the beleaguered travelers were heading west. Phelps recounted meeting other groups, including one "desperate" company that was trying to make its way east, "determined to explore their way, if possible, to Georgia, through wilds of hedious length, and dangerous passage . . . during the course of which almost all their women, children, and negroes died."[13] Indeed, the journey was considered so arduous in these early years that the presence of American women and children on the trails was somewhat uncommon. Other than Creeks themselves, single white men were the most frequent voyagers on the paths that led through the Creek Nation.[14]

For most travelers, the theft of provisions and property was a constant worry. Americans often remarked on the unpredictability of the Indians whose lands they traversed, finding that they would sometimes "plunder" them of horses and supplies and sometimes hospitably furnish them with food and shelter. Hawkins warned one surveying expedition that they "must travel light with as little baggage as possible that in case you are dismounted by a thieving party you will not be inconvenienced with baggage."[15] Some groups found themselves divested of their horses and whatever provisions the Indians could easily carry off. Occasionally they also lost companions. Some of these captives, both white and black, were rather easily recovered, but many others were not. In 1805, one claimant was still seeking restitution for the loss of his slaves to Indian raiders on the Tennessee River some ten years earlier.[16] Another slave owner spent almost thirty years trying to recover his slaves and "their increase" from Creeks.[17]

Conversely, southern Indians were widely known for their hospitality. Explorer and naturalist Bernard Romans remarked in the 1770s that a southern Indian "will share his last ounce of meat with a visitant stranger."[18] Lower Creek leader William McIntosh had declared that when travelers came to Creek towns or villages, they could expect that "we will do all we can to accommodate" them.[19] A French traveler similarly explained that upon arriving in the nation and being invited to smoke, "they ask from you the cause of your coming, and the time you spent on the road; what stay you intend to make among them, whether you have a wife and children."[20]

While the issue of a traveler's family is connected to Creek concepts of kinship, through which an individual's identity and position in the social order are determined, it was not a mere formality exchanged upon welcome. It was, in fact, a primary concern for the Creeks. As noted in chapter 2, Creek leaders were particularly opposed to the appearance of families on the paths through their homelands.[21] U.S. agents observed, "The General Idea in this quarter (which is authorized by the conduct of the Indians) is that they are averse only to families, or numerous parties passing with their property. Single passengers, or persons travelling without Effects, meet with no hindrance."[22] This policy may in part account for the disproportionate number of passports issued to single men in this era. Such passports typically contained a clause permitting them "to go into *and return from* the Creek Nation" (emphasis added) (see figure 1). Creek people recognized the difference between families who intended to settle somewhere in or near the nation and individual travelers heading west and usually back east again, often on business.

Travelers who made visits to the Tombigbee River region, to Natchez, or to New Orleans often did so to check up on family enterprises in those areas. These individuals were generally unimpeded in their journeys, provided they offered no interference in Creek affairs and minded the paths. Many of these lone travelers were also fortunate enough to procure Indian guides, whom men in the know thought indispensable. In fact, when Briggs pre-

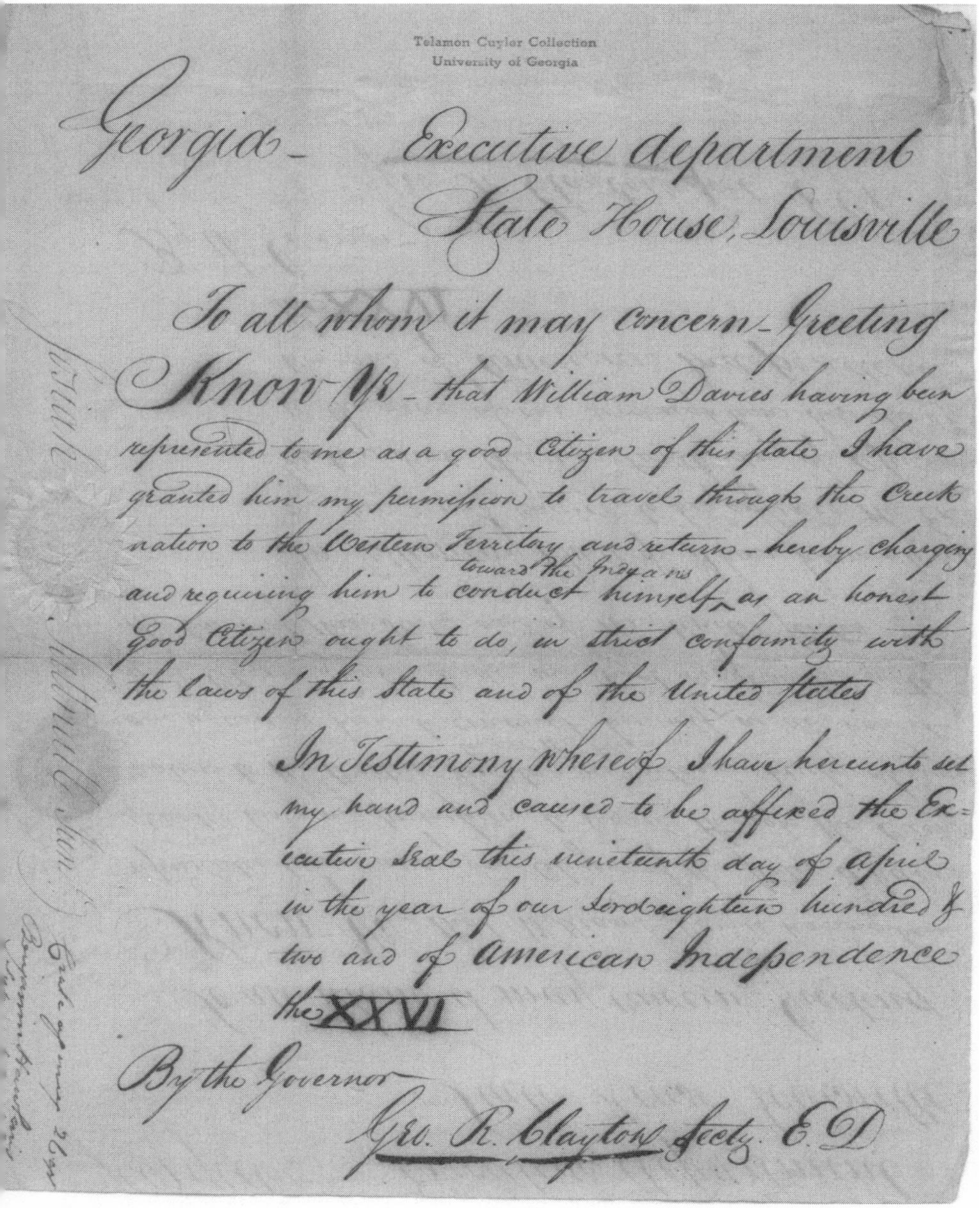

Telamon Cuyler Collection
University of Georgia

Georgia — Executive department
State House, Louisville

To all whom it may concern — Greeting

Know Ye — that William Davies having been represented to me as a good Citizen of this state I have granted him my permission to travel through the Creek nation to the Western Territory and return — hereby charging and requiring him to conduct himself toward the Indians as an honest Good Citizen ought to do, in strict conformity with the laws of this State and of the United States

In Testimony whereof I have hereunto set my hand and caused to be affixed the Executive Seal this nineteenth day of April in the year of our Lord eighteen hundred & two and of American Independence the XXVI

By the Governor

Geo. R. Clayton Secty. E.D.

Figure 1. A passport issued to William Davies by Georgia governor Josiah Tatnall in 1802 and endorsed by Benjamin Hawkins. The passport indicates that Davies, "having been represented" as a "good citizen," was granted permission to "travel through the Creek nation to the Western Territory and return" *(emphasis added). (Courtesy of Hargrett Rare Book and Manuscript Library, University of Georgia, Athens.)*

pared to set off to the west "without a path or a guide," the idea was "scouted and laughed at" in Georgia.[23] Thus, the vast majority of passports issued by the governors of Georgia in the opening years of the nineteenth century were for one or perhaps two men, typically in the company of one or at most two slaves.[24] Creek aversion to large traveling parties may help to explain why more families than single men found themselves in a "distressed situation," without horses, provisions, or guides.[25]

The primary enterprise of this era—the one that inspired the most authorized and unauthorized American travel—was cotton. While large numbers of travelers did return to the east, it was often to report their reconnaissance of available lands and cotton prices in the west. In some cases, they brought slaves and left them at western plantations in order to build infrastructure and clear fields, intending at a future date to bring more. John Cumins, who had only recently set up shop near the Chickasaw Nation, reported to his family back in Pennsylvania that he would never "leave this Country entirely, it is one of the finest in the world"; a farmer, he declared, needs only "4 or 5 Negroes" to make a good living off the land.[26] Eventually, once a plantation was deemed secure and solvent, these men would again make their way along the same trails with their families, including wives, children, and, most likely, more slaves.

As the first decade of the nineteenth century unfolded, passports began to reflect a marked change in the makeup of traveling parties. More and more of the passport applications requested permission to pass through the Creek Nation "with family," some of which were quite large. For instance, when Maurice Ronie set out for the Mississippi Territory, his party included his family, "ten in number, [and] Robert Hill and six negroes, Samuel Harvill and one negroe, and Morgan Clower."[27] Such a throng of travelers was sure to attract attention in the nation; its sheer size and composition betrayed its intended purpose and proposed permanence in or near Creek country. Even the presence of a single wagon could provoke serious concern among the Creeks, since it signaled the transportation of greater numbers of people. A broad wagon road was much more problematic than a simple horse path, only wide enough for a solitary traveler.[28]

At the same time, another demographic shift was taking place along Creek country paths. While enslaved people of African descent were increasingly seen along the trails in the company of American families, their relative mobility as individuals in this period is also notable. Since the founding of the Georgia colony, there had been prohibitions on traders taking slaves into Creek country, but these laws were difficult to enforce.[29] As some Creeks increasingly adopted chattel slavery, Africans and African Americans might be seen in larger numbers than ever before by travelers passing through. Frequently, these Creek-owned slaves were afforded considerable latitude in their daily tasks and were often known to travel great distances within the nation.[30]

The necessity of having slaves perform various long-distance tasks for American owners in the lower South was also undeniable, despite concerns over uprisings like the rebellions in Stono (1739) and St. Domingue (1791).[31] Timothy Barnard, trader and de facto agent among the Lower Creeks, employed at least one "negroe express" who conducted all sorts of business on his behalf, but was particularly involved in conveying messages between Creek towns and local officials.[32] He was but one of many southerners who found that the necessity of permitting slave travel usually outweighed the risks of escape or rebellion. Thus, enslaved Africans and African Americans could be found traveling in larger numbers than one might expect along the roads and trails of the lower South, including those inside the Creek Nation.[33]

In addition, though they were few, some free blacks also traveled Creek country roads in the early nineteenth century. One such individual, Moses Keating, intended to travel from Louisville, Georgia, to Natchez with a horse belonging to his employer, and, not unlike his white American counterparts, he sought a passport for his "safe and unintersecpted [sic] passage."[34] Some free black individuals also sought employment in the backcountry as boatmen, timber cutters, and cowboys. Thus, African and African American people moved through Creek territory not only as physical capital forced to migrate toward the westward cotton boom, but also as travelers with a modicum of personal freedom and individual mobility.[35]

Despite the necessity of travel by slaves and free blacks in the region, white American anxieties regarding African American mobility—as well as Indian mobility—began to surface in official channels. In discussing the regulations of the Post Office Department, Postmaster Gideon Granger made his views unmistakably clear to James Jackson, chairman of the Senate Committee on the Post Office. His message was revealing: "An objection exists against employing negroes or people of color in transporting the public mails. . . . Every thing which tends to increase their knowledge of natural rights, of men & things or affords them an opportunity of associating, acquiring, & communicating sentiments & of establishing a chain or line of intelligence must increase your hazard. . . . By travelling from day to day & hourly mixing with people they must, they will acquire information. They will learn that a man[']s rights do not depend on his color."[36] Granger's communication to Jackson indubitably linked the mobility of "people of color" with their potential freedom, both intellectually and physically. His cautionary words show the degree to which the roads and paths of the South in particular were considered information highways that connected geographically separate groups of people and had the potential to provide marginalized populations with a conduit for cooperation and resistance.

While these thoroughfares were considered vital to the U.S. government and its commerce, they represented a potential threat to the system of control that sought to keep people of color ignorant of the world around them. Roads like the federal post path functioned not only as official links connecting capitol to capitol (and capital to capital), but also as informal channels in which information and individuals might collide and collude. Such dissident possibilities were particularly plausible when the paths wound their way through Creek country.

While travelers of every description made their way in, around, and through the southern borderlands in the early nineteenth century, the federal government pushed forward with its efforts to regularize and regulate travel through the states and territories. The first great road project was the Cumberland Road, which, unlike the pioneer-blazed Wilderness Road, was a federal scheme undertaken after the formation of the Northwest Territory.[37] Although plans for the road emerged as early as the 1790s, little actual work was done on the route until after 1805.[38] By that point, the importance of the project had come fully into view. An appropriations recommendation for the project expressed the strong sentiment that connecting the Atlantic capitals in the east to the new territorial centers in the west was essential for the successful expansion of the nation.[39] Like many committees seeking financial support, this one waxed poetic in its appeal: "To make the crooked ways straight, and the rough ways smooth, will, in effect remove the intervening mountains, and, by facilitating the intercourse of our Western brethren with those on the Atlantic, substantially unite them in interest."[40] As advocates of internal improvement in both the Northwest and Southwest Territories soon discovered, however, straightening and smoothing the westward ways was inherently more difficult than imagined.

Even before these new federal plans could take effect and before the Treaty of Washington was negotiated, Benjamin Hawkins had been charged with the task of preparing and overseeing a modest mail service that would connect Georgia to Fort Stoddert.[41] As with many of the duties Hawkins had undertaken in the Creek Nation, this was no mean chore. Nearly every such effort required repeated assurances that the government did not intend to take the Indians' lands. In 1803, he had observed, "The Indians knew long before I came among them that the land on which they lived was theirs," and "it is not a road that they are afraid of as being asked for land."[42] Indeed, while Creek delegations begrudgingly agreed to allow the U.S. mail to pass through their lands, they rightly suspected that the Americans would soon ask for more.

In 1805, the Cherokees had also been informed that the mail would soon begin running through their lands. Once the post path had been improved, they were told, "[It] will bring money into the Country & we & you will then hear the news every week from Washington City & from the City of New Orleans."[43] The attractiveness of this proposition for the Cherokees, or the Creeks, is hard to gauge, but it became clear from daily acts of resistance that open communication between Washington and New Orleans was not as important to them as the preservation of their homelands. And Indian recalcitrance was not the only challenge to opening the postal routes. The difficult physical work involved in clearing the path, the potential for fraud or miscarriage in the post service, and the general incompetence of those contracted to open the roads and carry the mail all contributed to a rather haphazard effort to make the "crooked ways straight."[44]

After the Treaty of Washington, Postmaster Granger made his first attempt to establish regular postal service across the Creek Nation. He hired Virginian Francis Abraham to carry the mail from the prominent Lower Creek town of Coweta to New Orleans, directed him to cover the route in six and a half days, and agreed to pay $10 a mile. The fact that Granger did not provide Abraham with specific instructions on exactly how and when to proceed indicates that either Abraham was intimately familiar with the appropriate route or Granger was woefully ignorant of it. In either case, it is unclear if Abraham ever transported a single article of mail under this contract since no further mention of him or his service appears in the Post Office department.

By early 1806, Granger had become a bit more realistic about the challenges facing the project. His testimony to Congress indicated, "The path has never been cleared and is greatly obstructed by fallen trees. There are also twenty one creeks to be passed which are too deep to ride in time of freshes."[45] While the portion of the path between Georgia and Coweta followed the old Lower Trading route and was fairly well established, the southwestern portion proved daunting. Granger noted that causewaying would be required and the necessary timber would need to be taken from the adjacent woods. He recommended that five-foot logs be placed across the path where the ground was soft, making a crude corduroy road.

The mail was to run southwestwardly from the high shoals of the Apalachee River near Athens, through or near Coweta, along the southeastern edge of the Alabama River and on to Fort Stoddert, where the Alabama and Tombigbee rivers combined to form the Mobile River. According to the Treaty of Washington, this was to be a "horse path," four to six feet wide only—suitable for the conveyance of the mail by a single rider.[46] The post was to pass through Creek country at the rate of 120 miles every twenty-four hours, and Congress appropriated $6,400 for this purpose.[47]

Opening the route through a "country generally covered with a thick growth of timber" required a substantial amount of ax work, some of which was to be completed by soldiers from local garrisons.[48] Not only did the road itself have to be cleared but, as noted above, logs had to be cut for causewaying and for building bridges. The Treaty of Washington mentioned the need for "laying logs over creeks" but had made no provision for collecting the amount of timber that frequent causewaying and large-scale bridge building would require. While the road was under U.S. control, the timber still belonged to the Creeks, which would prove to be a thorny issue in the coming years.[49]

For work within the Creek Nation, Hawkins hoped to organize Indian laborers to assist the contractor. But, as he communicated to Jefferson, many in Creek country still sorely opposed the sale of the Ocmulgee lands and the entire road agreement. Hawkins reported that the "chiefs are yet divided, proud and jealous, full of intrigue. . . . The young men not yet accommodated to the sale of the Ocmulgee."[50] Understandably, his initial requests for Indian men to work on the road were not met with enthusiasm.

Another significant obstacle in opening the path was the issue of American settlers along the road. According to the Treaty of Washington, regular stands were to be established at which the post riders could refresh themselves and exchange their exhausted horses for fresh ones. Hawkins complained that the Creek headmen were not at all willing to permit white Americans to settle along the road.[51] And why should they have been? According to the treaty, the stands (as well as the ferries) were to be operated by Creek people, with the prices to be regulated by Hawkins or his successor, and the revenues collected by the Creeks. The issue of white Americans owning and operating taverns, stands, and ferries along the roads had been a sticking point in negotiations with all four southern Indian nations and would not be so easily overcome.

In addition to who might be allowed to settle on the road, the question of who would actually carry the mail was also a matter of concern. In September 1806 Hawkins reported, "Our present riders from Coweta [to Fort Stoddert] are half breeds, they are faithful and I have directed such to be employed in all things wherein they can be useful to us and this is necessary in the present stage of the business to the security of the mail as well as to settlers."[52] The implication was that, at least initially, post riders of Creek lineage were more acceptable to the Creeks and more likely to pass unmolested. Interestingly, this arrangement of the post directly contradicted the instructions Postmaster Granger had given to James Jackson that no "people of color" be employed in transporting the public mail.[53] But as Hawkins suggested, the realities on the ground were more delicate than Granger perhaps understood.

Although Hawkins was initially charged with opening the road, illness prevented him from carrying it out. In 1806, the responsibility passed to Joseph Wheaton, who was to oversee the route from Washington to Coweta, and Samuel Bloomfield, who would handle the route from Coweta to Fort Stoddert where the post would then be conveyed to New Orleans by water (assuming free passage could be arranged with Spanish officials at the port of Mobile).[54] Wheaton and Bloomfield were each responsible for clearing their portion of the path and contracting with post riders to actually carry the mail. They were also responsible for overseeing the various stands at which post riders could change horses and pick up additional mails brought along various cross-paths, like the one McIntosh opened and maintained between the Upper and Lower Creek towns.[55]

Soon after establishing the contracts, however, Granger lamented to Jefferson that while Wheaton could cover over one hundred miles per day, Bloomfield proposed to travel a mere twenty-three miles per day.[56] His dissatisfaction with Bloomfield's arrangements again conveyed his ignorance of the local situation. Wheaton had the advantage of an established road since his route roughly coincided with the Lower Trading path. Bloomfield was at a distinct disadvantage with the swampy route west of the Chattahoochee River. By this time, however, Granger had become nearly frantic in his efforts to have the path made passable. He confessed to Jefferson, "I cannot help entertaining a fear that the necessary operations of the road will not be made, and the necessary establishment of riders furnished so as to ensure a regular line in the manner contemplated."[57] Granger proposed contracting with Wheaton for the whole route, to be completed in just three months.

With this new arrangement established, the question of the federal post path seemed near resolution. But Wheaton's work was distinctly mismanaged. In addition to his failure to complete the road promptly and under budget, Wheaton perturbed the Creeks by stationing white Americans at the stages along the road, starting with the still controversial Ocmulgee lands. Wheaton either misunderstood or willfully ignored the 1805 treaty stipulations. He had even given unauthorized talks in the council square in Coweta, speaking in the name of the president.[58]

As Wheaton passed near Coweta, he met with McIntosh to discuss his plans. McIntosh reiterated that the stages were to be kept by Indians or "half breeds," and went so far as to rearrange his settlements so the path would strike them directly as it passed through the Creek Nation. Wheaton noted that McIntosh, Long Lieutenant, and others with whom he met "seemed anxious that it should be brought by McIntosh's house, & about one miles above the town."[59] Perhaps not recognizing that this privilege was, in fact, guaranteed by the treaty, he surmised that the request was designed to "disappoint" Marshall, a white man who lived lower on the Chattahoochee and had offered his house as the "place of refreshment."[60] Disregarding both policy and diplomacy, Wheaton determined that the lower route by Marshall's was the only passable one and that the route suggested by McIntosh was simply too swampy to be traversed. In addition to these blunders, Wheaton had entirely mislaid one portion of the route, in part because he felt unduly confident in his ability to proceed without local Indian guides. When David Meriwether took over the contract in 1807, Hawkins instructed him to abandon Wheaton's route and instead follow the path marked out by another contractor who had been assisted by two Creek representatives.[61]

The Cherokees were similarly divested of rights guaranteed in their road agreement when Americans opened ferries, or flats, along the road from Georgia through the Cherokee Nation and into Tennessee. As with the Creek treaty, the Cherokees had been guaranteed exclusive ferriage rights, and, like the Creeks, they were incensed to discover American entrepreneurs siphoning profits away from their nation. In late 1806, The Glass, prominent Chickamauga leader, spoke on behalf of Cherokee headmen in a complaint to their agent, Return J. Meigs: "What is the reson that Robber king [Robert King] will Cross travelers By forse you will Consedder the Bennefit of the Cherokees and Stop Robart kings [Robert King's] flat Landing if there is aney Bennefit to be got we out [ought] to have it of our one [own] Land."[62] The appearance of Americans at such places, seemingly intent on usurping the Indians' admittedly limited but nonetheless guaranteed rights, further heightened Creek and Cherokee suspicions. As with the establishment of "harmless" boundary lines, many southern Indians viewed the opening of these roads and businesses as ill omens.

In June 1807, Granger wrote to the judge and postmaster at Fort Stoddert, entreating him to "make every effort to quiet the Indians and to prevent a Stoppage of the Mail," suggesting that some Creeks had begun actively and aggressively resisting travel on the road.[63] Some Cherokees were apparently frustrated enough with the increased travel through their country that they occasionally greeted Americans on the path with rude treatment or worse.[64] At a meeting of the four southern Indian nations, the Creeks made their concerns known to Hawkins and the assembled delegations. Again they protested efforts to station Americans along the road. But this time, they went further in their objections: "There was a deliberate plan in operation on the part of the United States to get possession of their country, and they could now see their path with stages was cutting them in two."[65] Creek leaders were not necessarily averse to the running of a simple post service through their nation, but the sustained presence of travelers, especially families, and American-owned stands to supply them, was unconscionable.

Having white Americans settled along the road, with little or no oversight by the Upper or Lower headmen and no obligation to Creek clan or kin networks, was a threat to Creek security. Who would manage these people? If disputes arose between them and neighboring talwas, how would they be settled? Why should they profit from what were supposed to be Creek-owned and -operated enterprises?

The concerns of Creek leaders regarding the settlement of these white entrepreneurs may have also been connected to other hardships in the nation during the year. Hawkins reported to Dearborn that the 1807 Creek corn crop was exceptionally meager and that it had been "emphatically named the *hungry year*."[66] A severe drought had gripped the nation since 1804 and repeated crop failures had depleted public granaries, making subsistence for Creek families difficult enough without the intrusion of strangers and their stock.[67]

In late 1807, Little Prince, who had replaced McIntosh on the National Council, delivered a speech in which he offered some compromises on the issue of ferries (or flats) in an effort to resolve the confusion and avoid a crisis. Although the ferries were originally to be held by Indians, it was now agreed that the flat on the Ocmulgee River would be operated by an American, "on the white side," provided that all the profits would be "equally divided between the whites and Indians." At Flint River, the flat was to be owned and operated by an Indian with all the profits "belonging to the

Indians" and with "none to pass ferriage free but the post riders or people on public business."[68]

The sticking point, however, was still the issue of American-owned stands, or stages, in the heart of Creek country. The headmen would not agree to it. Their primary objection was that such places would increase the likelihood of horse theft within the nation, which would have wide-ranging repercussions. As has been discussed, if a Creek person stole property from an American and the property was not recovered, the theft could become part of the Creek national debt, added to a long list of claims against them and increasing pressure for another treaty and another cession of land. More urgently, Americans could be expected to retaliate with thefts or violence of their own. In either case, the Creek leadership knew that allowing the stands would probably beget further conflicts.

The problem of the post road and how it was to be used continued to plague Creek leadership over the next few years. At the end of 1809, the Creek headmen had explained to Hawkins that "they were greatly embarrassed at the repeated misunderstanding of the treaty stipulation relative to a post path thro' their land by every man who came from the Government and had any thing to do with the path or transportation of the mail. That the last had come on with his waggon and commenced building bridges contrary to what they understood their treaty stipulation with the President to be. It is not to be a road but a path with logs over the creeks."[69] It seemed that only the Creeks had any memory of what the controversial Treaty of Washington had actually established. The presence of a wagon signaled a more expansive road than the Creek delegation had approved and the appearance of bridges likewise implied far more extensive travel than a single post rider and his horse. The possibility that more families and perhaps even military detachments might use these more permanent structures to make their way across Creek country was extraordinarily disturbing.

In addition to these concerns, there were controversies regarding Creek travel and transportation. Numerous Creeks had been traveling to and settling on the shore of the Tennessee River in present-day northern Alabama, on lands still disputed by the Cherokees and Chickasaws. While these nations had their own anxieties about the Creek presence, it was the Tennesseans who seemed most distressed. In a talk to Cherokee leader Black Fox, Tennessee governor John Sevier chastised them for allowing the Creeks to pass through and settle in their nation, calling the Creeks "rogues" and demanding that the Cherokees "drive them from out of your Country." Sevier assured the Cherokees that his advice was simply "to enlighten your understandings that you may know how to take care of your own nation (if you wish to continue such)."[70] The Tennesseans were attempting to use the Cherokees to oust Creek settlements near the Tennessee River so that American settlers and traders could use the watershed for their own purposes.[71] This was neither the first nor the last time that the disputed lands around the Tennessee River would emerge as a borderland battleground.

In another situation involving Creek mobility, some Coosada Creeks complained to Hawkins that they were being taxed at Fort Stoddert on goods they brought from the Spanish territory via the Alabama River.[72] Both Hawkins and the Creek headmen found the practice to be patently unfair and potentially illegal. Dearborn responded to Hawkins's queries by informing him that the federal government had no objection to the Indians passing free of charge with their own goods, but that smuggling (particularly weapons) could not be permitted.[73] Indeed, some Creeks and Cherokees, along with Americans—white and black—who increasingly inhabited their homelands, were engaged in various forms of smuggling. Despite regulations regarding passports and "regular" or "authorized" travel, contraband goods and false papers were not uncommon. Much of this illegal commerce was conducted on the region's waterways where detection was more difficult.

In 1809, Creek leaders stopped a boat at Little Turkey's Town as it attempted to descend the Coosa River. Finding the passports irregular and the merchandise (alcohol and ammunition) illegal, the headmen sent word to Hawkins that they had detained the boat and its party—five Americans and a "half breed" Cherokee. They declared their intention to navigate the Coosa to the Alabama and descend to St. Stephens, insisting that their goods were sent by authority of the president to supply the garrison below. In fact, the smugglers were also carrying out a clandestine mission to "recoinnoiter the waterways here as far as the Bay of Mobile."[74] The Creeks recognized the passes as forgeries and seized the contraband goods.

In Hawkins's lengthy explanation of the affair to outgoing Secretary of War Dearborn, he blamed Cherokee agent Return J. Meigs for permitting the expedition and insisted on the Creeks' right to take such actions within their own nation. The smugglers tried to rely on the contested nature of the site of Little Turkey's Town (or Esenaca), and perhaps the identity of their Indian companion, to legitimate their presence in Creek country with illegal goods. But as Hawkins asserted, "The Creeks are to a certain extent an Independent people and treated as such by the United States[.] They claim and have long claimed the Jurisdiction of Coosau River. The Cherokees have admitted that the lands of Esenaca / Little Turkey's Town / were borrowed from the Creeks. The authority exercised by them is between them and the Cherokees."[75]

Creek and Cherokee leaders were opposed to the illicit trade passing along their roads and waterways, and either could detain smugglers on Coosa River. In fact, it appears that the Creek headmen actually turned the seized items over to Path Killer, the Cherokee leader then residing at Little Turkey's Town. Hawkins's defense of Creek sovereignty emphasized that they had a right to halt any commerce through their nation that they knew to be illegal. He also insisted that Creeks and Cherokees should be allowed to negotiate such matters for themselves on their own terms, an argument that contrasted sharply with Governor Sevier's demand that the Cherokees prohibit Creek travel through their lands.

Despite certain efforts to diminish it, the black market trade of alcohol, weapons, and ammunition, among other things, was thriving on the region's waterways. In many cases, American smugglers used forged licenses, old passports, and Indian guides to give their operations the patina of legitimacy. The presence of Indian collaborators is particularly interesting. Having a local Indian guide might make eluding detection easier, since he or she would ostensibly be more knowledgeable about heavily traveled routes. In addition, there was a sense that the presence of an Indian companion somehow legitimated otherwise illegitimate travel through the Creek Nation. The implication was that if an Indian person was willing to accompany and assist the party, then it must reflect the approval of the Indians in general.

The willingness of individual Creeks or Cherokees, including those of bicultural ancestry, to assist smugglers was usually prompted more by personal desires (to relieve debt or acquire wealth, for example) than anything else. Self-interested as they may have been, extralegal entrepreneurial endeavors like these nevertheless reflected the effort of enterprising Indian people to establish a middle ground between banditry and dependency. Smuggling and robbing travelers along the road were ways that disfranchised Creeks could profit from increasing American travel through their homelands, while simultaneously protesting the choices of those headmen who had agreed to give Americans greater access. In this and many other ways, the continued encroachment of Americans on Creek lands exacerbated political tensions emerging in the nation.

Smuggling was not the only way that Creeks might combine profit and protest. Speaking on behalf of the council, Hopoithle Micco revealed that they intended to appoint Creek representatives to visit all American settlements over the boundary lines and "demand rent for the fields cultivated, 25 cents a head for cattle and 50 cents for horses ranging on their lands, and the discontinuance of such unwarrantable conduct for the future."[76] The threat conveyed a revolutionary shift in the way some Creeks had come to view the nation's land. Rather than destroy the livestock and crops, as bands of young warriors were previously wont to do, the council proposed that they profit from these encroachments by treating the trespassers as tenant farmers.

Meanwhile, Creek young men resisted American migrants more directly. Their attacks ranged from straightforward physical brutality to extortion schemes. Bridges were popular targets. Several parties of warriors from the town of Cusseta seized small bridges near the Flint River and compelled travelers to pay a toll.[77] Like the plan to exact rent payments, requiring tolls to cross bridges might at first seem like a very American thing to do. But it would be a mistake to interpret such actions as simple greed rather than placing them within the larger context of Creek resistance to American intrusions. Creek headmen, sometimes trying to represent the discontent of their active young warriors, tended to appeal to Hawkins rather than confronting travelers directly. They increasingly complained not only about unauthorized bridges, but also about the appearance of other roads, as well as intrusions on their water rights, particularly on the Coosa, Tallapoosa, and Alabama rivers.

In 1810, Tennessee and the federal government decided to open a road and improve river navigation between Tennessee and Mobile. They were specifically interested in using the Coosa to gain access to the Alabama River, which would then take them to Fort Stoddert, where they could connect to the federal post path or the port of Mobile. Hawkins reported to recently appointed Secretary of War William Eustis that when the Upper and Lower Creeks met in Council in 1810, they had determined not to allow the Americans free navigation of the Coosa River. Hawkins further observed that this refusal seemed to be connected to "intrusions of our fellow citizens of the frontiers on the Indian rights; particularly on this frontier they have put over their stock to range on the Indian lands, have made fish traps, settlements and built a mill or two, in or connected with the river."[78]

Rather than responding to Hawkins's concerns, Eustis managed to exacerbate the situation by issuing orders to military detachments to begin surveying both land routes and water routes before even informing the Creek council. Accordingly, when General Edmund P. Gaines made his way northward, surveying a route from Fort St. Stephens toward Tennessee, he was "stoped by a party of Indians, after he had gone within sixty miles of the Little Turkey's town, and was under the necessity to return back."[79] Gaines should not have been surprised.

About a month before this episode, a party of Creeks had similarly detained John R. Luckett, who was charged with determining the feasibility of making a wagon road out of the federal horse path. Luckett was engaged in a centerline survey, starting near Fort Stoddert and proceeding northeastward toward the junction of the Coosa and Tallapoosa rivers, to determine the mid-point of the strip of land occupied by the horse path. The Creeks brought him to their council and told him that they had considered the question carefully and determined "that the measuring and marking of their country should be stoped."[80]

The marking of the landscape was particularly alarming and in this task Luckett was peculiarly prolific. He marked each mile of the survey by cutting Roman numerals into trees along the path, and because he eschewed the typical conventions for contracting large numbers, the ninety-ninth milepost tree was inscribed LXXXXIIIIIIIIII.[81] Such unannounced and unexplained surveys were disturbing to Creek leaders who already considered their concessions for the post path extraordinarily gracious. The prospect of even greater numbers of Americans moving north-south through their nation, as well as an expansion of the path already bisecting them from east to west, was most distressing.

By early 1811, it was apparent that the Upper Creeks in particular needed to be convinced of the mutual benefit of a north-south land route and the free navigation of the Coosa, Tallapoosa, and Alabama rivers. President James Madison addressed the issue in a talk to the Creeks: "Good pathways and roads are equally useful to his white and to his Red Children. Rivers & Water courses are made by the Great Spirit to be used by the Nations to and thro' which they run." He insisted that both Indians and Americans should have the freedom to travel through each other's territory, but it was especially important that the people of Tennessee be permitted to travel through Creek country to Mobile. As he explained to the Creeks, their neighbors to the north "have to go a great way to carry their produce and to bring home necessaries from the sea," and if a shorter way could be found, they should have it.[82] Nevertheless, the Creeks continued to resist such efforts, both through their national leaders and through individual protests, including those described by Secretary of War Eustis as "enormities committed by the Upper Creeks" against Tennessee settlers.[83] Eustis instructed Hawkins shortly after this talk that he was to "endeavor by every reasonable and proper means, to impress upon their minds the necessity, expediency, and importance to their own, as well as the interest of their White brothers, of having their rivers rendered boatable and good roads made through their Country."[84]

The Upper Creeks were particularly incensed at the possibility of Tennesseans having free passage through their country given that these Americans and their representatives had been aggressive and antagonistic opponents. Despite Madison's assurances that the United States had no interest in taking Creek lands or rights, the land and water surveys were contemporaneous with a renewed discussion between Tennessee and federal officials regarding "the extinguishment of the Indian claim to lands lying within the State."[85] As if to underscore their continued exasperation with their American neighbors to the north, a party of Upper Creeks seized and killed a Tennessee citizen along the banks of the Elk River in Franklin County in early 1811.[86]

In May of the same year, Creek speaker Hopoithle Micco tried to clarify the Creek position once and for all. In a talk to Hawkins and Madison he said succinctly, "You ask for a path an' I say no." As with the initial requests for the federal path from Georgia, one of the primary objections was the possibility of "mischief" that young Creek men might commit on the road. He warned that the headmen did not possess the coercive power to prevent crimes from occurring. In many ways, his language reflects established indigenous diplomatic rhetoric more than any particular aspect of the true internal situation. It is clear from the rest of his talk, however, that Creek frustration with the various road and travel schemes had reached a breaking point. What he described as the "mischievous" tendencies of Creek youth actually reflected the general feeling in the nation, where the increasing presence of American surveyors and travelers was widely protested. He continued, referring to Gaines and Luckett, "The officers must not be going through our lands to hunt paths[.] I spoke last Summer to you Colo Hawkins and to the President about paths through our Country I told you no, it would bring trouble. . . . My Chiefs and warriors now present will never say yes—I hope it will never be mentioned to us again."[87]

In order to make the reasons for Creek refusal of a north-south path and water route completely clear, Hopoithle Micco listed numerous American encroachments all along Creek borders, including several unauthorized paths already in common use. He concluded, "[This] is the reason we say no about the path—the white people are as difficult to be restrained as the red— and are constant habitual intruders on Indians lands."[88] Thus, the Creek speaker conveyed the interconnectedness of surveying, trespassing, traveling, road building, and security. Despite rhetoric of red and white brother-hood and mutual benefit, these concerns had come to dominate Creek inter-pretations of American intentions.

Nevertheless, the clamor for commercial routes to the Gulf and the in-creasing likelihood of a war with Great Britain ultimately made better and more accessible paths a fundamental necessity in the minds of American leaders.[89] Widening and improving the east-west federal horse path from Georgia to New Orleans into a military road, broad enough for wagons, artillery, and troops, was considered crucial. Despite the Creeks' distinct protests, Eustis told Hawkins that the administration was determined to open wagon roads through their country to Fort Stoddert.[90] He claimed that it was far better for the government to take charge of opening and improving roads through Creek country, rather "than that individuals should be left to seek their own way through the Indian Territory, which would be more apt to lead to the quarrels which they apprehend."[91] The improvement of the federal post path—which came to be known as the Federal Road—was as-signed to General Wade Hampton. Soldiers began the work of widening the path and erecting bridges in July of 1811 and were finished by the end of November.[92]

The new reality of the wagon road brought emergent Creek political ten-sions to the surface. The problems of the first decade of the nineteenth cen-tury—increased travel through Creek country, the enlarged and illegitimate presence of Americans in the nation, the changes wrought by the civilization program, and the sharpening debates over treaty concessions made by a priv-ileged few—all tended to magnify the growing dissent within Creek political and social life. There are many ways to characterize this split—progressives versus conservatives, young versus old, "mixed bloods" versus "full bloods," but all these dichotomies wear thin under close inspection. And truly, the situation on the ground was far more complicated than any binary descrip-tion can convey. What is most important here is the acknowledgment that there was a plurality of political positions within the Creek Nation, but they are unevenly represented in official records.[93] Those Creek people seeking the advancement of the Creek Nation through the adoption of plantation ag-riculture, chattel slavery, and American business models were often the ones who had the most contact with white Americans and were consequently the most likely to be directly involved in the formal negotiations surrounding such issues as the road and American travel on it. Those seeking to preserve the Creek Nation by resisting foreign social structures, including aspects of the civilization plan, were less likely to be invited to treaty talks and may have had to make themselves heard in more informal ways. Thus we often need to be more creative in interpreting their actions and their motivations.

Shortly after its inception, the federal road program became a visible target for the dissatisfaction of Creeks from multiple political persuasions. Those who had agreed to the road were incensed to find that the promises made to them in Washington were rescinded daily as the road proceeded through the woods and swamps of the Creek Nation. They had invested themselves in the principles of "civilization," believing that by fencing their lands, enlarging stocks of cattle and slaves, and engaging in private enterprises such as ferries and roadside stands, they could contribute not only to their own personal betterment but also to the increased stability and permanence of the Nation as a whole. Yet these opportunities were denied them. When the Creek majority learned of their concessions, the leaders of the delegation were dismissed (although not exiled). This was telling evidence that many Creek people did not believe that a secure future for them and their children lay in allowing more Americans into their homelands.

Creek men and women not involved in the treaty deliberations were more likely to feel alarmed by the increasing presence of white and black travelers in their country. Especially for young men, no longer effective in the deerskin trade and less able to distinguish themselves as warriors, the cotton fields creeping into Creek territory represented the loss of a manly future. Many of these individuals demonstrated their dissatisfaction by engaging in criminal acts along the roads and generally incommoding all but the most familiar travelers. Thus, the federal paths—scored and blazed on the landscape of Creek country—were themselves becoming a central battlefield in a contest for the Creek future.

By 1811 this brewing turmoil had reached a boiling point. The drought that had damaged Creek food crops since at least 1807 continued until the public granaries were empty. Traditionally, poorer Creeks relied on more fortunate kinsmen to help them through tough times, but the situation had become so dire that many of them asked Hawkins to supply them, only to find that his crops had also failed entirely.[94] Those Creek farmers who had adopted Hawkins's civilization plan had gradually resisted depositing crop surpluses (when they had them) into the communal supplies, choosing to sell them instead. The utter collapse of corn supplies in 1811 thus signaled both a sharp decline of Creek self-sufficiency and the divisive reality of the burgeoning market economy.[95]

Increasing difficulties along the federal post path and the emerging military roads from Tennessee and Georgia to the Tombigbee region also signaled the indelibility of the American presence in Creek country. American inhabitants of the lower South saw the expansion of the road and the struggles of the Indian nations bisected by them as providential. Cutting through the Indians' territory was a physical sign, a claim written upon the land, announcing that Americans had come to stay. One orator in the Mississippi Territory proclaimed triumphantly, "The forest falls before the axe of industry—the cabin of the whiteman is built—and the face of the country is every where covered with farms, smiling with harvest, and nodding with the rich produce of the growing year."[96] Contrast this writ of abundance with the void of drought and famine in the Creek Nation at the same time.

Into this tumult strode Shawnee warrior Tecumseh, or the Shooting Star, and his brother, the prophet Tenskwatawa, or the Open Door. The two men had formed a strong alliance of Indian followers in the Ohio Valley and had launched a religious and political revitalization movement destined, they claimed, to return the land to indigenous peoples. Tenskwatawa's visions were brought to him by the Master of Life and became the basis for his prophecies. Appearing dead to his relatives, Tenskwatawa had been transported to the spirit world where he was shown two paths. One led to a true paradise of abundant hunting grounds and fruitful forests and fields, while the other led to a place of fiery torture. Like Creek beliefs regarding the Spirits' Path, or *poya fik-tcálk innini*, the Shawnee prophet's vision showed that not all Indians would travel the road to paradise. Some would glimpse the glorious land of pleasures but would be forced to travel on the sinner's path leading to eternal suffering. Tenskwatawa's new chosen name, the Open Door, symbolized his determination to lead Indian people down the road to the paradisiacal Spirit World.[97]

In late 1811, Tecumseh left his base at the junction of the Wabash and Tippecanoe rivers and brought the prophetic message of revolution and revitalization to the southern Indians.[98] He met with the Creeks at the very same National Council meeting in which Hawkins was pushing the expanded Federal Road and brought them a war pipe and a bundle of red sticks.[99] Accepting the pipe and bundle would signify the intention of each community to join with the Shawnee prophets in their vision of an Indian world free of white people.

Although the message was new, the Creeks were not unfamiliar with the Shawnees generally, or with Tecumseh personally. According to Tustunnuggee Hopoie, a young headman from Tuckabatchee, both Tecumseh and Tenskwatawa were originally from his town, having been born there and departed some twenty years past; both Tuckabatchee and several other

Creek towns had long been home to a number of Shawnees.[100] Although it seems clear that it was actually the brothers' parents who hailed from within the Creek Nation, they nevertheless had social and perhaps also familial connections with the Creeks that intensified the effect of their message in Creek country.[101]

Tecumseh's appearance in the Nation coincided with the appearance of the brightest comet to cross the sky in hundreds of years. The spiritual and prophetic correspondence of these signs was not lost on the Creeks or their Indian neighbors. In general, however, the Shawnees' calls to war were not unanimously heeded.[102] But they did heighten the tensions already mounting within the Creek Nation. Sensing Creek ambivalence about joining his revolution, Tecumseh, in his final appeal to the National Council, threatened, "I leave Tuckabatchee directly and shall go to Detroit. When I arrive there, I will stamp on the ground with my foot, and shake down every house in Tuckabatchee!"[103] He left the Creeks wary of an all-out war against the Americans but aroused by the possibility of relief from famine, poverty, and dependency. Tecumseh's plan seemed to provide some hope. Having witnessed American troops cutting their timber and laying bridges across their rivers as the federal post path morphed into a military wagon road, the Creeks knew that dark days were dawning. But the thunder of ordnance rolling along the Federal Road was no match for the tremors to come.

On the morning of Monday, December 16, 1811, the ground convulsed as the mightiest earthquake ever recorded in the United States ripped through the land. One witness described the event thus: "The water in the Mississippi, near New-Madrid, rose in a few minutes twelve or fourteen feet, and again fell like a tide. . . . It cast up hillocks of white sand, of the size of potatoe hills. . . . The next day but one before the first earthquake, was darkened from morning to night, by thick fog; and divers persons perceived a sulphureous scent. The wind ceased and there was a dead calm, without the least breath of air, on the day of the earthquake. . . . The motions of the earth were undulating. The parts agitated quivered like the flesh of a beef just killed. They began just about the time the comet disappeared."[104] The epicenter was near New Madrid, Missouri, but the strength of the quake was so incredible that it toppled chimneys in Maine and rocked houses in Georgia like cradles. In the Creek Nation, still reeling from Tecumseh's dire warning, it was a moment of fantastic horror and realization—and for many it was the final and convincing call to revolution.

Chapter Four

WAR COMES TO THE CREEKS

When the dust finally settled from the New Madrid aftershocks, Creek people saw clearly that American travel through their homelands had increased since the end of 1811. The transformation of what was once a narrow post path to a broad wagon road meant that more people could enter the nation faster. At least 3,700 people passed through Creek country from October 1811 to March 1812, including 120 wagons, 80 carts, 30 chairs, and 3 four-wheeled vehicles.[1] Considering that this was all ill-advised wintertime travel, the numbers for the drier months (April through September) must have been even higher. While not all Creeks, nor indeed all southern Indians, would heed Tecumseh's call to war, all of them would soon experience its consequences. For many, the profusion of American roads through the Indian Country was a reason to take up arms, and the roads themselves would emerge as a theater of bloody battle before year's end.

Reflecting on a journey through Creek country during this era, Margaret Austill recalled, "As soon as we entered the Creek or Muskogee Nation, we could see the terrible hatred to the white, but as we advanced, we were joined by many movers, which gave us more security."[2] Her comment reflects two undeniable realities of American travel in the Creek Nation. Many Creeks were opposed to it and yet it continued to increase. Opposition was to be expected in certain parts of Creek country, especially in the Upper province where Hawkins and his civilization plan were generally less popular.[3] But even Creeks from previously American-allied talwas had begun resisting the intrusions of travelers by impeding them in any way they could.

When Hawkins reported that some Lower Creeks had occupied a bridge and stopped travelers, he attributed their actions to a "thirst for strong drink" rather than acknowledging the spread of discontent to the province. Nevertheless, his surprise was evident. As he explained to Secretary of War William Eustis, the perpetrators were from Cusseta, one of the largest towns among the Lower Creeks and one of the closest to the Georgia border. "Hitherto," he continued, "they have boasted of their friendship for white people."[4] For a leading town of Lower Creeks that Hawkins had consistently and confidently referred to as "friendly" to display such provocative conduct was a symptom of deep and abiding unrest in Creek country.

The Creek agent, however, should not have been surprised. At the very same Creek National Council meeting that witnessed Tecumseh's dramatic call to war, Hawkins had vigorously pressed the road issue, telling the assembled headmen, "The period has now arrived when the white people must have roads to market and for traveling wherever they choose to go through the United States."[5] Although Hawkins claimed he did not need Indian permission to expand the roads, the Creeks were nevertheless promised sundry "implements of civilization" over the course of several years, including 1,000 spinning wheels, 1,000 pairs of cotton cards, and a supply of iron for agricultural implements as part of the agreement.[6] This provision laid bare the relationship between the expanding travel routes through Creek country and the expansion of the civilization program Hawkins cherished.

Regardless of their various opinions about the roads, Creek leaders were expected to "prevent any improper conduct on the part of your young people" as well as providing cooperation, expertise, and support to troops working on the roads.[7] Headmen who assisted the troops were to be paid in cash and would have some say in the location of bridges and toll stations, at which they would be permitted to collect the required fees. Like the continued division between those who adopted the civilization plan and those who refused it, the split between those who accepted the road and those who opposed it was partly rooted in this system of patronage that Hawkins fostered. Creek leaders who accepted the roads and participated in opening them may have believed that the only real future for Creek people in the South lay in permitting American travel through their lands, accommodating them as far as practicable, and profiting from it whenever possible.

Despite pledges made by federal government representatives, the early months of 1812 found the Creek Nation awash in travelers but with none of the promised goods or tolls in hand. Hawkins was frustrated with the government's failure to live up to its promises, not least because they had come directly from his mouth. He complained on several occasions to Eustis, finally telling him in March, "It is high time a contract was entered into for the supply of [spinning] wheels under the conventions at Tookaubatche."[8] But as late as June of 1812, the goods were still not delivered even though the road was already "crowded with travelers."[9]

Meanwhile, some headmen had been assisting the road-cutting outfits and receiving pay, but the majority of Creeks were not benefiting from the increase in American travel. Men like Big Warrior, William McIntosh, and Alexander Cornells, who helped the troops widen and improve the road, stood to profit the most from the tolls and stages that would be established. Anti-American warriors, especially among the Upper Creeks, may have viewed these actions as traitorous, a perception that sharpened their determination to join the revolts being led by Tecumseh and Tenskwatawa or to join those sprouting locally, led by home-grown prophets such as Josiah Francis (or Hillis Hadjo), Captain Isaacs, Paddy Carr, and High Head Jim (or Cusseta Hadjo).[10]

The revolutions underway in the Ohio River Valley, as well as those to the south, had deep roots in Native eschatology and earlier revitalization movements.[11] Leaders like Neolin (or the Delaware Prophet) and Handsome Lake of the Senecas had brought messages of resistance and renewal to their communities in the 1760s and 1790s, respectively. Their movements often drew on a blend of traditional beliefs and imported philosophies to envision an Indian future based on reducing dependence on newcomers and reinvigorating traditional rites and rituals (although they frequently interpreted these traditions quite liberally). So while on the one hand revitalization prophecies called for a return to ancient ceremonies, they also borrowed from alien philosophies to envision a new world. Among the most important outside influences were those of European American Christian traditions and African American folk interpretations of those traditions. The apocalyptic tendencies of African American spiritual practice may have had a particular resonance with Creek people seeking to destroy the crooked, disordered world they inhabited and replace it with a straight, clean one.[12]

By the time Tecumseh came to the Creek National Council meeting at the Tuckabatchee square ground in late 1811, his Shawnee followers had already been engaged in a five-year effort to gain control of their own councils by identifying "accomodationist" leaders and weeding them out.[13] These imperatives were part of Shawnee prophet Tenskwatawa's vision for a new Indians' world—free from the influence of "civilizing missions" and "medal chiefs." Of particular concern were American expansionism and the subsequent loss of Indian land—often ceded in treaties signed by leaders they called "annuity chiefs"—a primary signal of which was the appearance of federal roads like the ones that were opened in both Shawnee territory and Creek country around 1805.[14] The opposition to American roads through Indian Country had become so intense that it helped to unite diverse and independent Native communities under a pan-Indian banner of protest and retaliation.[15]

The Creek leaders with whom Hawkins had the most contact vigorously repudiated the Shawnee call to war. He reported early on that "there has been sent to this nation a war pipe. . . . The object of the war pipe is to unite all the red people in a war against the white people. . . . The Chiefs here unanimously refused to smoke the pipe."[16] Similarly, a young warrior from Tuckabatchee initially informed Hawkins, "The Speaker [Tecumseh] talked much of conversations with God on Indian affairs. . . . But their opinion was the man was a mad man (Haujo Haugee) or a great liar or in fact both, and that as they did not understand them, to take no notice of their foolish talks."[17] But many Creeks, including some influential leaders, were inclined to take the "bloody talks" and join in the anti-American revolt. Those who did became known as Red Sticks for their antagonistic disposition and the red-painted war clubs they wielded.

By the middle of 1812, Red Stick Creeks were uniting with Seminole allies to the south to breathe life into a revolt against the American-allied head-men, the government agent, and especially the new roads. For many, the decision to go to war was complex and difficult. William Weatherford, a wealthy Coosada Creek who had largely adopted many aspects of Hawkins's civilization plan but nevertheless became a leader among the Red Sticks, is reported to have expressed his initial opposition to the war.[18] But, he reportedly said, "when it became necessary to take sides, he went with his countrymen . . . [because] to join the whites was a thing he did not think right."[19] For Weatherford and for many others in Creek country, choosing sides meant not only choosing between kith and kin, but also choosing a particular path.[20]

Meanwhile, the growing discontent in Indian Country both north and south of the Ohio River had become a particular concern for the federal government. But other problems of national security had also begun to emerge. One was the acquisition of the port of Mobile, the Mobile River, and the Floridas from the Spanish—a long-held ambition of the United States. Hawkins had once boldly asserted, "If you can get the Mobile all other things must come in course."[21] And indeed, by recommending a water route for the passage of the mail from Mobile to New Orleans, he yoked southern communication and commerce to American conquest of the Gulf.

A related set of concerns involved the increased tension between the United States and its trading partners in Europe. As American maritime mobility increased in the early nineteenth century, with ships plying both Mediterranean and Atlantic trade routes, U.S. ships stirred the aggression of the British, whose navy had been long engaged in defending its "belligerent rights" on the high seas. American ships—charged with supporting the French in their antagonisms of Great Britain—were repeatedly attacked by the British in the Atlantic and elsewhere; sailors were impressed into British service, their cargoes confiscated.[22] In an effort to protect the sanctity of its oceanic trade and mobility, by 1807 Congress had taken steps to prohibit intercourse with England.[23]

At the same time, the United States continued its push into the Northwest and Southwest Territories, largely by expanding westward roads and challenging foreign outposts, especially along the Canadian frontier. As noted, this American expansionism in the west was a central catalyst of the pan-Indian movements that were underway through much of the interior. Not surprisingly, the British acted quickly to extend support to western Indian nations, promising aid in their rebellions against American aggression. In so doing, they united their imperial imperatives with the growing indigenous insurgency.[24] As one observer put it, "If we have a British war we shall have an Indian war."[25] Thus, at the same time that Creek people were debating the right path for their country, the United States was entering a fight for its own national future.

Both the internal strife of the Indian revolutions and the external drama of American foreign relations further divided the United States along sectional lines. Many southerners felt that the trade restrictions against Britain were disproportionately harmful to the southern economy, benefiting only "New England navigation and fisheries" and detrimental to "the interests of Southern agriculture."[26] Some called openly for war with Britain to finally settle the conflicts. Opinions about a possible war largely corresponded with political party allegiances, with the mostly northern and eastern Federalists opposing martial action and the primarily southern and western Republicans favoring it.[27] The expansionist impulse along the northwestern and southwestern borders was similarly debated, pitting eastern against western interests, with many southerners falling somewhere in between. Too long had the welfare of the west been overlooked in favor of "eastern and mercantile interests," argued senators from Kentucky and Tennessee, and sympathetic southern statesmen like John C. Calhoun (South Carolina) and George Troup (Georgia) couldn't help but agree. "The rights of the former are every day shamefully sacrificed to the undue weight of the latter," Troup complained.[28]

In truth, the causes of the War of 1812 were complex and varied but can be traced in part to the aforementioned party politics between Republicans and Federalists, the Napoleonic Wars and their effect on maritime trade, particularly the use of blockades and the impressment of sailors, and the continued involvement of Great Britain in U.S. Indian affairs.[29] The chance to settle the Canadian problem and rid the Northwest of British meddling once and for all was a powerful motivator—as was the prospect of eliminating pernicious British influence among Indians in Ohio and the Northwest Territory who were working toward a "strong combination" with Native peoples to the south.

By June 1812, Republican war hawks, including Troup and Calhoun, succeeded in convincing Federalist foes and conservative members of their own party that only a war would settle the situation permanently.[30] In an interesting comment on the importance and difficulty of long-distance communication in this period, Great Britain had in fact agreed to last-minute concessions regarding the system of blockades that was driving the call to war, but the length of time it took to dispatch those decrees across the Atlantic meant that Congress had voted for war before the news arrived.[31] Once the United States declared war, however, Great Britain was quick to respond in kind. By July 1812 much of the east coast was in "the most dreadful state of alarm" as British soldiers marched toward Washington, D.C., burning and destroying everything in their path. One witness reported, "The roads are crowded with women and children flying from their desolate homes, who worn out with terror & fatigue beg every passenger they meet on Horseback to assist them in their flight."[32]

The start of the war had particular salience for Native peoples rebelling against American expansion and influence.[33] While they pursued their own agendas of reducing dependence, avenging themselves on American-allied leaders and wreaking havoc on settlers, the Indian revolutionaries also viewed the prospect of a British-American war as a sign that they would receive assistance in repelling the American invaders. British officials opportunistically seized the chance to gain local allies on many fronts in both the northwest and the southwest and nurtured the delusion, sending emissaries to visit the prophets and promising whatever aid was requested, independent of their ability or intention to deliver it.[34] The same strategy had been somewhat effective during the American Revolution and had generally kept the situation in Canada, and to a lesser extent on the Gulf coast, unstable ever since. Secretary of War Eustis recognized this strategy early on and quickly notified Hawkins: "War is declared against great Britain. Your vigilance and attention are rendered peculiarly necessary in your agency at this time, and no exertions or reasonable Expenses will be spared to keep the Indians quiet and friendly."[35]

Many Native people, however, were past the point of quiet friendliness. William Henry Harrison's aggressions after Tippecanoe, combined with the rejuvenation of British alliances and, most important, the rise of more indigenous prophets, galvanized many northern and southern Indians into pursuing the path to war. In Creek country, the Shawnee war talks had resurfaced in the spring of 1812, and some Red Sticks even traveled northward to assist their new allies in battles with American troops and attacks on settlers. By March, Hawkins had received information that Red Sticks and their allies along the Alabama and Tombigbee rivers were threatening settlers in the area known as Tensaw. In June, Tennessee governor William Blount reported that a party of Creek Indians, under the leadership of Little Warrior, kidnapped an American woman and killed several others in the vicinity while on their way back from campaigns in the Ohio River Valley.[36] Further south, parties of Red Sticks reportedly from the Tallasee and Autosee towns killed a traveler headed to the Mississippi Territory named Arthur Lott.[37] As the year wore on, the Autosees (whose name derives from *atássa*, meaning red-painted war club) would play a significant role in the development of the conflict— sheltering Red Stick Creeks from persecution and supplying warriors from their towns on the Tallapoosa River to battle Americans and their allies.[38]

Not surprisingly, a number of these early attacks took place on the roadways of the region. There were various bouts of "thieving" in mid-March near the Fort Stoddert portion of the Federal Road by "idle Indians in that quarter."[39] More seriously, in April an Autosee warrior assaulted two American men at a tavern along the Federal Road, killing one and wounding the other.[40] A few months later, a party of Seminoles from Alachua town took the scalps of two men traveling in the southern district. Hawkins reported, "One they say was an officer of the United States, the other a paper carrier (meaning post rider) a negro" and noted that runners bearing the two scalps had been sent to Big Warrior and Hopoithle Micco.[41] While mail carriers had previously been guaranteed safe passage on the roads, such aggression meant that American post riders and travelers, white and black alike, were equally unsafe on the public roads.[42]

On the one hand, roads and paths, especially the recently improved Federal Road, were arenas for such attacks simply because they were places where Creeks could be assured of finding Americans in increasing numbers. Hawkins noted that on a single day in April 1812, "six wagons, 4 carts, 12 chairs and 90 persons passed" the agency.[43] But attacks on the mail were of particular concern because they signaled an intention to disrupt the flow of information vital to American defenses. In fact, the capture of a U.S. mailbag near the Canada border had earlier provided the British with important information about American troop strength.[44]

Attacks on the southern mail revealed a two-pronged Red Stick strategy. They could inhibit American communication and mobility along the disputed thoroughfares while also potentially providing their European allies with valuable information in exchange for continued promises of support. Seminoles who attacked the mail carrier in Florida also seized the opportunity at hand and sent a revealing message to the Creek headmen along with the scalps. The British, they claimed, had promised to send four ships to St. Augustine, "with a little of every thing to help the poor red people."[45] As the crisis escalated, the paths on which such valuable information traveled through Creek country would also become a primary theater for bloody confrontations.

While these disparate attacks may not have led to an all-out war in the Creek Nation, the reactions of the American-allied headmen ensured that war would ensue. Hawkins had been putting increasing pressure on Creek leaders to punish those involved in kidnappings and murders along the roads and borders. Many of them, including Big Warrior, Little Prince, Alexander Cornells, and William McIntosh, complied as far as they were able. They were hopeful that swift punishment of offenders, or at least "taking measures to restrain them," might prevent harsher retaliation by local militias and the federal army.[46]

When the scalps of the traveler and post rider arrived in the Creek Nation, Alexander Cornells, sub-agent and close ally of Hawkins, seized them and "sent the runners back with orders to the chiefs of Aulotchewau to put the murderers to death, or this town would be cut off."[47] Hawkins thought it best to send a delegation of "distinguished Chiefs" to the Seminole town to urge them to punish the offenders. But both of these measures were largely ineffective since the Creek headmen were much less influential in the independent Seminole talwas than Hawkins may have hoped or believed.[48] Less than a month later, Hawkins reported that a party of Seminoles, apparently unwilling to heed the warnings of the Lower Creek delegation, had "stolen a great number of Negroes," probably intending to exchange them for arms and ammunition in Pensacola.[49]

Hawkins was determined to have the criminals punished, both to send a warning to the Red Sticks as well as to reconsolidate Creek political power (or attempt to do so) in the hands of his allies within the nation.[50] For example, after the murder of Arthur Lott, he supported William McIntosh in his effort to raise a detachment of pro-American Creeks and pursue the killers. Instead of delivering them to American authorities, bringing them to face the National Council, or handing them over to be dealt with by clan members in accordance with Creek custom, they shot the perpetrators on the spot. In other instances, these pro-American forces killed alleged criminals in surprise attacks, or pursued them to the very heart of "white" towns—which were designated as sanctuaries for Creek fugitives—and summarily executed them.[51] Big Warrior tried to punish the offending Autosees in a similar fashion but was unsuccessful, instead inciting them to take revenge on Creeks from his own talwa of Tuckabatchee.[52]

In addition, the headmen with an interest in the roads appear to have exerted as much influence as possible to keep Red Stick warriors from causing problems for travelers. Indeed, Hawkins repeatedly, though somewhat disingenuously, claimed during this period that "traveling is quite safe."[53] For some Creek leaders, like Big Warrior and William McIntosh, a major incentive to prevent depredations against travelers was the income promised to them as part of the road agreements. The actions of the Red Stick Creeks not only threatened the peace and security of Creek country, but also jeopardized their personal investment in its expanding road network. While their enforcement of Hawkins's directives may have been motivated by an earnest desire to restore peace and calm to Creek country, it was likely interpreted as a final sign that they had only their own interests (and those of the Americans) in mind. The willingness of the American-allied headmen to take decisive action against their kinsmen and neighbors in response to hostilities against Americans further galvanized the Red Stick party against them.

When the scattered attacks threatened to turn into a civil war, the "Road Indians" and their allies closed ranks.[54] The Tuckabatchees fortified their settlements to defend themselves against the Red Sticks, largely from neighboring towns in the Upper Division and along the western edge of the Creek Nation. The linguistically distinct Alabama towns, whose settlements were bisected by the lower portion of the Federal Road, were particularly receptive to the prophets' movement.[55] Other towns were essentially split and many who may have hoped to remain neutral were forced to abandon their homes and seek refuge among Lower towns and at the Creek agency.[56]

Complicating the chaos within Creek country was the growing conflict further north. After the fall of Detroit to the British in late 1812, American forces attempted to regroup and focus their attention on securing the rest of Michigan. In January 1813, British regulars along with several hundred Native warriors, including many Creeks, defeated a large detachment of American soldiers at the River Raisin, killing many of the remaining wounded the next day. On their way back to the Creek Nation, a handful of the Red Sticks, under the leadership of Little Warrior, attacked a group of white settlers at the mouth of the Ohio River. The combination of these two events prompted the states of Tennessee and Georgia to call out their militias and begin preparations for war against the Creeks.

In his talk to the Creek headmen, Hawkins made it clear that he considered the Ohio River murders the work of the entire Creek Nation. Speaking, as he often did, as a member of the nation, Hawkins warned, "The northern nations have a back country to go to, we have none. What do we want with war? do we expect to drive [out] the United States and take their country? This is impossible. Have the United States taken any land, or threatened to take any from us? They have not. They have secured our lands so that it can only be purchased fairly from us; they have at great expense taught us to clothe and feed ourselves. . . . You have a public road through the country on which the travelers leave a great deal of money every year. . . . We are brave men and can die in battle, but is it not better to live and enjoy our property and the fine prospects before us, arising out of the plan of civilization?"[57] Hawkins's speech emphasized the impossibility of returning the lands "fairly" purchased from the Creeks to Indian hands, as many of the prophets promised to do, and impressed on them the futility of pursuing a war when Creek country was surrounded by American settlements on every side. He spoke particularly to those leaders who had accepted the civilization program, reminding them what they risked should the nation descend into total war. He focused specifically on the revenues brought into the nation each year by American travelers. Wealth and progress, he argued, were more valuable than pride.

Before the Creek council even had an opportunity to react to Hawkins's address, two more white Americans were attacked by Red Sticks on the Federal Road.[58] American-allied leaders, fearing reprisal from within the nation, wrung their hands until finally in the spring of 1813, they embarked on a campaign to punish the perpetrators of these most recent roadside murders.[59] Ultimately, a joint party composed of participants from both the Upper and Lower towns captured and executed two Okfuskee men guilty of the Federal Road killings and a woman who harbored one of the accused.[60] With these actions, the Creek civil war officially began.

By this time, Hawkins's allies within the Creek Nation had put themselves in a particularly tricky position. By enacting swift and decisive punishments against the Red Stick Creeks who had committed murders and other attacks across Tennessee and along the region's roads, Big Warrior, Little Prince, Alexander Cornells, McIntosh, and others essentially ensured the opposition of any Creeks who found themselves torn between factions. But American-allied headmen risked losing control of the funds and supplies (however irregular) that flowed from treaty negotiations if they did not pursue suspects in attacks like those along the Federal Road.[61] For example, newly appointed secretary of war John Armstrong advised the Superintendent of Indian Trade that the goods and payments due the Creeks according to their most recent treaty agreements should not be transmitted, "until they deliver up to the authority of the United States the perpetrators of the murders and outrages."[62] In fact, even the executions described above did not satisfy the Americans, as Armstrong later communicated: "Nothing short of taking & delivering over the Murderers to the Custody of the Governor of the State in which the offences were committed, (to be there dealt with according to law) will satisfy the united demands of policy & justice."[63] The headmen's actions not only violated customary Creek norms of justice, but also failed to measure up to American standards of law and process.[64] Rather than being handed over to the Americans to be dealt with dishonorably, the suspects were dealt with dishonorably by their own leaders—a course of action that ultimately satisfied no one.

In addition, given the connection between British and Spanish officials and the Red Stick Creeks, as well as northern Indians, Hawkins's allies knew that anything other than complete opposition to the Red Sticks would be viewed as consorting with the United States' foreign enemies. In fact, these leaders already faced accusations of collaborating with the British as well as false reports of depredations that continually undermined their efforts to preserve peace. Hawkins referred to the constant rumors as a "dreadful mania" and reported in March 1813, "They [American-allied headmen] complain, 'that the current of misrepresentation against them from their white neighbours seems to be generating hostility which is to jeopardise their peace and safety . . . that their nation is not only charged with what their wicked young people do although they without delay give satisfaction to it, but with whatever every idle, worthless vagabond choose to invent and circulate against them."[65] Cornells was more succinct: "I never saw nor heard so many lies as white people bring from Georgia."[66]

The spread of such lies inflamed the passions of southern Americans and had an impact on the daily lives of Creek people as well. One American resident on Alcovy Creek, a small river on the Georgia border, reported on the reluctance of a Creek man to accept assistance in landing his canoe: "His behavior was doubtless occasioned by reports which had been current on the river that the People of Georgia had intended to make war on his nation."[67] Hawkins himself recognized the perverse power of "calumnious reports" and even accused the secretary of war of withholding the Creek annuity on the basis of falsehoods, "fabricated in Tennessee and Tombigbee aided by a mite from the frontiers of Georgia."[68] Pathways like the Federal Road thus brought not only travelers, but also their misconceptions, suspicions, and lies into the Creek Nation. These same roads also functioned as conduits for eastwardly mobile misinformation, and Hawkins noted in late 1812 that travel "has been mostly from the west."[69] Recent time spent "in the Nation" gave travelers' accounts, however false or misleading, a veneer of authenticity and veracity, igniting calls for war among an already indignant southern population.

Despite credible news from the Creek Nation that "many of the reports respecting Indian hostility, [are] totally unfounded, & those founded in truth, much exaggerated," the American-allied headmen knew that the situation was slowly unraveling.[70] In April 1813, Big Warrior and Cornells expressed their deepening concerns to Harry Toulmin, a federal judge in the Tensaw, a rich delta district of the Mississippi Territory settled with American, Creek, and mixed ancestry planters and ranchers.[71] They were particularly concerned about the conduct of Little Warrior, who lived on the Black Warrior River and had commanded the party responsible for the killings in both the Ohio River region and along the Tennessee border. They advised Toulmin that Little Warrior had nothing to lose and was likely to continue attacking Americans, "as he is now out lawed in his own country and men are out in all directions to take or kill him." They expressed particular concern for the safety of the inhabitants of the Tensaw district and travelers on the north-south road between Fort Stoddert and Tennessee.[72]

Big Warrior and Cornells also used the occasion of their communication with Toulmin to distance themselves from Little Warrior's actions. They explained that his behavior was not sanctioned by the Creek council, emphasizing one point above all others: "You must not think from any conduct of the Little Warrior that the chiefs are any foes to the Whites. . . . Do not by any rash means fall upon our villages, that are above you, for they are friendly."[73] The threat from Red Sticks in the area was certainly real; one official reported, "Many of the families residing near the Indian boundary line are preparing to leave their farms and retreat down the river for safety."[74] In an attempt to ensure that area settlers and local militias would not take such depredations as cause to "fall upon" peaceful Creek towns in the vicinity, the headmen struggled to differentiate themselves from their Red Stick foes. In so doing, they also insinuated that the reaction of neighboring white Americans might be equally precipitous and damnable.

As it turned out, the Red Sticks fell upon Creek towns before the Americans did. In mid-summer 1813, a traveler noted, "The Rebels have shot all the horses in the neighborhood of Tuckabatchee," and Big Warrior confirmed, "The[y] have not left me A horse to ride."[75] Hawkins similarly reported that the "prophets party" had killed all the livestock and fowl in several of the Upper towns.[76] The apparently indiscriminate slaughter of stock animals may at first seem perplexing since it bespeaks incredible waste during a time of continuing famine. Some Red Sticks were also successful ranchers and commercial farmers who made personal sacrifices to bring the prophets' visions to fruition, so it would be a misrepresentation to see attacks on livestock as purely a reflection of backwards-looking, anti-agrarian sentiment. Acting on the revolutionary prophecies required them to reorder their world by destroying signs of American influence and invasion, including homes and other property, alive or not.[77] For some Red Sticks, killing Big Warrior's horses and destroying other Creeks' accumulated wealth in the form of houses, slaves, and stock signaled a rejection of the "civilized" path these headmen had chosen for themselves and the Creek Nation, but for others, it was simply an efficient way to hit them where it hurt the most—in the pocketbook.[78] Furthermore, killing horses and livestock and leaving the meat otherwise untouched was one way that the Red Stick faction could inscribe their revolutionary ideals on the very contested landscape they hoped to retain. It became a sort of bloody calling card, with the rotting flesh symbolizing the spiritual decrepitude of the nation as a result of the infiltration of American ways.

As might have been expected, American travel through the Creek Nation became increasingly problematic during these tense spring and summer months of 1813. In addition to the numerous murders on the Federal Road, there were persistent troubles along the waterways of Creek country as the

Tennesseans pushed for free navigation for their goods to Mobile, now under American control. Although recently installed Secretary of War John Armstrong urged Hawkins to force the Creeks to accept the free movement of goods and traders along the Coosa River, the agent recognized that his Indian allies were skeptical of the plan. He told Armstrong that he had endeavored to explain to them the necessity of "viewing the navigation of Coosa River as a common right to all persons within the United States," but that they feared an increase in the whiskey trade from Tennessee would "bring ruin on their nation."[79] The chiefs may have been overtly concerned about the alcohol trade, an enterprise that was in fact crucial to the economic development of early Tennessee, but they must also have been apprehensive about the possibility of continued hostilities by those Creeks determined to escalate the war. Like the nation's roads, the watercourses of Creek country would become a primary theater for surprise attacks and murders no matter what the "common right[s]" were presumed to be.

In addition, the American-allied Creek leaders were likely frustrated with the renewed pressure to open the Coosa to free navigation when promises made to them in exchange for improving the Federal Road had not been fulfilled. According to the 1811 agreement, the United States "were to build bridges and flats, to regulate to tolls and to give 1,000 spinning wheels, 1000 pr. cotton cards," but only four bridges and two flats were made, and by May 1813 the Creek annuity, along with the promised goods, had still not been delivered. The American-allied headmen may have looked on the new demands for navigation from the north as particularly unjust, given the disappointment of these earlier agreements, from which they hoped to profit personally and politically. And they further had to contend with Hawkins's opinion that while the Tennessee people must be allowed to come "down the Coosa with their produce to market," it was not proper "to let your people go on that [Tennessee] frontier. They [the Tennesseans] are exposed on one side to the incursions of Indian war parties from the Northwest and are strongly prejudiced against you, which your people have given cause for."[80] Interestingly, this line of argument directly contradicted his earlier statement to the Creeks that their hemmed in situation was a reason to preserve peace with their neighbors. Because the Tennesseans were surrounded by Indians, he now argued, they were rightfully inclined to wage war on the Creeks if their borders were breached. The Americans, it seemed, should have greater mobility to and through Creek lands while the Creeks were to stay home and peacefully welcome Americans in their country.

Just as the headmen had feared, the opening of the wagon roads and the push for expanded access to waterways inaugurated a new era of smuggling. In April 1813, Georgia governor David B. Mitchell (who would later become known as a smuggler himself) was alerted that "a contraband trade has commenced between Pensacola and the upper parts of Georgia; The old post road which enter's Jasper County is the line of Communication." This black market commerce added to the growing confusion in Creek country since some of the smuggled goods—many of which were being transported by wagons on the recently widened road—were being stored at Creek homes in the nation.[81] Like their worries about Creek youth stealing horses at roadside stands, the idea of increased commercial travel that might entangle desperate Creeks similarly concerned Creek leaders. Thus Tennesseans were permitted to travel the length of Creek country by water, Georgians were permitted to travel its breadth by land, and smugglers were suffered to pass largely unmolested both ways, but the Creeks, even those who viewed themselves as allies of the Americans, found their individual mobility constricted.

The Red Sticks were not content to sit idly by, however, and let Americans rule the roads. Their growing need for arms and supplies resulted in an increase in the smuggling traffic and illicit travel on the part of Creek warriors themselves. The paths between Creek country and Pensacola were particularly well used during this period, as Red Stick Creeks moved back and forth passing weapons and information between their towns and their European supporters on the Gulf. Pensacola remained under Spanish control, but British traders also maintained a strong presence there as well and both had reason to undermine Creek-American relations.[82] The Red Sticks sought arms and ammunition from their allies in the old Gulf city and were rewarded for stolen slaves they brought with them from the frontiers of Georgia and Tennessee. American observers were aware of the perils such a relationship might engender. One Tensaw inhabitant noted that if the Red Sticks are "supplied with arms and ammunition from the Spaniards . . . we shall be in a dangerous situation here."[83] High Head Jim declared that the Red Sticks had received a letter from a British general that would enable them to receive ammunition from Pensacola. According to High Head Jim's claim, "they calculated on five horseloads for every Town."[84] Now under the leadership of an influential headman known as Peter McQueen, the Red Stick party did in fact make frequent appeals to the Spanish governor at Pensacola for assistance—sometimes receiving it and sometimes returning to their towns disappointed.

Emboldened with the support of their European allies, however sporadic, the Red Sticks occasionally engaged their foes on the trails between their towns and the Gulf ports. Big Warrior informed Hawkins in August 1813 that McQueen had gone to Pensacola to get ammunition and kidnapped the wife of American-allied James Cornells on his way. On the return of McQueen's party to the Creek Nation, they were intercepted by a force that included a number of Americans as well as American-allied Creeks from the Tensaw district. The ensuing fight, known as the Battle of Burnt Corn Creek, lasted several hours, with the Red Sticks emerging victorious. The battle galvanized both the Red Stick and the American-allied parties since the former felt vindicated in their prophecies after defeating a much larger detachment and the latter felt compelled to redeem themselves in battle.[85] McQueen's party also destroyed the property of Sam Moniac, a planter, rancher, and tavernkeeper of mixed Creek-American parentage.

Sam Moniac's situation reveals how deeply divided the Creek Nation was and how frequently these struggles played out along intimate physical and familial paths. Moniac lived in the Tensaw district and had several properties, including a settlement and store along the Federal Road.[86] One of his brothers-in-law was Red Stick prophet Josiah Francis, whom Moniac referred to as "pretends to be a prophet."[87] He stated that when he went to take some of his considerable livestock to market, his own sister and brother "joined the war party came and got off a number of my horses and other stock and thirty six of my Negroes." When he returned, he encountered a group of Red Sticks camped near his house on the Federal Road and was asked by High Head Jim whether he would join them. Perhaps to save the rest of his family from reprisal, Moniac later testified that he told them he would sell his property, buy ammunition, and join their movement. For the benefit of his American listeners, he later added, "Many . . . who had been induced to join them to save their property were very desirous to leave them but could not." When Moniac duplicitously assured High Head Jim that he would side with the Red Sticks, he was in turn assured "that the war was to be against the whites & not between Indians themselves, that all they wanted was to kill those who had taken the talk of the whites viz. The Big Warrior, Alex'd Cornell, Capt. Isaac, Wm. McIntosh, the Mad Dragon's son, the Little Prince, Spoko Hauge of Tallasee Thicksico." They burned Moniac's house and destroyed most of his livestock anyway.[88]

In addition to targeting American-allied Creeks, especially along the Federal Road, parties of Red Stick Creeks increasingly used the roads as a means for disrupting American travel and mobility. One white American memoirist recalled that their party was often forced to cross large creeks on small bridges the Creeks had themselves erected, "which they demanded toll at a high price for every soul that crossed a bridge." The men of the traveling party often refused these bridges and "would make their negroes cut trees and make a bridge, which gave the Indians great anger, and they would threaten us with death."[89] Similar incidents occurred throughout this period and remind us of both the necessity of dangerous river crossings in Creek country and the symbolic nature of the water's edge as a border space bristling with possibilities.

Elijah Gordy informed Georgia governor Mitchell that while traveling on the Federal Road with a number of other men, women, and children headed for the Mississippi Territory, they were stopped at one of the new bridges by a Creek man who demanded that they pay a toll to cross. Gordy reported that, with the aid of an interpreter, they told the Indian man that "the Rode and bridg was Purchased by the United States." To this, the Creek man responded, "The rode Was and the bridg was built by us but of his timner [timber]." They pushed past the man but were stopped again at the next river crossing, where he had returned with a number of his kinsmen. Gordy explained, "By that Time their was About 30 indions and the Women and Children Would have been in danger or We Would have forst our Way but We had to pay him before We Could With Safety Go on the Cumpeny."[90] All in all, the Indians managed to extort $7.50 from the party.[91]

What is particularly interesting about this incident is that the Creeks demanded money rather than simply killing or kidnapping the travelers, their children, slaves, or horses. They could have easily destroyed the bridge as well. Instead, the Indians repeatedly insisted on being paid for the privilege of passing. It is impossible to determine whether these Creeks were aligned with the Red Sticks or if they were just in search of quick income or both. It is highly suggestive, however, of the ways in which Creek people could profit from the turmoil in the nation.[92] It also reminds us of the ways in which bodies of water that had been customarily considered places of great importance and great danger in Creek cosmology could be invoked. Like the Tie Snake stories, such encounters represent the water's edge as a place of potential peril where one might harness the awesome power of another realm either to help or harm others. In fact, home-grown prophet Captain Isaacs claimed he had received his prophecy from the Tie Snake he encountered after diving down to the bottom of a river. He insisted that it was the powerful serpent from the watery Lower Realm who had shaken the ground beneath the feet of Creek people in the momentous New Madrid quakes. And his visions from the water's depths would now shake the foundation of Creek country to remake the broken world.[93]

Like water crossings, travel itself also appeared in Creek stories as an occasion for increased awareness and potential danger. The Red Sticks seemed determined to exploit this time of potential chaos and confusion by targeting Americans who continued to push through their homelands. And as American travel through the Creek Nation became more and more perilous, the passage of the mail continued to be a particular concern of the region's inhabitants.

Despite earlier assurances that the Indians had "pointedly disavowed any hostile intentions . . . and that travelers would be as safe as ever,"[94] two Tensaw settlers communicated their belief that the mail carrier on the Federal Road had been killed by Red Sticks.[95] Judge Toulmin clarified this report when he informed Brigadier General Ferdinand L. Claiborne that "the post-rider who was supposed to be killed has returnd. He was robbed of his mail by a party of Creeks going to Pensacola. He was afterwards fired upon & had his hat shot off and his horse killed under him—but escaped unhurt."[96] It is clear that many of the Red Sticks were unable to read or write English (or Spanish), so the theft of the mail might at first seem somewhat odd; but, as noted above, it was oftentimes a strategic policy encouraged by the British and perhaps by the Spanish, despite their assertions to the contrary, and yielded a prize worthy of the Red Sticks' attention as well.[97] In addition to the fact that the mail often contained cash, harassing post riders was yet one more way that Red Stick Creeks could demonstrate their deep discontent with the opening and operation of American roads through Creek territory.

As the summer wore on, such confrontations became more frequent as the "Alabama prophets" went on with their magic and the revolution gained support within the Creek Nation. Not surprisingly, their efforts were often concentrated on the nation's roads.[98] Georgia governor Mitchell claimed that the Federal Road itself was the "line of separation" between the Red Stick and American-allied Creeks, which, although not entirely accurate, nevertheless reveals the way such a road could operate as a border space— between peoples and worldviews.[99]

One observer noted, "The hostile Indians were way-laying all the paths leading to Tuckabatchee with intention to kill McIntosh," who had gone there to rescue Big Warrior.[100] William McIntosh, headman of Coweta and signer of both the New York and Fort Wilkinson treaties, had emerged as public enemy number one for the Red Stick Creeks for repeatedly ceding lands and agreeing to roads that brought so much trouble to the Nation. But Big Warrior of Tuckabatchee was almost equally despised.[101] He wrote to Hawkins in mid-July and described his unenviable position: "I never expected a civil war among us, the Council house . . . is destroyed . . . the town was surrounded and we fired on. Our friends from Cowetau were with us and urged the besiegers not to destroy us, but in vain. . . . They fired seven days and an half on the town. . . . My friends brought me to Cowetau, and there I have left my Miccos women & children." In revealing his distress to Hawkins, Big Warrior said that such hostile actions should be thrown "out of the path of peace."[102] Although he was largely falling back on established diplomatic rhetoric describing the relationship between Creeks and Americans, his choice to frame the conflict as one that darkened or disordered the path recalls the importance of the concept of the Creek "sacred path" and again reminds us of the intense referential power of roads and paths in Creek epistemology.

Fully understanding the internal divisions within Creek country and interpreting the factors that motivated individuals to choose different paths is perhaps impossible at this remove, not least because the spiritual dynamic of the war is often missing or submerged in the historical record.[103] While several superficial distinctions, like mixed Creek-American heritage, immediately rise to the surface, the division between Creek factions had as much to do with the influence of American alliances than any particular degree of mixed ancestry. Bicultural individuals like William Weatherford and Alexander Cornells, who ended up opposing one another during the conflict, are but two examples of how complicated the divisions really were for individual Creeks. Nevertheless, as the fighting intensified, many participants and observers tried desperately to decode the logic of the war for one another.

In the summer of 1813, one observer reported of the Red Sticks, "Their language breathes vengeance on the white people."[104] Red Stick leaders frequently stated that they did not wish to make a general war on their own people—only those who had "taken the talks of the whites," meaning those who had adopted the plan of civilization and subsequently abandoned Creek ways. Judge Toulmin said of the Red Stick faction, "As to the half breeds, the revolutionists have no original quarrel with them. If they fall into the new order of things; it will be well. They will remain unmolested:— but if they take part with white men; they will meet with the fate of white men."[105] A month later he reported that the Red Sticks had committed "the most destructive outrages on the persons & property" of those Creeks "known to be well attached to the United States, & on the ground of that attachment."[106] Despite his own suffering at the hands of the Red Stick party, Sam Moniac, of Creek-American ancestry himself, believed that their primary goal was to attack white Americans. But he also told Judge Toulmin that they planned to execute eight of their own headmen in order to effect a "complete revolution in the government."[107] Thus, it seemed that only white Americans and their Creek allies had anything to fear. As James Cornells testified, "They have uniformly declared their determination to cut off all Americans & their friends, and to burn & destroy as they go."[108]

Hawkins's reaction to the increasing hostilities prompted this harsh talk to the "Fanatical Chiefs," under the leadership of Hopoithle Micco, which is worth quoting in detail: "I hear you have begun the war dance, made your war clubs, and are for war with the white people. . . . Do you not know the prophets talk will be the distruction of the Creeks, and give joy to your enemies? . . . You may frighten one another with the power of your prophets to make thunder, earthquakes, and to sink the earth. These things cannot frighten the American soldiers. . . . The thunder of their cannon, their rifles and their swords will be more terrible than the works of your prophets."[109] In Hawkins's interpretation, the Red Sticks were putting the entire nation on a path to ruin by choosing a war with the Americans. His threats certainly carried weight, but his willingness to recruit American-allied headmen to deliver the talk to Hopoithle Micco likely strengthened the Red Sticks' resolve to oppose them both. Indeed, "Youholau Emaultau Haujo Chief of the Autosee" responded to the talk Hawkins sent with the Cusseta chiefs by saying, "I will not receive it or any other talk from Col. Hawkins or the white people. I am done with him and his talks."[110]

Trying a different strategy, Hawkins enjoined Big Warrior to make it known that anyone who accepted the "prophets talk" would be put to death.[111] As a result, Big Warrior found himself again in the position of having to be rescued from Red Stick aggressions. He wrote to Hawkins in early August 1813, requesting immediate assistance from the Americans: "Come along as you have a public road to come in our nation.—We are very scarce in Arms & ammunition, We hope you will bring that along to furnish our people with it."[112] Thus, the "friendly" faction themselves characterized the Federal Road as a war path, optimally designed for the transport of ordnance and weaponry into the Creek Nation to put down one part of the Creek people.

The Americans had, in fact, already become increasingly involved in the conflict. Secretary of War Armstrong reported that same summer that the governors of Georgia and Tennessee had each been requested to raise 1,500 men into militia regiments to move into Creek country without delay.[113] But it was not until September 1813 that local outrage reached its peak and American preparations began in earnest.

On August 30, a party of Red Stick Creeks, under the leadership of William Weatherford, among others, surrounded a small garrison just north of the Federal Road known as Fort Mims, named for Samuel Mims who owned a ferry at the nearby confluence of the Tombigbee and Alabama rivers.[114] Despite warnings from slaves who had spotted the Red Stick warriors in the vicinity and a report from a scout to the same effect, the fort's commander, Major Daniel Beasley, neglected to take defensive measures.[115] Though accounts vary and exact numbers are impossible to determine, approximately 400 people, including white Americans, allied Creeks, African American slaves, and Red Stick warriors, perished in the battle. The Red Sticks also took about 100 captives and a large number of scalps in their retreat. The carnage shocked a frightened southern public, though reports of the battle were slow to trickle across the Creek country roads because the vast majority of eyewitnesses had been killed.[116]

While the Red Sticks were fulfilling their prophecies and bloodying the paths of the Creek Nation, the region's militias were thundering along the same routes, bringing their vengeance and their weapons of war across the widened roads and newly constructed bridges. Civil war among the Creeks may not have been particularly alarming to outsiders, but the increasing violence against Americans along the borders and on the paths, as well as rumors of continued British interference, was a call to action. Hawkins had warned the Creeks during the summer of 1813, "If the white man is safe in your land, you are safe. If the white man is in danger in your land, you are in danger and war with the white people will be your ruin."[117] While the fate of Americans in and near the Creek Nation, like those who had taken shelter at Fort Mims, was a primary cause for the invasion of militias from surrounding states, the appeals of American-allied Creeks did not go unheeded. From Augusta, Elijah Clark reported to his brother on the Mississippi River, "The peace party having applied to their White Brethren for assistance & protection, the State of Georgia are preparing to march a large detachment into their Country. Tennessee and the United States it is said, are making similar preparations."[118]

Also of concern to both eastern and western southerners was the line of communication with New Orleans and settlements in the Mississippi Territory. Some southerners, like Clark, had made significant investments in the western lands and probably felt as he did: "The Extraordinary state of things in the Indian nation, by preventing any Communication between Orleans & this Country, has given me much uneasiness." But he, like his southern neighbors, also looked forward to the war's end when he felt confident that white Americans would either gain possession of the Creek territory or would finally be permitted to establish garrisons along the Federal Road, "so as to insure perfect safety in travelling, and regular communications between Orleans & the Atlantic States."[119]

The very action that had aroused so much Creek hostility—opening more and better American routes through their homeland—was also the best possible outcome of the war itself as far as white southerners were concerned. The restoration of peace through the deployment of state and federal troops thus weighed heavily on the minds of white southerners, and was intimately linked to their fears and fantasies about the cotton boom and their individual and collective stake in it. But it was not only commercial concerns that spurred southern interest in the war.

American enthusiasm for entering the Creek War had surged since the Fort Mims incident and militia enrollment increased dramatically in those states that felt most threatened—especially Tennessee and Georgia. Accounts of the battle commonly referred to it as a "massacre," a scene of "inhuman butchery,"[120] and a "bloody, burning conflict."[121] Men like Samuel Dale and Davy Crockett would earn lasting fame for their "heroic" roles in the war and would carry their southern brand of patriotism with them as they pushed west in the years to come.

In the region's newspapers, blame for the "havock" was largely placed at the feet of Benjamin Hawkins, who was almost universally considered an enemy of the southern states by editorialists. Despite everything Hawkins had done to render American travel through Creek country safe and secure, many southerners branded him a champion of the Indians and complained of the tenuous line of communication across the nation. One Knoxville paper denounced Hawkins, along with Judge Harry Toulmin: "For years have the two former gentleman been the apologists of the murders & robberies, committed on our innocent fellow citizens by the creek Indians! In so much, that in times of profound peace, it was dangerous to travel through the country!"[122] The growing frustration of the southern public with these federal representatives and their Indian policy reflected a widening rift between southern and national interests that would inflame the passion for Indian Removal in the 1830s and contribute to increasing southern sectionalism.

By October 1813, local newspapers were filled with excited news of troop movements and militia musters.[123] Tennesseans, long having viewed themselves as neglected westerners, "in the midst of an immense wilderness, trembling for our homes and houses," heeded these calls to action like no other.

Andrew Jackson, commander of the Tennessee militia and ever-interested speculator in Indian lands, made a plea to his fellow "Brave Tennesseans!" telling them, in a sensational published message, "Your frontier is threatened with invasion by the savage foe! Already do they advance towards your frontier, with their scalping knives unsheathed, to butcher your wives and children, and your helpless babes."[124] In a private communication to Georgia governor Peter Early, Jackson betrayed a similar tone and a foretelling unwillingness to differentiate between the Red Sticks and the American-allied Creeks. "The Creeks," he insisted, "must be destroyed." In order to complete this mission, he continued, "[and] thereby secure a permanent place to our Southern frontier, we must take possession of Pensacola."[125] It was clear to Jackson that British and Spanish aid flowing in through the Gulf—or at least rumored to be flowing in—continued to impede American development of the region.

One strategy that Jackson and his comrades pursued in their drive to "destroy" the Creeks was to open, improve, and utilize roads through Creek country. Naturally, the unimpeded movement of troops across enemy lines is of concern during any armed conflict. But given the nature of the ground to be covered in the Creek Nation and the unreliable character of many of the roads, it was quickly deemed necessary to expand and improve the old paths into roadways suitable for the transportation of ordnance and supplies.[126] Thus, the palimpsest was scored again as the trading paths, post roads, and travelers' routes were rutted with commissary wagons and heavy weaponry.

Not long after arriving in Creek country, Jackson sent out a fatigue party to begin cutting a road along which he intended to move with the main body of his troops.[127] He was involved in opening several roads, including a short route linking the Tennessee and Coosa rivers at Fort Armstrong that was eventually extended to meet the Federal Road further south. They later built another road that passed from central Tennessee to New Orleans and became known as "Jackson's Military Road."[128] Georgia governor Mitchell likewise initiated an effort to open a path southeastwardly from the town of Hartford on the Ocmulgee River to the St. Mary's River, an area subject to frequent threats by Seminole Red Sticks.[129] Similarly, hundreds of troops, along with their weaponry and some supplies, moved along the Federal Road from Georgia, grimly proving, as the treaties creating it had predicted, that the road would be "indispensable" for the movement of soldiers and munitions in time of war.[130] Just as Elijah Clark had hoped, the Federal Road itself became the location of new military garrisons that, while not essential, were nevertheless useful to quiet "the fears of the Pusilanimous" who lived near them, especially in Georgia.[131]

As the war moved on through the winter of 1813–1814, however, the problem of supplying American troops and moving them from one theater to another actually worsened. One Tennessee soldier wrote of great dissent in the ranks on receiving news of another long march on "a very muddy road with several large Creeks to wade," later adding, "There is much Sickness . . . one or more dies every day."[132] A North Carolina volunteer informed his mother that notwithstanding "the troops in camp are very sickly," they had just endured another "fatiguing march."[133] Another Carolina soldier exclaimed that the road being used to provision a new American fort on the Tallapoosa River "exceeds any thing of the Kind I have ever seen." He explained that they had more than two hundred wagons bringing supplies to the garrison but the poor condition of the road meant that each one could only carry four barrels of flour, even with six to eight horses pulling each wagon. Even so, the fifteen-mile trip from the supply fort to the new post took four days.[134] The problem of provisioning the troops was also one of both supply and communication, as the war effort's central commander explained from his post at Fort Hawkins. General Thomas Pinckney complained that due to difficulties receiving mail in the area, he had not received word of troop relief and warned that the delay would likely result in "fatal consequences."[135]

The waterways of the Creek Nation were similarly put to military use, primarily for the transport of supplies and munitions from Tennessee to outposts along the Coosa, Tallapoosa, Alabama, and Chattahoochee rivers. One famous incident of the war, although among the most difficult to substantiate, took place in a canoe on the Alabama River. Samuel Dale, "the Daniel Boone of Alabama," engaged a handful of Red Stick warriors in dueling canoes, his own piloted by an enslaved man named Ceasar, without whose help Dale would have surely perished.[136] Except for this celebrated episode, most of the river transport was less exciting but nevertheless perilous, and absolutely essential to the war effort.[137] Another soldier later recalled an ill-fated mission in which his detachment was to march along a trail so poor that no supply wagons could travel it and eventually meet their boatloads of provisions, which were being sent up the Alabama River. After becoming thoroughly lost and missing the place at which they were to meet the boat, the commander took off in a canoe with three others in search of the landing spot. But all they managed to do was "upset" their canoe and "all their ammunition, except a few cartridges some of them had in their pockets, got wet, and one musket lost overboard." After an attack by the Red Sticks, the party was reduced to just two men, who twice tried in vain to cross the waterway and find the Federal Road—the only polestar in their attempt to reunite with the rest of the troops. In the end, a lone man survived to report the events.[138]

Despite the hardships of travel through Creek country, the American troops managed to gain control of the situation. By the middle of 1814, the position of the Red Sticks had worsened considerably as troops under the command of Andrew Jackson, John Coffee, and Ferdinand L. Claiborne began to squeeze them from all sides. In addition, several hundred Cherokee warriors and headmen, as well as a significant number of Choctaw fighters, had joined the Americans and American-allied Creeks in their effort to re-take the Creek Nation and proved to be formidable adversaries for their neighbors.[139] One soldier wrote that Georgia troops, having already engaged the Red Sticks, warned his detachment that they would "find the creeks to fight desperately," but General Jackson's large assemblage of Tennessee volunteers, along with troops from the Carolinas, were poised to "strike the final blows."[140]

Just three days later, on March 27, 1814, the Red Sticks suffered a serious and devastating defeat at the Battle of Horseshoe Bend on the Tallapoosa River. Nearly 600 Red Sticks were killed after Jackson's troops, including his Indian allies, surrounded them on a peninsula formed by a distinctive horseshoe-shaped bend in the river. Within a month, Jackson was preparing the terms of a peace treaty to be offered to the Red Sticks, despite the fact that masses of "hostiles" were still active among the Seminole towns and along the southern Georgia frontier and word of British assistance to the Red Sticks was still heard throughout the region.[141]

The provisions of the preliminary agreement emphasized the unrestricted movement of Americans into and through Creek country. In addition to retaining "as much of the conquered territory as may appear to the government to be a just indemnity for the expences of the war," the United States also reserved the right to establish military posts and trading houses, "and to make and use such roads as they may think necessary, and freely to navigate all the rivers and water courses in the Creek territory."[142] Although this draft of the peace treaty was never adopted, the implication was clear. The Americans, through their conquest of the Red Sticks, had earned the right to traverse Creek country whenever and however they wished. Fearing that they could not remain in their homelands and anticipating the renewed

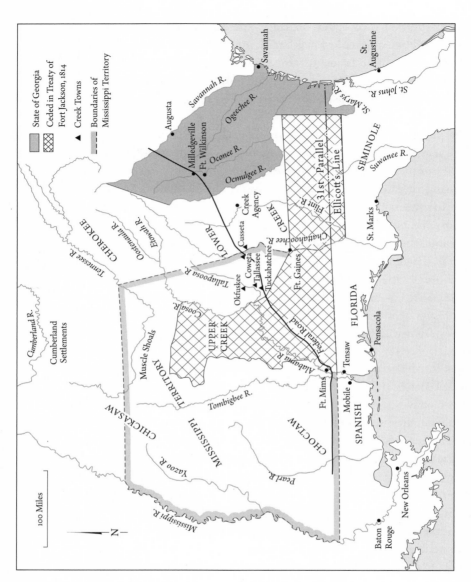

Map 3. Creek cessions in the Treaty of Fort Jackson, 1814

influx of Americans, large groups of Red Stick Creeks began to flee to the relative safety of Seminole settlements in Florida.

On August 9, 1814, General Jackson met with the American-allied Creek leaders to settle the terms of a treaty ending the Creek War—at least on paper. The Treaty of Fort Jackson resulted in the loss of nearly 23 million acres of Creek land, including much of that claimed by American-allied towns, as well as several million acres claimed by Jackson's Cherokee allies (see map 3). The terms of the treaty are among the most punitive and destructive ever recorded in American-Indian affairs, and Jackson's personal involvement in crafting the treaty reflects his deep personal opposition to the persistence of Native peoples in the region.

The opening of the treaty emphasized the "unprovoked, inhuman, and sanguinary" nature of the war and reminded the Creeks of the murders committed along the Federal Road, among other locations. As in the proposed peace terms from June 1814, the United States reserved the right to "establish military posts and trading houses, and to open roads within the territory, guaranteed to the Creek nation by the second article, and a right to the free navigation of all its waters," ensuring their permanent presence in Creek country. The Americans claimed these rights as a consequence of their victory, "in conformity with principles of national justice and honorable warfare."[143]

Although a number of Creek headmen signed the treaty, including Big Warrior and William McIntosh, almost none of the Red Stick leaders were among them. In fact, Hawkins predicted that "as soon as our new line of limits for the Creeks is known it will rouse up and combine their whole force in that quarter [southern border of Georgia] against us."[144] While the situation in Seminole country continued to deteriorate, as Hawkins feared, with Red Sticks continuing to "do mischief against our posts on the road" as well as stealing or freeing slaves from Georgia, McIntosh reported that many of the "Red Club" leaders within the Creek Nation were laying down their arms and asking for forgiveness from their kinspeople.[145] President Madison later blandly referred to the persistent problems on the southern frontiers as "restlessness," but the continuance of attacks, particularly along Georgia's southern border, signaled a deep and abiding hostility for the Americans and their allies in Creek country.[146] The intensification of hostilities on the Georgia-Florida border would ultimately ignite another several years of warfare, known as the First Seminole War, that centered less on access and acquisition of Seminole lands and more on the recovery of slaves stolen or escaped from plantations in Georgia.

By the end of 1814, however, Andrew Jackson had already left the Creek War theater. He moved west toward the grand port of New Orleans—the jewel of southwestern commerce and navigation—to put an end to the War of 1812. Fighting with a motley force against superior numbers of British troops, Jackson managed to secure New Orleans in January 1815, though the war had already ended on Christmas Eve with the signing of the Treaty of Ghent.

Like the close of the Revolutionary War, the end of the War of 1812 and the earlier "end" to the Creek War brought punishing results for the Native peoples involved. Both allies and enemies of the Americans were divested of their lands and caught in the midst of an imperial battle for abstract "rights of conquest" that had little to do with the realities on the ground. The Treaty of Ghent provided for a restoration of lands as they were held in 1811, which if strictly applied would have meant that the lands ceded by the Creeks in the Treaty of Fort Jackson four months earlier would be returned to them. But American officials contended that the treaty clause did not apply to the Creeks since the two wars (the Creek War and the War of 1812) had occurred independent of one another. This was an about-face from their previous claims that British incitement of Indian aggression was a primary cause of the Red Stick rebellion, which fomented the Creek War.[147] Hawkins was instructed to "sedulously counteract any impressions that may be attempted to be made upon them [the Creeks], that the stipulations of the late Treaty with Great Britain, have any relation whatever to the Treaty made by Genl. Jackson with them."[148] He told his own staunch Creek ally Alexander Cornells, "There is nothing in that treaty [Ghent] to do away with the one called Jackson's."[149] The debate over this interpretation continued until the ratification of the Treaty of Fort Jackson in February 1815, but the problems did not end there.

With ongoing encouragement from the British in Florida, small bands of Seminoles and Creeks continued to perpetrate attacks on the southern borders, focusing their energies on the roads. Hawkins reported in April 1815, "I find the hostile Indians in small parties continue their plundering and murdering on the road."[150] Less than two weeks later, he noted, "A banditti of hostile Indians of Fowltown fled into East Florida have infested the road through the agency since peace and attacked our waggons four times."[151]

In addition, the attempt to run the new boundary line established in the Treaty of Fort Jackson occasioned many difficulties, with one of the most controversial aspects being that it took for granted the boundaries between the Creeks and the Cherokees, Chickasaws, and Choctaws. The government representatives relied on the word of the Creek leaders who signed the treaty regarding the limits of their territory. It quickly became apparent to the federal officials, however, that "the boundary lines between the Cherokees, Creeks, and Choctaws depend entirely upon tradition, and that there is no record [or] evidence of them."[152] The Cherokees were particularly concerned about their lands having been included among those ceded by the Creeks in Jackson's treaty.

As discussed previously, southern Indians had distinct beliefs about the extent of their respective territories, based on their mythologies, intertribal agreements, and traditions of usage. The sticking point for the Americans was that there was no map, no authoritative record of the location of these boundaries on which they could base the treaty. Ultimately, it was necessary to convene delegations of Creek, Cherokee, and Chickasaw leaders to create a documentary record of the limits of their respective nations so that the United States could determine the true boundaries of the Fort Jackson cession. In their discussions about the borders that separated their nations, representatives from the four Indian nations recounted not only their treaty histories but reached back to the stories of their origin and migrations to try to clarify their limits for the Americans.[153]

In addition to the continuing disturbances on the Georgia boundaries and between the Creeks and their Indian neighbors, the American-allied Creeks emerged from the Creek War with very little that showed them victorious. The Creeks had not received their annuity since 1811 and the American-allied headmen had not been compensated for their considerable expenditures and losses in support of the war effort. Far more serious was the complete devastation of Creek crops and stock holdings.[154] The combined result was a near-ruinous famine. Hawkins sent this alarming report to the governor of Georgia: "Provision is very scarce and the Indians in the country are living altogether on alligators."[155]

Big Warrior, literally watching his people starve around him, decried the injustice to those who had fought so loyally with the Americans in the war. When they could receive food, such as at the newly established Fort Mitchell on the Federal Road, it was not issued as rations, as the Treaty of Fort Jackson had stipulated, but sold to them at exorbitant if not criminal prices. The Tuckabatchee headman pleaded to Jackson, "You told me that you would feede me, I looked for it until I was near perished to death. You told me you loved me, and would feed me. The people towards sun rise were to bring on provisions—I do not know why they did not, bring them on, when the provisions was Brought to Ft. Mitchel, We bought and paid for it. Yes it is so, We sold negroes for Flour also horses and Cattle."[156]

Such extreme economic hardship combined with the loss of nearly eight million acres of their land disgusted the American-allied leaders. In a speech to the assembled headmen at the council square in Tuckabatchee, Big Warrior explained their untenable situation: "General Jackson . . . threatened us and made us comply with his talk, when we were not satisfied. I told him to wait. I did not want to talk about the land. The first thing he talked about was the land. I told him the enemy had raised arms against me. . . . Before they were conquered the General talked about land."[157] Big Warrior went right to the heart of the matter. American involvement in the Creek War, he now believed, had little to do with the British or Spanish or with attacks on the roads. Those things were all pretext for the acquisition of land. And as Jackson had hinted in his wish to "destroy the Creeks," at the end of the war it mattered not whether the land belonged to his allies or his enemies.

Believing the boundary lines established by the treaty to be patently unjust and entirely unacceptable to the Creek Nation, Big Warrior concluded his talk with an old but established strategy of resistance. He refused to send men to attend the running of the boundary line that would take more than half of the Nation and throw it open to white American settlement. "It is well known we are a small nation," he told Hawkins and Jackson, and "it appears you would shove us off, and take what little we have got. . . . It appears you are taking it away from us. . . . We were all raised on this Island. If that is the law you have made to rob us, if it is the law you must go on with the [boundary] line. I will sit still and hold down my head."[158]

Chapter Five

A NEW WAVE OF EMIGRATION

On his journey through the southern states in 1817, writer James K. Paulding remarked, "I had heard much of the continued migration from the Atlantic coasts to the regions of the west. . . . I have now had some opportunity of witnessing the magnitude of this mighty wave which knows no retrograde motion, but rolls over the land, never to recoil again."[1] Indeed, the period following the close of the Creek War was one of massive and continued emigration into the Trans-Appalachian region. In this increasingly agrarian west, the primary enterprises were cultivating staple crops like cotton, corn, and sugar and raising hogs and cattle. Nearly all these products were transported on rivers and newly opened roads to and from the market hubs of the south and west, places like Natchez, New Orleans, and St. Louis.[2] Eastward migrants saw the availability of recently acquired Indian lands as an opportunity to stake their claim in the new economy, and they proceeded by the wagonload into even the most suspect of western cessions and "purchases." They set forth in record numbers on the new and recently repurposed roads that cut through the heart of Creek country.

Even before the Treaty of Fort Jackson boundaries were surveyed, the lands ostensibly ceded were "rapidly settling by the whites."[3] The state governments were largely powerless to stop this onslaught, and Creek leaders, particularly those who had allied with Americans during the war, were horrified to find their lands and villages overrun by the most backward of backwoods settlers. The federal government planned to use the millions of acres gained in the war to promote public land sales and was also concerned with the mass movement of unauthorized migrants pouring into the western lands along "the Indian Road."[4] As Secretary of War William H. Crawford put it, "The effect of these settlements is to place the very worst part of our citizens in possession of the very best part of the public lands upon pre-emption principles," thus depriving the government of the purchase value. Emigrants traveling past the Creek Agency were warned that they would not be allowed to settle on the new lands unless they had purchased them, but that hardly staunched the flow.[5]

Many white southerners felt they had already purchased these lands with blood spilled in the recent war.[6] Volunteers from North Carolina, Tennessee, and Georgia had spent much of their time marching through the forests and floodplains of Creek country with an eye for the best and most desirable lands. They performed this resource reconnaissance as they pursued the course of war, and more than a few had signed up for service with the specific belief that the hostilities would lead directly to their possession of some part of the Indians' land. One Tennessean told his wife, "In the Creek Nation there is abundance of good land,"[7] and a North Carolina volunteer reported that the land on the rivers of the Creek Nation was said to be of good quality.[8] And indeed, the spirit of emigration was high, not only among veterans but throughout the country. Alabama fever began to infect the eastern states, and great numbers of migrants headed out, or started, for the former Creek lands. Of this trend one correspondent wryly observed, "When people set out to go any where in this country, it is called *starting*. Thus they start to the westward —for the people of this country are the most active in the world and do everything by a start."[9]

By mid-1817, prospective settlers from as far away as Kentucky were pestering the surveyors of the Creek cession for information on the boundary lines, indicating their eagerness to emigrate.[10] "Men of small capital" tended to head for the edges of the many waterways that crisscrossed the region, because they provided the most abundant cane range necessary for cattle grazing.[11] Livestock were a particularly suitable commodity for less wealthy settlers because they could be taken to market "under their own power," unlike cotton or other products that had to be transported in wagons or sent on pole-boats.[12] Men of greater capital were better able to push along the Indian roads with wagons and carts full of their possessions, including slaves. The influx of settlers of both great and small means was one of the most influential events in the period following the Creek War.

The death of Benjamin Hawkins in 1816, just over a year after he had tendered his resignation as Creek agent in protest of the Treaty of Fort

Jackson, brought another significant postwar transition in Creek country.[13] Although Hawkins had biased notions of Creek cultural practices and was one of the harshest critics of the Red Sticks, in many ways his presence had tempered the predatory intentions of the surrounding states. Moreover, his authority as a federal agent assured a level of control, albeit uneven, over the intrusions of squatters and criminals who pressed along the edges of Creek country. His death, coming as it did around the same time that the Fort Jackson treaty was ratified, must have struck Creek leaders as forcibly as the unjust treaty had struck Hawkins. Indeed, as a party of Creek headmen explained, "The president pointed Col Hawkins to see justice done in our nation & we lost him & the nation was at a lost [sic] for some time."[14]

Former Georgia governor David B. Mitchell took over Hawkins's position in 1817, but he was no stranger to the Creeks. Creek leaders probably did not imply affection when they referred to him as "a man we know very well."[15] As governor, Mitchell had been a determined foe of Creek sovereignty, often clashing with Hawkins, whom he considered "overzealous" in his attention to Creek treaty rights. As agent, he speculated in Creek lands and ran a variety of illegal trading and smuggling operations.[16]

In addition to his personal and professional shortcomings as Creek agent, Mitchell also found himself embroiled in a variety of complicated internal conflicts he had inherited from his predecessor, including decades of Creek political turmoil. But some of the challenges facing the Creek Nation were unique to the postwar era. One of these new difficulties was the problem of the Seminole frontier. Large numbers of Seminoles inhabiting towns just below the Georgia-Florida border were still engaged in conflicts with Americans, particularly between the lower Altamaha and Flint rivers. Their ranks were swelled by an influx of former Red Sticks who had fled Creek country after the defeat at Horseshoe Bend, and, perhaps more significantly, by large numbers of escaped slaves.

During the summer of 1817, U.S. Army Commander Edmund P. Gaines reported that he was assembling a force to "adjust our differences with the Indians."[17] Paramount to Gaines's mission was the construction of a new road heading almost due east from Fort Montgomery (site of present-day Montgomery, Alabama) to Hartford, Georgia. The new road, to be completed by troops under Gaines's command, was part of a consolidation effort to provide better routes between military outposts established in accordance with the Treaty of Fort Jackson. Gaines asserted that "by the old road [the Federal Road], the traveller is compelled to pass near 150 miles through an Indian Country," but the new road would shave 100 miles off the time spent in Creek lands.[18] Along with John Coffee, Gaines had completed a similar military road leading from near the Muscle Shoals on the Tennessee River to the Cotton Gin port on the Tombigbee River in the middle of 1816. Thus, opening new roads and repurposing old ones was one of the most visible transformations of the Creek landscape in the postwar period.

As the military continued to open and improve roads in and around Creek territory after the Treaty of Fort Jackson, some Creeks continued to seek reprisal along the routes. In late 1817, on the road leading south from Fort Hawkins, Gaines found two men "just slain," one of whom had been scalped. The location of the incident convinced Gaines that Seminoles committed the crime, but it is difficult to know for sure.[19] So many Creeks had taken refuge to the south following the Red Stick defeat at Horseshoe Bend that a number of Seminole towns were home to a diverse population that included former Red Sticks and fugitive slaves, as well as long-time Seminole residents. Mitchell warned the governor of the Alabama Territory that with "two men having been killed a short distance from Fort Gaines by some hostile fellows from below . . . it will be unsafe to travel in the direction of Forts Scott and Gaines."[20]

In addition to the new roads and forts built after the end of the Creek War, the demands of new emigrants heading into the Alabama Territory and toward the newly created state of Mississippi (established December 20, 1817) required significant improvements to the Federal Road—still the primary route for both military and civilian travelers.[21] But because of repeated failures on the part of the federal government to ensure that Creek leaders received the remuneration guaranteed them, many were less than eager to welcome new travelers. Secretary of War George Graham noted, "The citizens of Georgia and travellers complain much, not only of the road, but of the impositions which they are subjected to by the Indians. As the Chiefs of the Creek nation have refused to permit our citizens to establish public houses and ferries on the road within their limits."[22] And indeed, the Creek headmen had reminded Graham in March 1817 that the right to such establishments and the profits to be had from them were guaranteed to the Creeks in the 1805 Treaty of Washington. As they had before, they explained once again, "You have got a road, a public one, on our land and country on which we do not want the white people to settle or live, for we believe we are able enough to furnish the travelers with corn and provision."[23] Nevertheless, Graham suggested to Mitchell that he conduct a new treaty with the Creeks stipulating their responsibility to establish and maintain public houses and ferries.[24]

For his part, Mitchell had already broached this topic with the Creek headmen and received less than hoped for results. Big Warrior and Little Prince told Mitchell, "You mention to us about the rode not being fulfill to the treaty but we will try to furnish all the road as well as we can & if you will say nothing more about the rode we will say nothing about mills in the oakmulgee as this is a part of the treaty between us."[25] With the turmoil and famine caused by the Creek War still pinching the nation, it is no wonder that they might have been unable and/or unwilling to erect and supply stages and ferry landings so soon after the outbreak of peace. In addition, it was the responsibility of the federal government to establish the ferry landings and bridges at which Creek owner/operators would collect tolls. The Creeks were perhaps reluctant to shoulder the expense of creating such facilities when it was clearly a responsibility of the United States. Neglecting this "obligation" also provided one way to retard the advance of Americans along the new and newly improved roads through Creek country. And, as the headmen implied by their reference to illegal American mills in the Ocmulgee River, they were not the only ones falling short of their promises.

Despite these setbacks, by 1818, American travelers were taking to westward roads like never before. Augustin Harris Hansell recalled his boyhood on the Federal Road near Milledgeville, Georgia: "We met almost daily, caravans of fifteen and twenty one-horse covered carts, going westward; each containing a whole family and with a spinning will on the back and usually a dog underneath, and the boys would question the men as to where they cam from and where they were going, with an almost unvaried reply: 'From Anson County, North Carolina,['] bound for the 'New Purchase,' or bound for the 'Alabam.' "[26] While not all the westbound migrants were in fact from North Carolina, many were from one of the Atlantic states, including Virginia, the Carolinas, and Georgia, and they "made a fair start" along the Indian roads, taking their families, black and white, to a "new world which promises so much to industry & enterprise."[27] In nearly identical terms, a travel guide of the era remarked, "Alabama presents a most desirable field for youthful enterprise."[28]

The number of emigrants heading for the "New Purchase" was so great that the Goode family was forced to wait their turn with a horde of other families at no less than three river crossings on their way through Creek country. At the Chattahoochee River, they discovered "the flat was gone, the rope broke . . . and [the] river high!" Waiting on the riverbank were twenty-two wagons and carriages, as well as several hundred cows and hogs.[29] Indeed, the population of the Alabama Territory grew at an extraordinary pace, increasing from about 10,000 in 1810 to over 120,000 by 1827, and of this total population nearly 50,000 were slaves.[30] Future governor of Alabama Israel Pickens described a "monstrous number of emigrants pouring into the Alabama Country"[31] and noted, "We passed many waggons & other carriages . . . such is the crowd of strangers."[32] More than one old-timer must have thought, like Thomas Ritchie, "If I were young, and unincumbered with a family I would certainly strike for the West."[33] But as Hansell's memoirs and countless travel diaries testify, having a family, while certainly an encumbrance, did not stop others from heading for "the Land of Promise in the West."[34]

The claims of promotional literature and travel guides notwithstanding, the trip across Creek country was still exceedingly dangerous. To say it was also uncomfortable would be an understatement. The larger the party, the more likely it was that someone would not survive the journey. Even along the best roads, the trip was difficult and the problem of river crossings was a persistent one. So remarkable was the Goode family's preservation along their route that the patriarch deemed it necessary to detail their good fortune at great length.[35] Most others were not so lucky; even the positive Mr. Goode couldn't help but remark on the "bad roads which were truly desparate." Pickens likewise complained, "The road was bad beyond conception," and recalled passing innumerable wagons and carriages stuck in the mud along the way.[36] Despite the recent improvements on the Federal Road between Georgia and New Orleans, Pickens described the route as one of "miserable dreary wilderness" (see figure 2).[37]

John Owen, migrating from Norfolk County, Virginia, to Tuscaloosa, Alabama Territory, repeatedly recorded the "infernal Roads," "bad roads worst I ever saw," "roads intolerable," "roads very bad," and "broken Roads." The condition of the roads was so deplorable that their wagon was stuck several times, the wagon tongue broke, and on at least one occasion the entire contraption was overturned. The difficulty of the trip—a distance of nearly 775 miles that took nine weeks to complete—was so exhausting that Owen remarked more than once, "My wife more fortitude than myself—ashamed of it."[38] For other emigrating families, the hardships of the trail were far more serious. One party removing from North Carolina to Alabama had their wagon overturn in a rut along the road, causing the death of a thirteen-year-old child, who perished when a heavy barrel of flour was tossed from the wagon onto her head.[39]

As a result of such frequent difficulties, the condition of the roads leading through the South, including those passing through Creek country, was a

Figure 2. A portion of the Federal Road in present-day Pintlala, Alabama, near the border between Montgomery and Lowndes counties. The closeness of the trees and the ubiquitous presence of Spanish moss along this part of the road suggest Israel Pickens's description of the route as one of "miserable dreary wilderness." (Photo by Mark Dauber, © 2009.)

topic of considerable public discussion during the decade following the Creek War. An editorial reprinted in the *Georgia Journal* complained that the public highways were in a constant state of disrepair and observed, "To hasten their crops, people are very willing to neglect the very roads along which the produce must pass to market." This incongruous lack of interest in the roads meant that it was "ten times as easy to hit a stump as to miss one . . . and the ruts are so deep that one might imagine the wheels to be semi-circles." The editorialist concluded his rant by advising all travelers setting out for a distance of fifty or more miles to take out an insurance policy and "thank his stars for any fortunate combination of circumstances that is able to keep his soul-case from being shattered to pieces."[40]

The subject of internal improvement—building roads and canals, in particular—generated considerable interest and discussion during this period, not only in the South but also nationwide.[41] Politically, the construction of roads was debated as a constitutional issue and more than a few bottles of ink were expended arguing about the federal government's authority to undertake such improvements.[42] The Federal Road from Georgia to New Orleans had been constructed under the auspices of the Post Office Department, and though it had been improved into a wagon road for travelers, it was still officially regarded as "intended principally for the transportation of the mail through the wilderness."[43] The labor used to open these roads was primarily derived from contractors who supplied hired laborers and Creek men who acted as guides. The various military roads constructed by Andrew Jackson, Edmund P. Gaines, and John Coffee during and after the Creek War and the War of 1812 came under the aegis of the Department of War. Soldiers stationed at local garrisons were the principal source of the labor used to construct and repair these roads, such as the one between the Muscle Shoals and New Orleans.

On the state and local level, the condition of travelers' and market roads was left largely up to the local governments.[44] The state of Georgia amended its road laws in 1818, providing for greater state oversight of the construction of new roads and improvement of old ones. They further required that all men aged sixteen to forty-five years, including "mulattoes and free negroes, and all male slaves," participate in yearly work on roads, causeways, and bridges. Like the Indian trails of earlier decades, these roads were marked with posts or other identifying markers to assist travelers on their way.[45]

In addition to state initiatives, numerous private turnpike companies were formed to open new roads across the region. One such outfit, the Unicoy Turnpike Company, proposed to establish a road from the edge of the Cherokee boundary to Franklin County, Georgia, and open stages and inns that would be operated "by white men and their families."[46] Thus, not only would the roads connect planters and ranchers to markets, but they would also be sources of revenue in and of themselves for inhabitants living on the Indian boundaries.[47]

The fever for faster and more efficient transportation seemed to be spreading during the late teens, and many portions of the country were witnessing a boom in steamboat navigation as well as a rise in the profitability of flat boats, especially on the larger, deeper rivers of the Mississippi and Ohio valleys. By 1819, steamboats even plied the shoaly Oconee River in Georgia, though it was no easy undertaking.[48] It was also during this period that Scottish inventor John L. MacAdam introduced his practical process for the "scientific repair and preservation of public roads." Although the process, later known as "Macadamizing," was not widely adopted in the South for several years, this theory of preparing roads with crushed stones of decreasing size—largest on the bottom, smallest on the top—was peculiarly suited to both the "naturally moist and soft soil" of Britain and the swampy ground of the interior South.[49] These various internal improvement impulses derived their force from the growing clamor to unite the Atlantic states with the Trans-Appalachian states and territories, by crossing, circumventing, or removing the Indians who lived between them.[50]

In addition to the issue of sovereign Indian nations in the west, the question of slavery and westward expansion became a political powder keg during the late 1810s. Some eastern and northern politicians began to openly advocate prohibiting slavery in the new territories, but their efforts were largely in vain.[51] To many southern statesmen, it was unimaginable that slavery should be prohibited in the new western states. Indeed, for many of the families moving into the Alabama Territory, or perhaps pursuing an even more westerly course, the worldly possessions they packed onto wagons and trucked along the roads included slaves.[52] The great profits to be gained from migrating to the newly secured lands in the Alabama Territory relied on the labor of these forced migrants. One emigrant directory asserted, "Labor is almost exclusively performed by slaves," and estimated that a "good negro" would command anywhere from $800 to $1,200 and could tend to approximately three acres of cotton. After deducting the expense of feeding and clothing these laborers, it was estimated that "the clear profit of the full grown male slaves will average about 200 dollars" if employed in cotton cultivation.[53]

Some of the wealthier emigrants set out on tours through the ceded

Creek lands to determine the best location for their farms, anticipating the public land sales that would take place on terms "so perfectly easy" that there could be "no possible difficulty" in obtaining as much as desired.[54] Like other men of great capital, Pickens sent his slaves on to Alabama in the care of an overseer to settle on the farm "which we had engaged for." For men like Pickens, slaves, particularly experienced men, functioned as a sort of venture capital—sent out at no small risk to form the first layer of investment in the new western lands. Their success or failure would determine the potential growth of the entire enterprise. He referred to the group as "our colony" and surmised that they were "some where in the Creek country on the march."[55] Others, like Virginian John Owen, brought his "three or four slaves" along with him and his family on his overland journey to the Alabama Territory. Once there, he "added to his slave property."[56] On his journey from Richmond, Virginia, toward the southwest, English correspondent William Tell Harris observed, "We are continually passing families, sometimes in large bodies, removing with their furniture and negroes to the Alabama."[57]

These enslaved peoples were westward emigrants of a kind, but unlike the white migrants who moved along the same paths they were "westering without hope."[58] Large parties of slaves were sometimes forced to travel with slave traders determined to make their fortune in the "New Jerusalem" like the planters they hoped to supply.[59] The image of slaves driven by traders in coffles along Creek country roads emphasizes the degree to which they were conceived of as property, like livestock, hogs, or horses—sent along the southern roads under their own power and utterly necessary to the economic development of other transportable wealth in the form of staple crops. Indeed, the slave trade was crucial to the development of southern commercial routes in the postwar years.[60] One observer exclaimed, "There is no branch of trade, in this part of the country, more brisk and profitable than that of buying and selling negroes," and remarked that there was constant speculation in slaves as well as livestock.[61] Although vast numbers of slaves intended for sale in the southern market were later transported by sea and sold in New Orleans and other ports, this was an expensive method of transport and at least until the 1830s, "bringing them through" was considered preferable.[62] Despite fears that they might escape into the Indian towns along the way, bringing them on foot was not only cheaper but also believed to permit a gradual adjustment to regional climactic differences.[63]

The men were typically chained together in coffles, with women and children occasionally allowed to ride in wagons; they often numbered in the hundreds.[64] The sick, the elderly, and the very young were often absent from

Figure 3. An engraving of a slave coffle being driven from the upper to the lower South captures the great peril of forced overland migrations that included frequent river crossings. Although the image contains highly stylized and somewhat inaccurate figures popular in contemporary illustrations, James Buckingham claimed to have witnessed this very scene near Fredericksburg, Virginia, in the 1830s. The image appears in Buckingham's The Slave States of America, vol. 2 [1842], facing page 553. (Courtesy of Cushing Memorial Library and Archives, Texas A&M University, College Station.)

these traveling flesh marts, although pregnant women might be included because of the higher prices that could be demanded for them. Long trains or "droves" of slaves like these were a common sight on the roads that led from Virginia to the southwest through the rolling southern landscape, through Creek country, and beyond (see figure 3).[65] An early historian of Alabama noted that while the period from 1817 to 1830 was one of "rápid immigration" to the area, the increase in the white population paled in comparison to the increase in the number of "colored inhabitants."[66] Indeed, the slow change from Creek country to cotton country might be most accurately mapped in terms of the number of African-descended peoples forced to populate former Indian lands.[67] Thus, the winding trade paths of the

Creek Nation that were remade and remapped as post roads, military roads, and market roads now became paths of bondage, instrumental in the forced migration of thousands of enslaved Africans and African Americans.

Many of these enslaved individuals were separated from their families, resulting in vast broken or damaged networks of kinship that stretched from the mid-Chesapeake southwest to the lower Mississippi River.[68] When Charles Ball's mother was sold to a Georgia trader after the death of their owner, he recalled, "My father never recovered from the effects of the shock, which this sudden and overwhelming ruin of his family gave him."[69] To prevent his own sale southward, Ball's father eventually escaped and was never heard from again. Another desperate slave resolved to break his own leg using an ax so that he would not be sold southward to a trader.[70] Although it is impossible to calculate statistics on the phenomenon, at least one observer claimed that suicide provided a way of resisting removal to the South: "Self-destruction is much more frequent . . . than is generally supposed."[71]

Enslaved people traveling in the company of a family fared somewhat better than those spurred on by slave traders, but not always.[72] One traveler reported that some families displaying the "migratory disposition" removed toward the southwest with their slaves in a "frequently pitiable" condition: "Where they have betrayed any intention of running away, they are chained to the waggons; when there is a gang of from twenty to a hundred, the poor creatures are arranged two abreast, secured by a long chain that passes down between them, and in this manner are driven forward; all prospect of escape being cut off, by the loaded rifles on either hand."[73] Even when greater care was taken with a family of slaves, accidents and misfortunes could just as easily befall them as other members of a traveling party. Israel Pickens lost an enslaved woman to illness after a perilous winter trip by water and an adolescent girl perished during a hazardous river crossing the following year.[74]

The roads were not merely symbols of their enslavement, however. Some slaves used these very same roads and paths to obtain their freedom.[75] Moses Roper used both the rivers and roads of the Lower South, including one built by Andrew Jackson during the First Seminole War, to navigate his way from the Florida-Georgia line into freedom, even obtaining a false passport along the way.[76] On his own long journey after being sold southward from Maryland, Charles Ball memorized all the rivers he crossed and the "order which we had reached them." With this furtive geography in mind, he was later able to make his escape northward.[77] Similarly, folklorists have recorded a song called "Follow the Drinking Gourd" that contained specific references to the rivers of the interior South, to human-made marks on trees, and to the stars. Following these natural and artificial signposts, fugitives kept one eye on the ground and one on the night sky to "follow the drinking gourd" (a folk reference to the Big Dipper).[78] The song enjoined escapees to follow the marks of a human foot and a pegleg side by side on the trees along the Tombigbee and the Tennessee rivers, then northward to the Ohio River and into freedom.[79]

In addition, though it was somewhat less common by the late 1810s than during the height of the deerskin trade, African-descended men continued to serve as messengers, wagoners, and boatmen through Indian country.[80] Alabama governor Israel Pickens occasionally sent his "servant" from the seat of government in Cahaba to his home in the hinterland of Alabama, "to see my children & know how all are doing."[81] Charles Ball traveled with his owner into Indian Country to purchase livestock and "Indian horses."[82] An enslaved man known as America was embroiled in a legal dispute when he attempted to obtain passage at a ferry crossing and was inexplicably beaten by the ferryman. Signaling how frequently his slaves traveled independently, America's owner complained that he had paid in advance for them to use this particular ferry and it was a hardship for them to cross elsewhere.[83] In addition, African-descended men continued to serve in limited capacities as "cowboys," driving large herds of livestock to market along the rutted southern roads.

Larger numbers of fugitive slaves than ever before had also begun to ply the southward trails into the swamps and thickets of north Florida, seeking the refuge of Seminole and Creek towns there or establishing their own maroon communities, ensconced in hard-to-reach wetlands.[84] Others continued to travel furtively along the roads and trails of the Old Southwest, as noted above, often thought to be headed for "the Nation," either as outright fugitives or with passes of varying levels of legitimacy.[85] An enslaved couple known as John and Hannah may have had "passes to enable them to get through the Creek Nation," and their Alabama owners surmised that they would head eastward along the Federal Road toward Georgia, "the usual route through the nation."[86] Some were recovered in the Creek Nation, either by American slave catchers or Indians seeking a monetary reward.[87] Others ended up enslaved in the Creek Nation or tangled up in legal disputes between putative white and Native owners.[88] A lucky few managed to secure their freedom after traversing Creek country, sometimes relying on the kindness of Indian people they met along the way and sometimes avoiding contact with them altogether.[89] Still others actually headed deeper into the Old Southwest, perhaps seeking a reunion with family members who had been "sold South."[90]

The "crowd of strangers"—white and black—that pressed into the Old Southwest during the late 1810s through the early 1820s depended on the fantasy of free or cheap land vacated by the Creeks after the termination of the war. Of course, it was not merely fantasy. Many millions of acres had indeed been given up to the United States as part of the Fort Jackson treaty agreement, but Creek people had by no means given up their claim to their homelands. Despite the hopes and fears of the white and black outsiders who came to the region, the land was not simply destined to become the "Cotton Kingdom." Much of this interior region was still Creek country and Creek men and women continued to make it their own, even as wider roads and freer rivers brought more and more outsiders to their lands.

The presence of greater numbers of travelers in the Creek Nation also meant that there were expanding opportunities for Creek entrepreneurs. Travelers (and often surveyors as well) needed supplies, provisions, guides, and lodging, and Creek men and women were sometimes called upon to provide these necessaries. In addition, some of the best-positioned Creeks managed to make handsome profits by operating ferries and stages along thoroughfares like the Federal Road. While the Creek War and the continuing difficulties along the Seminole frontier were indubitably devastating for much of Creek country, men and women of the nation continued, as they had done for generations, to adapt and exploit the new conditions they faced.

A number of problems conspired to frustrate Creek attempts to maintain national sovereignty in this period, however. One was the Fort Jackson treaty and the boundaries it proscribed. Only one former Red Stick leader actually signed the controversial treaty and many of the American-allied signatories were themselves disgusted with the outcome. In addition, it was extraordinarily difficult to determine the exact boundary lines to be run according to the vague specifications of the document. These two issues made travel and settlement in and near Creek country perilous for American migrants hoping to establish themselves in the "new cession," as Creek men and women resisted their presence through both formal and informal means. Meanwhile, increasing numbers of Creeks, as well as fugitive slaves, continued to travel southward to join the Seminoles in a massive internal migration.[91]

While Creek men and women had always traveled widely through their territory (on winter hunts, to see family, and for trade), the havoc of the Creek War led to a dispersal of clans and families and subsequently ensured that members of the confederacy would now travel even greater distances to remain in contact with one another. One surveyor in lower Georgia reported that a company of Indians "made many enquiries of us . . . whether or not the low Country Indians would be permitted to visit those in the up Country & C."[92] And as noted, large numbers of former Red Sticks had departed for the Florida towns of their kinsmen and allies. Edmund P. Gaines reported, "I am assured by the friendly chiefs that the hostile warriors of the Towns on the Chatahotchie have been for some time past moving off down the River to join the Seminoles."[93] The strongholds of these southerly talwas were the settlements around the Apalachicola River, located to the south of American-allied towns like Coweta. While this internal migration conformed to an older southeastern Indian custom in which dissidents typically departed from their communities rather than try to enforce their will at large, it was cold comfort to Americans along the southern Georgia border. The exodus may have also been unsettling to those Creeks who remained in the nation but did not necessarily want to see political power consolidated in the hands of the American-allied leaders like William McIntosh, who stayed behind when the Red Sticks departed.[94]

As the First Seminole War raged, Red Stick Creeks and Seminoles battled not only American soldiers but also the emigrants pressing on the borders of their remaining lands. Numerous accounts of attacks on travelers appeared in the winter of 1817–1818. In December, Mitchell informed Georgia governor William Rabun that two male travelers were killed "by the hostile Indians" on the road leading from Fort Perry (just east of present-day Columbus, Georgia) southward to Fort Gaines (along the lower Chattahoochee River).[95] Although McIntosh had been ordered to muster a party of warriors to protect travelers on the public roads, Mitchell reported another "daring outrage" against an American family traveling near the lower Chattahoochee River in early 1818. Mitchell soon recommended that a military force be stationed nearby to protect agency property and "scout occasionally on the public road." The agent claimed that there was not "the least danger" in traveling along the Federal Road from Georgia to Fort Mitchell, but advised against traveling more southern routes such as those near Fort Gaines unless accompanied by an armed guard.[96]

Such attacks are reminiscent of similar assaults on families traveling along the federal horse path in the period preceding the Creek War. But whether or not they were committed by former Red Sticks, assaults on travelers represented a continued, growing resistance to American travel and were at least partially successful in impeding it.[97] One correspondent noted that because of the "troublesome hostile" Indians and the "impassible" nature of the un-improved roads, "it was impossible to procure baggage waggons at any price to enter the nation."[98] Again, the roadways became a primary site for enacting resistance and demanding respect.

The Treaty of the Creek Agency, signed hastily in 1818, only exacerbated such tensions in Creek country. Like the Treaty of Fort Jackson, this agreement was signed only by American-allied headmen, including Big Warrior and William McIntosh, and provided that in exchange for a tract of land ranging from the high shoals of the Apalachee River to the "shallow ford" of the Chattahoochee (a fairly small parcel), the Nation was to receive $120,000 (see map 4 at the start of chapter 6). In addition, the United States would furnish blacksmiths and strikers to the Creeks for a period of three years. Like earlier treaties, this document secured the elite status of American-allied leaders and cemented the civilization plan that Benjamin Hawkins had first introduced some thirty years before. And like those past agreements, the Treaty of the Creek Agency was not approved, witnessed, or signed by any of the dissenting leaders of the Creek Nation. Despite the fact that the cession was comparatively small, it was yet another wedge between McIntosh's party and the remaining anti-American inhabitants of Creek country. That both Big Warrior and McIntosh agreed to sign the treaty masked a growing division within the pro-American party.[99]

The subsequent effort to delineate the boundary lines pursuant to the still disputed Treaty of Fort Jackson and, to a lesser degree, the new Treaty of the Creek Agency not only hindered peace in Creek country, but also slowed American settlement in the ceded lands. As in earlier decades, Creek resisters used a variety of strategies to antagonize surveyors and reinterpret the boundary lines. Referring to the Fort Jackson line, Surveyor William Green reported, "Those below Flint River say positively that the land on the lower side of the River shall not be Survey'd, as they never sold it."[100] In addition, Green notified Georgia governor Rabun that the expedition had been repeatedly delayed by Little Prince's unwillingness to supply an escort. The dissimulation of reputed American allies at this juncture signals the depth of Creek frustration with both the treaties and attempts to enact them.[101]

Green's anger about the surveying delays only grew as Little Prince and his compatriots bided their time, demanding greater pay and more rations, and generally inconveniencing the expedition. The surveyor complained to Rabun that both his funds and his provisions were nearly exhausted "by the enormous time concerned waiting on those worthless fellows."[102] He had hoped the American-allied Creeks would act as a security force against the possible attacks of those whose land was about to be parceled off. At one point, he was approached by a Seminole leader who "enquired after we had drank together by whos authority I was running the line."[103] According to one observer, "The best informed White men say that it will not be done without bloodshed."[104] Indeed, Green confessed that rumors of violence were common and some Creeks spoke openly of their disdain for the purchase and the survey. "I was completely deserted," he continued; "not a man or boy would accompany me."[105] It should not have been surprising that when the time came to mark the land, the treaty signers were less than eager to put their hands to the trees in the same way that they had put their pens to the paper.

Once Green and his surveying party were able to have some conversation with the "lower Indians" along whose towns the new boundary line would pass, the depth of the Creek internal political division became painfully apparent. Far from planning attacks, one leader assured him, they were busy deflecting threats from McIntosh (who said he would "put hell upon them" for disturbing the expedition) and simply trying to preserve their communities from ongoing famine.[106] He implied that when "red club refugees from the upper towns" stole livestock, horses, or other provisions from surveyors or travelers, they were simply trying to help their families survive. But the very real concerns of famine might also have provided convenient cover for deliberate acts of resistance. Another government representative testified to the purposeful destruction of the marked survey lines in his district just east of the Flint River. In what appeared to be an effort to erase or overwrite the new boundary between the Creeks and Georgia, he discovered "several of our Corner posts destroyed and the numbers cut from some of the Station trees on our lines as well as newly blazed trees Crossing and Intersecting with my lines which from every appearance and circumstance must have been done by Indians."[107] Here was a distinct attempt to revise the writing on the forest walls. And given the close proximity of several settlements of intermixed African Americans, Creeks, and Seminoles, this effort may have represented not only a Native but also a hybrid response.[108]

For some Creeks, however, the push to delineate new boundaries and permit increased travel signaled the emergence of new economic opportunities. The ability to create and exploit these opportunities varied widely depending on one's position among the political divisions and emerging social classes within the Creek Nation. For instance, William McIntosh was able to operate highly profitable stages, taverns, ferry landings, and plantations, all of which catered to American travelers and officials. This was largely because McIntosh himself agreed to land cessions, partnered with American businessmen and representatives, and ultimately welcomed, if not always American people, at least American money. He was willing to lop off great parcels of former Red Stick lands, for example, in the treaties following the Creek War with the dual purpose of punishing the faction that opposed his control of the National Council and enriching himself by securing lucrative contracts, reserved land, and annuity payments. Similarly, he was willing to facilitate American movement through Creek lands if it meant that travelers would pass his plantations, taverns, and stores, buy his goods, and keep him well connected to the southern market.[109]

Those Creeks who were most closely involved with American trade establishments naturally profited most handsomely from the commerce of westward travelers. McIntosh went into business with Creek agent Mitchell, supplying the agency with foodstuffs, horses, and various forms of transport, as well as running at least one separate store for travelers heading along the Federal Road into Alabama.[110] The agency and the associated stores often charged exorbitant prices, largely because of the absence of significant competition. Thomas Stocks recorded his journey along this southwesterly route in 1819 and noted, "Traveled 30 miles to the agency and spent the Night. (here we paid a most Extravagant Bill.)"[111] In fact, the entrepreneurial possibilities that accompanied increased travel through Creek country were reportedly part of the reason that McIntosh and others agreed to consider to ceding additional lands bordering Georgia in the Treaty of the Indian Spring in 1821 (see map 4 at the start of chapter 6).[112]

Although the Treaty of the Indian Spring involved a significant cession of land (almost seven thousand square miles between the Ocmulgee and Flint rivers and bounded on the north by the Chattahoochee River), part of the impetus was settlement of Georgia claims against the Creeks for stolen or destroyed property. Slave owners in Georgia clamored for compensation for enslaved people escaped or taken into the Creek Nation, demanding in addition "requital for loss of services." Considering that some of the enslaved people named in these claims had lived in the Creek Nation for more than twenty years, Georgians expected a considerable sum.[113] U.S. commissioners agreed to pay Indian debts, primarily associated with alleged thefts of slaves and horses, up to $250,000, but also demanded a cession of land.

McIntosh was the chief architect of this agreement, and in the months after the treaty was signed Creek people began to protest the terms of the treaty.[114] In addition to their frustration about the location of the cession's boundaries, it seems likely that rumors of McIntosh's personal gain also spread through the nation. The Coweta headman profited tremendously from the treaty, receiving two reserved parcels of land, including the very location of the negotiations, and an indeterminate amount of cash.[115] By reserving the right to continue operating his Indian Springs tavern, McIntosh maintained his role as gatekeeper to Creek country. His was the preferable place of refreshment on the start of any westward journey through the Creek Nation.[116] But Mitchell's departure from the agency and the arrival of John Crowell, an entrepreneur in his own right, presented a distinct challenge to McIntosh's reign. Within a year, the two would be competing rather than collaborating to supply travelers.[117]

Only McIntosh and other American-allied Creek businessmen like Big Warrior, Alexander Cornells, and George Lovett were wealthy enough to establish and run public houses and other facilities for travelers. As a result, they benefited the most from improvements to local roads, including the still prominent east-west route, the Federal Road. Big Warrior maintained a stand on the road whose daily operations were overseen by his slaves. Alexander Cornells often hosted travelers at his plantation, also situated alongside the Federal Road.[118] Not to be outdone, McIntosh began construction on a new road from Kimulgee, on the Coosa River, to one of his plantations on the Chattahoochee River. An advertisement of the new route emphasized the great benefits to American travelers: "There are good ferries and bridges, so that travellers need not be apprehensive that they will be detained on the road by high waters. The accommodations on the road will be good; and as the Indians have made large crops, there is no doubt that corn may be purchased at any time on the road for less than one dollar per bushel."[119] The "Indians" referred to in this newspaper notice were probably not the individual Creek men and women engaged in small-scale daily exchanges with travelers, but were instead the large-scale producers engaged in plantation-style agriculture with crops tended by African-descended slaves and surpluses not earmarked for a talwa granary.

Less elite Creeks did manage to participate in the changing economy of the Lower South, however. Whereas in decades past they had hunted for subsistence and to supply skins for the credit-driven transatlantic deerskin trade, Creek men and women were now enmeshed in a small-scale cash economy. Of course, as American settlement around them increased, these Indian entrepreneurs faced growing competition to supply westward travelers.[120] They couldn't compete with men like Clement Freeny, who owned a "large, commodious, and well situated public house . . . on the great state road [Federal Road] leading from the Atlantic states to Mobile and New

Orleans . . . being one of the best stands for business in the southern states," or with other white Americans who had gone into business alone or with Creek headmen to set up profitable taverns, stands, or ferries outside the bounds of the law.[121] But non-elite Creeks do seem to have been engaged in selling supplies and provisions when they could spare them.[122]

There is also evidence that Creek people managed to earn or extort money from travelers in the form of tolls. According to Lukas Vischer, a Swiss businessman and artist who traveled the Federal Road through Creek country in 1824, his party was stopped at nearly every river crossing and required to pay a fee to cross. The typical cost was fifty cents, but on at least one occasion they were required to pay double. Vischer claimed that these tolls, and the similarly flexible ferriage fees, were deposited in the Creek "national treasury" in the form of annual taxes levied on toll bridges and ferries. But it also seems likely that a significant amount of the money collected in these daily transactions never made its way beyond the toll collector, some of whom may not have been authorized to assume such a role. Although Vischer occasionally referred to "toll officers" without further remark, he was also accosted at one small bridge by a boy, "half Indian half Negro," who demanded seventy-five cents, a sum the diarist later discovered was quite apart from the norm.[123] Although there is little additional evidence about these toll takers and how they operated, it is certainly possible that river crossings continued to function not merely as places of latent power, where Creeks could seize or be seized by the forces of a lower realm, but also places of profit, where travelers could be pressured into paying more than the usual fare.[124]

Despite the growth in Creek commerce as a result of increased travel, by the early 1820s the outlook for Creeks in the South had darkened considerably. The number of emigrants continued to increase, as did the pressure to cede more land. A wholesale removal of the eastern Indians to lands west of the Mississippi River had been discussed since the turn of the nineteenth century, but with the tremendous success of the market economy in the eastern seaboard states, the meteoric rise in cotton production in the interior South, and the rapid expansion of U.S. territory since 1819, the topic received renewed interest. Georgia statesmen began to remind the federal government and the Creeks of the import of the Georgia Compact of 1802. If the federal government would not uphold its part of the bargain and remove Indians from the lands within Georgia's limits, then Georgia was within its rights to demand restoration of the western lands ceded in that agreement.[125]

A public notice in late 1824 conveyed the powerful disgust that even American allies like Big Warrior felt toward further cessions: "The Chiefs were unwilling to listen to any propositions of the kind: representing that their present limits are too small for their population.—that they wish to live and die in the country which they now inhabit."[126] In December of the same year, the principal leaders of the Creek Nation, including Little Prince, Opothle Yaholo, and William McIntosh, appealed to U.S. commissioners that ceding remaining lands in the state of Georgia, as they were now being steadily pressured to do, would bring their "downfall and ruin." They objected to the argument that the cession of these lands was necessary under the decades-old Georgia Compact (1802) and justly complained that they were never a party to that agreement since it was negotiated between the United States and Georgia.[127] But as with previous treaties, it was bribes, patronage, and perhaps threats that eventually convinced McIntosh and a handful of other signatories to cede all remaining Creek lands in present-day Georgia.

The Treaty of the Indian Springs, signed in February 1825, is by far the most transparently fraudulent, self-interested, and deceitful of all the treaties conducted between the United States and the Creeks to that date. Like the 1821 treaty, this one was signed at McIntosh's thriving tavern in Georgia under the watchful and approving eye of U.S. and Georgia commissioners. McIntosh and his party received a significant payment for the cession and agreed to be the first to take up lands across the Mississippi.[128] They sent a "farewell address" to the Georgia state legislature, presaging the language and sentiment of the Indian Removal debates that would characterize the next fifteen years: "You are like the mighty storm, we are like the tender & Bending tree, we must bow before you, you have tore us up by the root, but still, you are our Brothers & friends, you have promised to replant us in a better soil, an to watch over us, and nurse us."[129] Even those who had sided with McIntosh in the recent Creek War, the Upper Creek Tuckabatchees under Big Warrior and Lower Creeks in his own province were horrified at this surrender.[130]

McIntosh's rift with Big Warrior and Little Prince had been growing since at least the negotiation of the Treaty of Fort Jackson, which the latter saw as patently harmful to the Creeks and which they accepted only after Jackson repeatedly threatened to renew the war and punish them without mercy. But headmen from both the Lower and Upper divisions were especially scandalized by McIntosh's willingness to sell so much Creek territory at once, particularly in light of recent laws of the Creek Nation that mandated execution as punishment for anyone who ceded additional Creek land.[131] To them, the idea of removing to the west was still untenable, no matter what the payoff.

Members of McIntosh's party, long aware of their fragile position, clung desperately to the guardian/ward rhetoric of U.S. Indian policy and begged their "Father" to protect them from the recrimination of other Creeks. Just days after agreeing to the treaty, Etomme Tustunnuggee and other signatories pleaded: "We have been trying to [gratify?] the wishes of our Father the President, and we hope he loves us as his Red children, and hope you love us as friend of justice as friends of good order and friend of Harmony, Remain your affectionate, Children. PS And wish to know from you, in writing wether you could protect us if it should [illegible] with us."[132] Indeed, McIntosh had insisted that the 1825 treaty include a provision guaranteeing protection for him and his supporters.[133]

A party of headmen opposed to the treaty, represented by Opothle Yaholo and including Menawa, an infamous and battle-worn Red Stick leader, vigorously protested through both formal and informal channels. The treaty party's actions united former Red Sticks with disillusioned former American-allied Creeks (like Big Warrior) in an uneasy partnership that was nevertheless determined to undo what the increasingly self-interested Coweta leader had done. They sent a talk to newly installed secretary of war James Barbour in which they stated, "The Creek nation declares the treaty of McIntosh and certain Indians and the United States Commissioners at the Indian Springs on the 12th February last to be counterfeit." They reiterated the National Council's position articulated at Broken Arrow earlier in the year that "they had no land to sell" and asserted that when the U.S. commissioners convened the meeting at McIntosh's Indian Springs tavern, their sole object was to conduct a minority treaty that was against the wishes of the majority of the Council.[134]

The later parts of the petition were more blunt. They named Little Prince and Big Warrior as the rightful leaders of the Creek National Council and repudiated McIntosh's authority to make such a treaty. Insisting on the sovereign status of the Creek Nation *as a nation*, they asked, "Would such a treaty stand, made by a Nobleman of France or Britain unauthorized either by a written or verbal power and would it be insisted upon as lawful?" The petitioners made clear that they would not touch the money appropriated for the cession and demanded, "What excuse can the Congress of the U. States make to itself in confirming a bargain which our nation has not sanctioned and for which they have not value received?" In closing, they placed

Creek dispossession alongside the wave of American immigration through their lands and vowed, "As fast as we are knocked in the head, the throats of our wives and children are cut, by the first tide of population that know no law, we will then afford the United States a spectacle of emigration, which we hope may be to a country, prepared by the Great Spirit for the honest and unfortunate Indians."[135]

The flood of emigrants that had washed into Creek country in the aftermath of the Creek War not only brought free and unfree American travelers, but also deepened the divisions seething within the Creek Nation. The pressure exerted on the Creeks by Georgia and later Alabama to continually cede more land and constrict the borders of their already shrinking nation, combined with the constant friction of settlers and slaves scoring the landscape with footfalls, wagon wheels, and cattle hooves, were second only to the despair of a nation still reeling from a bloody civil war.

In the spring of 1825, after decades of slowly but consistently turning his back on his people for a price, Coweta headman William McIntosh finally learned the ultimate cost of his betrayal. On Sunday, April 30, a party of Creek men appeared at McIntosh's commodious home at Lockchau Talofa, or Acorn Town, on the Chattahoochee River. After evacuating the women and children, they set fire to the house. When McIntosh finally emerged from the blazing building, he was shot repeatedly. According to one account, "Every man shot a ball thro his head body or legs—until they burrow'd up the ground with their balls."[136] His friend and ally Etomme Tustunnuggee was also shot and killed. Jane Hawkins, wife of another McIntosh ally executed that day, reported to U.S. commissioners that "more than One hundred ball[s]" were shot into the bodies of the victims "to attone for their Constant friendship, to both your Nation and our own."[137] The executioners were primarily former Red Sticks from Okfuskee and Tallapoosa, but the plan was carefully scripted by Opothle Yaholo and Little Prince and was widely reported as a "public execution."[138] It was not unexpected. McIntosh had desperately called on his first cousin, Georgia governor George Troup, for protection from his rivals just days before the attack.[139]

To relieve the fears of white Americans who might have seen the execution of an ally as yet another call to war, the headmen who ordered the killing reportedly stated, "No danger whatever is to be apprehended by persons travelling through the nation . . . and [we] wish them not to be alarmed at this execution, which is only a compliance with the laws that the great Chiefs of the nation made at Pole-Cat Spring."[140] While many of McIntosh's foes rejected and resented the constant overtures made by the United States and

Georgia, they were unlikely to risk another all-out war. This was a Creek national affair. The law that justified McIntosh's execution stated that if the members of the offender's town did not act, members of other towns would be enjoined to put the law into action. And so it was that his executioners all came from towns other than Coweta, reflecting the national will to punish the offending headman.[141] For McIntosh, the roads that passed his taverns and plantations symbolically led all the way west across the Mississippi, where he intended to travel with his supporters after signing the treaty. Instead, the west came to him, as his executioners traveled from the western and northern reaches of Creek country on the very roads he had helped to open.

Chapter Six

REMAPPING CREEK COUNTRY

Continued American expansion into former Indian homelands north and south of the Ohio River sparked a renewed passion for what American politicians called "internal improvements." In addition to roads, canals seemed particularly promising. In 1825, the opening of the Erie Canal heralded a new era in commercial transportation, and nearly overnight it made Cleveland an Atlantic port by connecting it to the valuable New York trade network. Equally significant were the improvements in steamboat navigation that united Cleveland's rival Cincinnati with New Orleans in a tight bond of corn, pork, and cotton exchange. The push for improved roads to connect local producers to commercial depots also strengthened in the mid-1820s, as men of "small capital" and those of greater means all sought to tap into the new wealth that seemed to be sweeping the Trans-Appalachian region. In many cases, the path to this new wealth was a literal path—a canal or a road that would provide direct access to commercial ports—whether on the seacoast or on one of the Trans-Appalachian riverine highways.

Viewing the success of their more northerly neighbors, the states of Georgia and Alabama hurried to enact new laws and provisions for public works that would improve their own internal transportation and communication. Among other potential projects were a canal and a railroad linking the rivers of Tennessee with those of Georgia and a canal cutting across the peninsula of Florida.[1] These and many other visionary schemes in the South were designed to promote the "disposal of the products of the soil," especially cotton. As the Georgia Board of Public Works put it, the state of Georgia was primar-

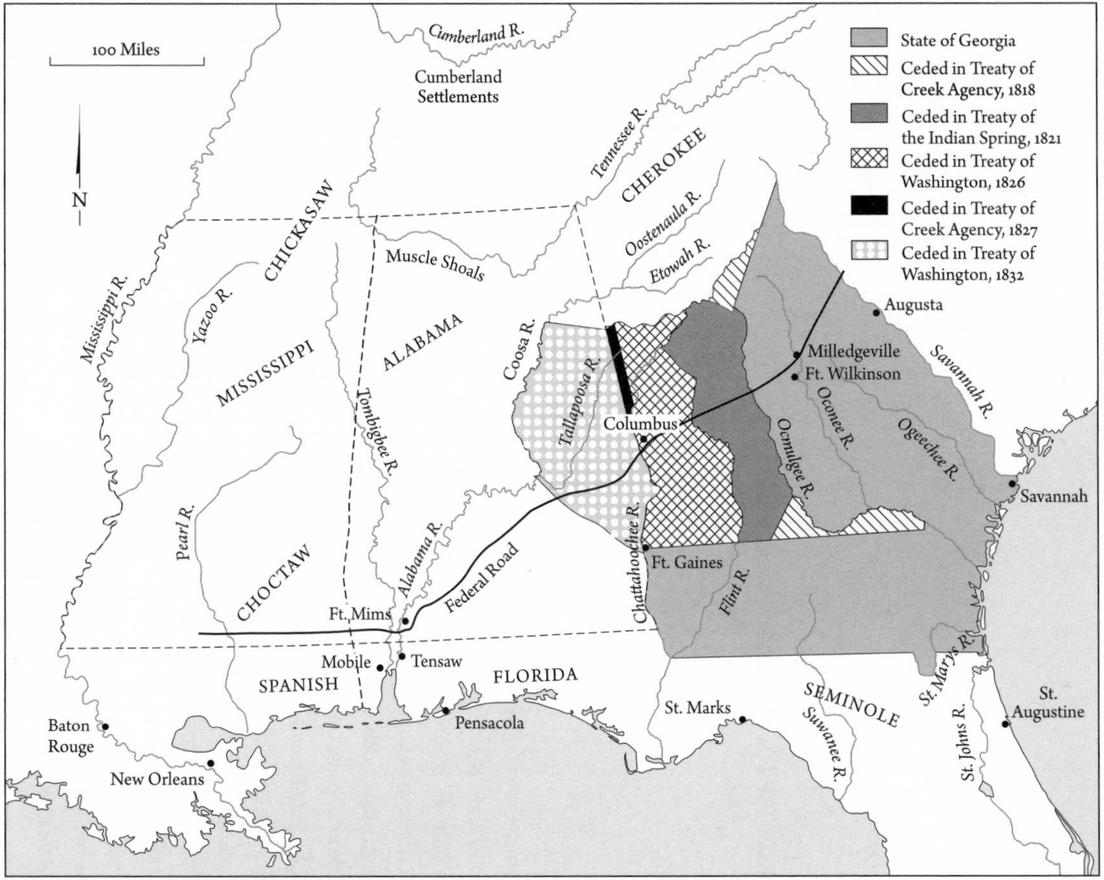

Map 4. Creek cessions, 1818–1832

Legend:

- State of Georgia
- Ceded in Treaty of Creek Agency, 1818
- Ceded in Treaty of the Indian Spring, 1821
- Ceded in Treaty of Washington, 1826
- Ceded in Treaty of Creek Agency, 1827
- Ceded in Treaty of Washington, 1832

100 Miles

N

Places and features labeled: Savannah, St. Augustine, Augusta, Savannah R., Ogeechee R., Milledgeville, Ft. Wilkinson, Oconee R., Oconee R., Ocmulgee R., Flint R., SEMINOLE, Suwanee R., St. Johns R., St. Marys R., St. Marks, CHEROKEE, Tennessee R., Oostenaula R., Etowah R., Columbus, Chattahoochee R., Ft. Gaines, FLORIDA, Pensacola, Cumberland R., Cumberland Settlements, Coosa R., Tallapoosa R., Federal Road, Muscle Shoals, ALABAMA, Alabama R., Tensaw, Mobile, SPANISH, Ft. Mims, Tombigbee R., CHOCTAW, Pearl R., MISSISSIPPI, CHICKASAW, Yazoo R., Mississippi R., Baton Rouge, New Orleans ily agricultural and the "obvious policy" of internal improvements in the state should be that which would promote this central source of "power and wealth."[2] For Georgia, as for other southern states, the persistence of southern Indian nations, particularly the Cherokees and the Creeks, presented a distinct obstacle to the development of these "improvement" schemes and by extension to the economic development of the region as a whole.

By 1825, the federal government had also undertaken a series of surveys, both topographical and epistolary, to determine the best overland route for a new "National Turnpike Road" to be made from Washington to New Orleans. This contemplated thoroughfare would replace the system of interconnected roads that culminated in the Federal Road from Georgia to New Orleans through Creek country and was the subject of intense regional debate. Three possible routes emerged as contenders, one coinciding roughly with the extant Federal Road, one along a similar upper route but cutting through Cherokee country in northern Georgia and then southwestward, and one leading through the same upper route but crossing the Appalachians north of the Cherokee Nation and descending through Tennessee, past Nashville, and south to New Orleans.[3]

Some of the correspondence directed toward the president regarding these competing routes suggested that only the third route would be of "great national purpose." These complainants, mostly from Tennessee, Kentucky, and parts of Alabama, argued that devising yet another road to pass along the east side of the Appalachians and cross through central Georgia would unfairly provide additional commercial assistance to Atlantic states that already had sufficient maritime and overland trade routes.[4] Other correspondents suggested that bringing the road through the heart of Cherokee country would be most beneficial. It is unlikely that the majority of Cherokees agreed with this assessment, though powerful elites like Major Ridge and the Vann family, who owned roadside taverns and ferry landings, certainly stood to profit from such a route.[5] Not surprisingly, most local white residents believed that the best route for the new road was the one that passed closest to them, and they mustered a wide variety of arguments to support their diverse contentions—revealing the degree to which access to stable transportation routes was deemed essential, on both a local and a regional level, to commercial development of the South.[6]

Meanwhile, greater and greater numbers of free and unfree southerners had been plying the roads and waterways of the region, in a continual process of making and unmaking homes and communities. Immense numbers of white Americans abandoned their homes in the Atlantic coast states of the

Chesapeake and Upper South and headed for the "new purchase" to the southwestward. One enslaved man recalled during his forced march through Maryland and Virginia, "Industry, enterprise, and ambition, have fled from these abodes, and sought refuge from sterility and barrenness in the vales of Kentucky, or the plains of Alabama."[7] The Americans pressing into the Creek Nation included not only cattlemen and planters, but also missionaries hoping to capitalize on the spiritual vulnerability of a "defeated" Native population. Secretary of War William H. Crawford had suggested that establishing a school for Indian children would do more for the "civilization of the Creek Indians" than all Hawkins's efforts over the previous thirty years.[8] By 1827, there were at least three missionary schools for the education of Indian children, two of which, the Withington and Asbury missions, were located within Creek country itself.[9]

The American settlers who poured into the Old Southwest during the 1820s were dreaming the great western dream that had steadily strengthened its grip on the American psyche. In Alabama, Mississippi, Louisiana, and places farther west, they saw the Jeffersonian promise of vacant fertile lands and economic opportunity for all. Of course, this dream was mostly fantasy, as speculators and land companies took up the lion's share of available lands and those that remained were complicated by Indian title. That did little to stem the tide of emigrants spurred on by promotional writings. Although it had recently gained momentum, such boosterism had been present since before the settlement of the Georgia colony.

In 1717, Sir Robert Montgomery had described the southern lands as "the most amiable Country of the Universe. . . . Nor is this Country yet inhabited, except those Parts in the Possession of the English, unless here and there a Tribe of wandering Indians, wild and ignorant, all artless, and uncultivated, as the Soil, which fosters them."[10] After having commented extensively on the various Indian populations of West-Florida and Louisiana, Thomas Hutchins incongruously remarked in 1784 that "this immense continent will be peopled by persons whose language and national character must be the same," in effect rendering the native inhabitants something less than people —and perhaps more akin to the landscape itself.[11] Despite the very real presence of Native peoples in the interior South, such wishful thinking on the part of European-descended settlers would persist as long as there was presumed *vacuum domicilium* to the west.

Promotional writings depicted American settlement of and profit from the land ceded after the Creek War as inevitable. One 1818 advertisement for the sale of lots in a new Alabama town to be called "Florence" vigorously asserted, "There *must*, in the natural course of things, spring up one of the largest commercial towns in the interior of the South-Western section of the Union."[12] According to the trustees of the town, the success of the new settlement related directly to the roads established through the locale by Andrew Jackson during the recent war. Though unstated, the ad implied that the town's success hinged on both the presence of the U.S. military and the absence of the Creeks.

Other accounts were somewhat less oblique in their reference to Creek dispossession and its impact on the profitability of American settlement in the region. A piece in the *Blakeley Sun, and Alabama Advertiser* claimed: "But yesterday, these lands were darkened and overshadowed by the wilderness; to-day they are reclaimed from their rude and forbidding state, and clustered with towns and villages, and decorated with the enchanting embellishments of taste and cultivation."[13] Here, the former presence of Creeks near the settlements of the lower Alabama River was decried a wild specter now banished from the region. Interestingly, this piece asserted that the land had been "reclaimed" for American settlement and posited the presence of "towns and villages" as evidence of its legitimacy—both of which claims implied that the Creeks were never the rightful proprietors of the land and that during their tenure, they never settled in fixed or permanent residences. Fundamental to claims about the newly available lands in travel guides, promotional literature, and celebratory accounts was their potential as commercial centers, linked in a burgeoning transportation network. Nearly every advertisement for land sales or new towns emphasized their proximity to the roads or waterways that would enable the transport of various agricultural commodities, especially cotton, to the "great marts" of the country and the world.[14] Thus, the estrangement of the Creeks from these lands was directly connected in the minds of American promoters (and the emigrants who bought their pitches) to the commercial agrarian development of the region and the opportunity for individual prosperity. Emigrating Americans were actively reimagining Creek places as empty spaces, overlaying the Creek world with new meanings and purposes.

Although the Creeks were still embroiled in bitter political turmoil over the "breaking" of William McIntosh and the spurious Indian Springs Treaty of 1825, they were also trying to preserve their homelands, often by surprising means. Almost one year after the negotiation of the first Indian Springs Treaty, the Creeks who had protested so forcefully against it signed another treaty with the federal government. The Treaty of Washington, signed January 24, 1826, unequivocally declared the Treaty of Indian Springs to be "null and void" because it was "signed on their [the Creeks'] part by persons having no sufficient authority to form treaties, or to make cessions."[15] Unlike the 1825 treaty, this new treaty did not cede away all lands remaining in the state of Georgia, but only those lying to the "east of the middle of the Chattahoochee River" and another small portion lying just below the Creek and Cherokee boundary line.[16] The lands restored to the Creeks were not terribly large (see map 4). In fact, Georgia state commissioner James Meriwether communicated to the governor that "we shall lose but a very small part of our land by the ratification of this new treaty[.] This however does not change the principle if we are entitled to any we are to the whole."[17] The fundamental difference between the two treaties was who negotiated them and how.

The Treaty of Indian Springs had been signed between a small group of marginal Creek representatives under William McIntosh who essentially agreed to leave Creek country for a price. The Treaty of Washington was conducted under the leadership of Opothle Yaholo and contained no such stipulation that the Creeks remove from their lands (although those who still desired to do so would be paid and protected in their emigration west of the Mississippi).[18] Whereas the 1825 treaty was signed under duress at McIntosh's tavern within the limits of Georgia, the replacement agreement was signed in Washington by a delegation of Creeks who were deemed the true representatives of the Nation.[19] In effect, the treaty was less of a Creek victory regarding lands than it was a statement of their continued sovereignty, particularly their ability to designate their rightful leaders.

The state of Georgia, under the leadership of William McIntosh's first cousin, Governor George Troup, was in no way prepared to accept this reiteration of Creek autonomy. This was especially the case since state officials had already attempted to survey and lottery off the land that had been ceded in the Treaty of Indian Springs. To receive word nearly a year later that the men who executed "the unfortunate, but gallant minded McIntosh" had been honorably welcomed in Washington was simply more than Troup could bear. That they were also allowed to negotiate an entirely new treaty that reestablished their rights to remaining lands and contained no provisions for removal nearly drove the governor to hysterics.[20]

The situation exploded into a full-blown debate on the rights of states versus the rights of the federal government, with the rights of the Indian nations coming under full attack. Troup portrayed the controversy in both legal and familial terms when he claimed that the federal government, particularly the executive branch, had defied the principle of state sovereignty and jurisdiction, giving "open proof of the fact, that it will become the ally of the Indians against one of its own family."[21] He raged at this "monstrous doctrine" and asserted that with regard to the sovereign rights of states, "There is such a radical difference of opinion between the authorities of Georgia and those of the United States, that the harmony and tranquility of the two Governments, so much to be cherished by all good men, can never be maintained uninterruptedly until those Indians shall have been removed."[22]

Troup was particularly incensed that Georgia surveyors engaged in running boundary lines pursuant to the Indian Springs Treaty were halted by Creeks *and* threatened by federal representatives—a move he characterized as a direct assault on the state's right to carry into effect its laws within its limits.[23] The fact that Georgia surveyors had entered the cession before the agreed-upon date and that the Indian Springs Treaty had ultimately been declared void by the U.S. government seemed beside the point. Such obstructions actively prevented Georgia citizens from taking their "rightful" place on these newly acquired lands, postponing white settlement and throwing the entire enterprise of Indian dispossession into disarray. Years before the Cherokee Supreme Court cases that would render the issue of state jurisdiction over Indians a national debate, Troup and the Georgia legislature openly declared: "Georgia owns exclusively the soil and jurisdiction of all the territory within her present chartered and conventional limits, and . . . claims the right to exercise, over any people white or red within those limits, the authority of her laws."[24]

Equally disturbing to southern statesmen was the effect that acknowledging Creek national sovereignty had on the state's ability to pursue internal improvement projects. As noted, enthusiasm for internal improvement projects increased tenfold in this era. Alabama governor John Murphy declared, "The State of Alabama has had in constant contemplation, the uniting of the Waters of the Tennessee, with the Waters which flow through the State into the Gulf of Mexico," and corresponded with Georgia governor Troup on the possibility that the abrogation of the Indian Springs Treaty might become an obstacle to such projects.[25] Connecting the Tennessee River with the waters of the Coosa, Chattahoochee, Alabama, and Tombigbee rivers depended on the absence of the Creeks from the shores of those waterways. Some in Georgia were particularly excited about the possibility of opening a "direct water communication from the Atlantic Ocean to the River Mississippi," and quite openly envious of the "ease, speed, and cheapness of transportation now enjoyed by the citizens of the State of N. York" since the opening of the Erie Canal.[26] Just as the continued presence of the Creek Nation was seen as a potential obstacle to Alabama's development of canals and railroads through that state, the persistence of both the Creeks and the Cherokees was likewise troublesome for supporters of similar improvement projects in Georgia. For example, the state Board of Public Works complained of Cherokee interference in conducting a survey of the practicability of an Atlantic-Mississippi canal or railroad and asserted that when, not if, their land was acquired in its entirety, such a project would finally be feasible.[27]

Not surprisingly, the newly negotiated Treaty of Washington contained provisions regarding transportation. Article 15, for example, allowed for American citizens to own the ferriage rights at crossings *into* the Creek Nation (while Creeks were to have exclusive rights of ferriage *out of* the Creek Nation). But ultimately this was small change compared to the vast and largely unrealizable public projects that had captured the imagination of local and national politics in 1825 and 1826.[28] Troup declared, "The great work of Internal Improvement is suspended, and all because Georgia is not in possession of her vacant territory—A territory waste and profitless to the Indians—profitless to the U. States; but in possession of the rightful owner a source of strength, of revenue and of union."[29] The Georgia legislature passed a series of resolutions decrying the effects of the Treaty of Washington on development within the state and concluded by stating, "The assertion that we have no right to enter the Indian country within our own limits . . . with the peaceable objects of Internal Improvement, without the consent of the Indians, is a doctrine which this State will not admit."[30]

The degree to which these imaginative internal improvement schemes were reasonable and practicable, given the "execrable" state of the region's extant roads, reveals an interesting problem in the legislature's vision of Georgia's future. The state's politicians railed so vociferously against the southern Indians as obstacles to internal improvement writ large (canals, railroads, and other grand designs) that they seemed to forget that the state roads were in dismal disrepair and neither a canal nor a railroad would be useful to planters who could not get their produce to the riverside or the depot.

As late as 1828, a Massachusetts traveler described travel in Georgia as such: "But little pains is taken to make roads, and if a tree should fall across the path it is not removed, unless absolutely necessary—but turn out and drive round it. . . . Good roads and bridges would, I think, in this country, be a luxury."[31] The overland wagon routes that crossed Creek country and had caused so much dissent, debate, and dispute just a few years before were neglected in favor of more ambitious improvement projects. One traveler wryly observed, "If, Instead of expending their money so lavishly on splendid but visionary schemes of canals & railroads the Georgians would mend their important highway avenues the public would perceive some palpable advantages in their expenditures, but now all is chimerical & profitless."[32] And yet, the Creeks were labeled the primary obstacle to the development of transportation and commerce in Georgia and Alabama.

Some southern leaders also felt that the intervention of the federal government on behalf of northern and western internal improvements represented a distinct prejudice against the economic development of the South as a region. And yet many southern politicians opposed federal support of internal improvement projects within and between the states as unconstitutional since the power to make public roads and canals was not expressly granted in the founding document. Thoroughfares like the Federal Road had been approved under the provision granting the Congress the power to regulate the post, since these routes were initially designated for the transmission of the mail. Appropriating treasury funds for transportation routes not expressly related to the postal system raised concerns for strict constructionists and by extension southern republicans.

An editorial in the *Southern Recorder* distilled the problem for southern politicians, asserting that while it was true that the southern states objected to the unconstitutional nature of federal spending on internal improvements, doing so risked leaving the region completely underdeveloped. "May we not," the writer asked in explicitly sectional language, "while protesting against the principle, consistently claim our fair share of the public expenditure? If it be of importance to the Union to connect the Eastern and Western waters at the North, is it not equally so at the South? While millions on millions of the common treasure of all the States are expended on Roads and Canals for the benefit of the Eastern, Middle, and Western States, the South is altogether neglected."[33] While many southerners generally objected to the extension of congressional powers to projects like roads and canals, they were nevertheless perturbed that when such unconstitutional concessions were made, they were uniformly not for the benefit of the southern states.[34]

Georgia leaders also argued that the federal government was errant in its support of Indian sovereignty to the injury of southern state sovereignty. In many ways, this debate was a dress rehearsal for the enormous Cherokee removal controversy to come in the 1830s. Georgia state senator Augustin S. Clayton articulated the state's primary complaint, arguing that not only had the Indians not been removed from the limits of the state, as prescribed by the Georgia Compact of 1802, but in fact they had been encouraged by both government agents and missionaries to take up the "arts of civilization" and become settled farmers within the state's limits. Again emphasizing the victimization of the South by the North (and hinting at the presumed role of Christian missionaries from New England, as well as federal "meddlers"), Clayton continued, "This is done too by men drawn from other states, where the Indians have been literally exterminated. . . . And now all at once the very godly given, and grace abounding pinks of piety, think that Georgia *alone*, ought to christianize the balance of the Indians."[35]

John Quincy Adams was specifically accused of repeatedly overstepping his authority as president and trampling on the rights of the states. Returning to the case of the 1825 Indian Springs treaty, one Athens, Georgia, editorialist wondered on whose authority the old treaty was superseded and the new one negotiated, remarking that if it was by Adams's hand, "his cup must soon overflow."[36] As noted earlier, this debate represented both an upsurge in state rights versus federal responsibility rhetoric, as well as the makings of a distinctly sectional controversy. Troup asserted that Georgia had the same right as her "sister states" to run boundary lines and pursue improvement projects on Indian lands within their limits.[37] A North Carolina newspaper sounded support for the beleaguered governor: "Georgia has been rudely dealt with in this transaction. . . . State rights have been invaded—power, has triumphed over justice."[38] As southern state leaders like Troup and Clayton would increasingly claim in the following decade, the interventions of the federal government on behalf of Indians were a sharp departure from the modus operandi that had allowed the enormous economic development in the northern states and in the Ohio Valley. Southern statesmen saw this as prejudicial and disproportionately damaging to the development of the South as a region and the state of Georgia in particular, especially where the issue of state boundaries and transportation across them was concerned.[39]

Interestingly, the major impediment to establishing Georgia's boundaries was not in the Treaty of Washington, but in the fact that the exact limits of the state had never been determined. The treaty itself declared that the lines of the Creek cession were contingent on the boundary line between Georgia and Alabama, "it being understood that these lines are to stop at their intersection with the boundary line between Georgia and Alabama, *wherever that may be*" (emphasis added). Despite the fact that Alabama had been a state since 1819, the border between the two states had never been amicably settled, primarily because a significant portion of it ran directly through the Creek Nation.

The issue of the unresolved boundary was at least as old as the Georgia Compact of 1802, which adjusted the western limits of Georgia in exchange for settling the Yazoo scandal and the promise that the federal government would remove the Indians within the limits of the state on "peaceable and reasonable terms." The two states set out to remedy the border problem on their own around the same time that the Treaty of Washington was being ratified in the middle of 1826. The boundary project was explicitly connected to Georgia's desire to see all the Indians within the state's putative limits removed. What better way to exercise complete authority over the Creeks (and the Cherokees) than to establish once and for all that they lived within the geographical and jurisdictional boundaries of the state?

But settling the boundary was not so simple. Almost immediately, a difference of opinion arose between the states of Georgia and Alabama as to the rightful location of the line. The controversy focused on the "contradictory and bewildering" language of the Compact of 1802 and the place at which the western boundary of Georgia began.[40] At issue was whether the boundary was to begin at the "Great Bend" of the Chattahoochee where the river changes direction from southwest to due south or whether it was to begin at the confluence of Uchee Creek with the Chattahoochee—a location several miles to the south of the "Great Bend." The Georgians maintained that the boundary began at the lower location, whereas the Alabamians declared that the upper location was the true one.[41] It seemed not to matter that the land in question was located in the heart of the Creek Nation.

Richard A. Blount was one of the principal officials appointed to represent the state of Georgia in its efforts to settle the Alabama boundary. While in the field, he remarked of the disputed tract, "Surely if all Georgia cou'd see those sterile stony knobs, they wou'd not contend strongly with Alabama for a narrow slipe of such land west of Chattho-hoche separated by such a river, or be so solicitous to dispossess the forlorn sons of the forest." Considering the weeks spent tracing and retracing this same debated but in his estimation overvalued ground, Blount complained, "My patience is tried with a foolish contract."[42] Even while he was engaged in the daily work of running the line designed to slice down the center of remaining Creek lands and determine the jurisdiction of either Alabama or Georgia over the Creeks, he digressed: "How or whence did we get a right to extend the charter'd limits of Georgia far to the West over their [the Creeks'] territory—By a grant from George King of England—And what gave him the prerogative to grant charters for the land of a people, rightful owners of the soil and tenants in possession from time immemorial?"[43] In effect, even as he surveyed their land, Blount questioned the basic principles that undergirded the remapping of Creek country. Ignoring for a moment the Georgia Compact of 1802, he rather astutely wondered where Georgia got the right to extend its original charter all the way to the Mississippi in the first place.

Creek leaders had asked the same question on numerous occasions, and the rising clamor of Georgia voices calling for action on the Georgia Compact raised these concerns once more. Of course, Creek people were not merely passive spectators of the boundary survey. As protestors, guides, entrepreneurs, and town leaders they alternately empowered and impeded the survey according to their own needs and desires. The Creeks were keenly aware that the future of their nation was intimately connected to the deeds and doctrines of the states that surrounded them. Many were opposed to the running of yet another line of demarcation on their lands, especially one so fraught with the recent memory of McIntosh's betrayal and the constant encroachments of Georgia settlers on the eastern edge of Creek country. The problem of intrusions onto Creek lands had continued unabated through the entire treaty controversy, only worsening as the Treaty of Washington was being negotiated and settled. Incidences of border theft were serious enough that even former members of the McIntosh party protested strongly that whites from Georgia were stealing their property and were actually organized into "a company of horse & cow thieves."[44]

The leaders of the Creek National Council also made clear that they were "much disturbed at the idea of the Surveyors entering the Country" before the new treaty had gone into effect.[45] And although there were not the same sort of attacks that halted the survey in Cherokee country, local parties of Creeks were clearly dissatisfied with Blount and his men measuring sight lines and carving letters and numbers into their trees.[46] In addition, on more than one occasion, Blount encountered a distinct Creek preference for the Alabama commissioners' construction of the boundary line—perhaps revealing their belief that to be ultimately included in that state's boundary would be preferable.[47] And despite the fact that the surveying party was not frequently confronted, the Creeks were clearly aware of their every move.[48] Given the situation in Cherokee country, Governor Troup was eager to see the Creek line continue with no interruptions and repeatedly ordered out troops to support Blount, so that "those misguided people shoud reconsider their conduct."[49]

As in years past, Creek opposition to a new survey line may have been tempered by the hope that this line would finally put an end to the trespasses they had suffered for so long. Others may have believed that either the survey expedition or the settlers who would follow would provide them the sort of entrepreneurial opportunities that sometimes accompanied Americans traveling into their homelands. Seizing on the possibility that not all Creeks were opposed to the boundary line then being run, Clayton claimed, "The Indians do not care about it; indeed they would prefer its survey, as thereby they will have a ready market for every article they would wish to sell."[50] Nevertheless, some Creeks and most Cherokees were extremely dismayed with this line being run through lands they had been solemnly guaranteed on repeated occasions.

Just as they had done for decades during Benjamin Hawkins's tenure, Georgia politicians tended to fault federal officials stationed in their midst for the refusals and protests of the Indians. Creek agent John Crowell, who had taken over after Mitchell's dismissal in a slave smuggling investigation, now received the lion's share of the blame.[51] But northern missionaries were also coming under increasing attack by southern statesmen and sympathizers. Blount remarked on his journey through the Cherokee country, "So long as the Cherokees are fully furnish'd with missionaries from Connecticut, we shall never get the territory by purchase."[52] And it was not just the politicians and officials who evinced such a strong disgust for the perceived assault on Georgia state sovereignty. On his expedition, Blount encountered an elderly white woman living in Georgia who similarly complained. In response to the opinion of a northern missionary who said, "We had as much right [to] run a line thro' England as thro' this [Indian] nation," she replied that "England was not within their limits."[53]

Individual Creek men continued to act as guides for Blount and other boundary surveys as they had to varying degrees since the earliest European explorations into Creek country.[54] Whether they participated solely on the basis of remuneration, or in order to exert some measure of control on the outcome of the expedition, or some combination of the two, cannot be precisely determined. They were certainly there nearly every step of the way, whether invited or not, as the Georgia-Alabama boundary came into relief against the southern landscape. Blount's party circled around and around the area near where Uchee Creek empties into the Chattahoochee River trying to determine whether they had located the true place for the departure of the boundary from the river, but they frequently relied on the expertise of either Creek collaborators or other local inhabitants hired along the way.[55]

Little Prince had provided Blount's party with a guide, Cho-chus Micco, which tends to suggest that the Creek leader intended through him to exert some influence on the location of the boundary. Blount certainly saw it that way since Cho-chus Micco consistently "manifested his predilection in favor" of the Alabama commissioner.[56] Indeed, Blount believed that many of the Creeks were hostile to the expedition and that "nothing but fear of the power of Ga. sav'd us from destruction," although few incidences of violence were recorded during his reconnaissance.[57] One tense situation did arise near the end of the expedition, when Blount and his companions were accosted by several Creek men who appeared to be intoxicated. The Creeks inquired of the guide "who the Comrs. were as they intended to kill one . . . and they upbraided him for being our pilate."[58] Clearly, the long-lived tensions between those who were willing to help the Americans and those who wished to hinder them had not dissolved. But it is important to avoid oversimplifying the motivations of those men who consented to act as guides, guards, or companions to the surveyors. Many of these Creeks were responsible for helping the party procure supplies from the local Indians, and Blount expressed his frustration that he was often forced to pay "the highest prices for whatever we bought," whether honey, chickens, beef, or corn.[59] Such actions suggest that Creek men frequently took advantage of opportunities, however small, to support their communities whenever they presented themselves.

Likewise, Creek women operated in such encounters as both enterprising entrepreneurs and political actors in their own right. Blount recorded numerous instances of purchasing watermelons, corn, honeycomb, meat, and other supplies from Creek women and children along the route, as well as their attempts to sell other sundries that the party was typically disinclined to buy.[60] These were by and large amicable exchanges in which Creek people, women in particular, were viable producers engaged in the same small-scale market economy that many of their new American neighbors were enlarging. But there were also tense and revealing encounters in which Creek women displayed their frustration with the surveying party's presence. On one occasion, Blount and his party attempted to procure melons from some Indian women but could not make themselves understood, even after drawing one on the ground. Given the frequency with which they had been supplied with melons heretofore and Blount's suspicions that one of the women had been educated at a missionary school, he concluded, "It produces very unpleasant sensations. . . . They pretended not to comprehend us."[61] In another incident, an elderly Creek woman directed a young boy to take up the green corn shucks that were scattered about near the party's horses so that they would not be able to eat them. A small gesture of resistance, to be sure, but Blount interpreted it to mean that "they were inimical to us or our object." It was likely both.[62]

When the surveying party moved into Cherokee country, they were eyed with similar suspicion. Like the Creeks, the Cherokee men and women the surveyors encountered supplied the expedition with sundries necessary for their subsistence—frequently at high prices. But as evidenced by the controversies described above in which Cherokee leaders halted other Georgia reconnaissance efforts, the Cherokee people Blount encountered appeared openly dissatisfied with his presence and his mission.

Blount had spent nearly five weeks traipsing through Creek country, cutting hatch marks, initials, and scores of roman numerals into the skin of trees in order to mark the boundary and so-called experimental lines before heading north. An encounter in the Cherokee Nation with a leader known as White Man Killer revealed the depth of Cherokee concern with this expedition. Although the headman could not speak English, he "talk'd freely & fluently in Cherokee" to Blount, who could not understand him. Blount described an annoyed charade in which White Man Killer took an axe and began to blaze stumps in the same way the surveyors blazed the timber along their line. Walking around Blount, the Cherokee man said again and again, "No good—no good."[63]

Meeting later with another Cherokee leader, Blount tried to explain to him that "blazing & marking a line will not damage your timber—We did not come to damage your timber, your stock or your corn." But the damage was not in the actual cuts on the trees; it was in the remapping, the active reimagining of Indian lands as state parcels. The Cherokees, like the Creeks, knew that the recontextualization of their homelands, through surveying, marking, and renaming, was more often than not a prelude to Indian dispossession. As one Cherokee headman put it to Blount, "It look'd a good deal like taking our land away."[64]

Indeed, the effort to redefine the land of southern Indians was not merely an abstract exercise in representation. It was an attempt to know, name, and obtain the land. As discussed earlier, the creation of transportation routes, both grandiose and mundane, was seen as vital to the development of the region both economically and politically and required well-defined boundaries as well as networks of roads that crossed them. But equally important was the produce that would be transported on those newly reimagined and repurposed pathways. Cotton promised to make New Orleans "the emporium of the produce of a great portion of the western states" and led investors to dream of the Mississippi as the site of the "most extensive inland navigation on the globe."[65] In a widely available travel guide to the region,

Timothy Flint elaborated, "Cotton is the grand staple of Alabama. The growing of this article has increased in this state in a ratio even greater than that of the population."[66]

Since the early part of the nineteenth century, the lands in and around Creek country had been valued and assessed in terms of their suitability for agriculture, and while there were considerable stretches of pine barren and swampy lands, much of the area was well suited to the cultivation of cotton.[67] The boosterism associated with the western lands of the South was bolstered by the American acquisition of Creek lands after the Creek War and the treaties signed in the subsequent decade. As one hyperbolic account proclaimed, "In the 'Chattahoochee region,' rich land can be obtained, so rich, it is said—so rich—so very rich, that, as we are credibly informed, a man one evening after using an iron handspike, usually called a crow-bar, stuck one end of it in the ground, and left it;—and in the morning when he returned to his work, lo and behold the crow-bar was covered with ten-penny nails, that had sprouted out during one single night."[68]

Despite such claims, the cultivation of the rich and fertile lands of the lower South required tremendous labor—usually that of slaves. There were small producers, who cultivated the necessities of their subsistence and raised only small quantities of cotton to sell as surplus, but their opportunities for acquiring land were limited by their inability to purchase slaves and the potential for excessive debt if they tried.[69] Much more prominent in the reimagining of the southern landscape from Indian Country to cotton country were the large-scale producers who depended on the toil of enslaved people of African descent. In many cases, the men of small capital saw themselves as such only temporarily, believing that the elimination of the Indians would open up the possibility of acquiring greater capital, meaning more slaves, and thus producing, selling, and profiting on a larger and larger scale. Traveling through the South during this era, British writer Basil Hall commented that slaveholders in the Upper South had made it their business to "rear as many negroes as possible" for sale to the southwest since the emigrants headed for the interior region were "unceasing in their demands for more labourers."[70] Another observer similarly noted, "The increased demand for slaves led many farmers in Virginia . . . to turn their attention to raising slaves, if I may so term it, for the south-western market."[71]

Remapping Creek country thus meant not only expanding internal improvement projects, but also replacing southeastern Indians with people of African descent. The effort resulted in a major demographic shift that enabled the spread of profitable cotton cultivation throughout the region. As cotton prices rose and cotton fever reached its highest pitch, the calls for the wholesale removal of the Creeks and their Indian neighbors rang loudly through the halls of southern capitol buildings and the columns of local newspapers. Persistently sovereign Indian nations within the states of Alabama and Georgia, it was said, not only prevented the development of those states' resources, but also perpetuated the possibility of slave escapes to Indian lands. For the Creeks, the intense pressure to cede their small holdings remaining within Georgia's claimed limits, combined with a desperate commitment to preserve as much of their sovereignty as possible, led to the negotiation of yet another treaty in late 1827. The Treaty of the Creek Indian Agency provided for the cession of "all the remaining lands now owned or claimed by the Creek Nation . . . within the chartered limits of the State of Georgia."[72]

The treaty was the result of a yearlong public debate between the states of Alabama and Georgia, on the one side, and the federal government under John Quincy Adams on the other.[73] Still unwilling to accept the authority of the Treaty of Washington (1826), Georgia and Alabama had extended state law over the lands ostensibly ceded by the Creeks in the annulled Treaty of Indian Springs (1825), and the state of Georgia had issued hundreds of land lottery tickets to its citizens for parcels. President Adams and Secretary of War James Barbour had taken steps to prevent the survey and settlement of Indian lands in the South that had not been ceded under the Treaty of Washington, even going so far as to order out regular troops to defend the Indians' lands.[74] Meanwhile, Adams's representatives struggled to prevent the states from enacting their will over the Creeks while they labored to convince newly emboldened Creek leaders that the issue would not go away. Ceding the Georgia lands was the only way to quiet their clamorous neighbors.

John R. Vinton was given the unenviable task of traveling from Washington to Georgia to communicate Adams's position to Governor Troup. Upon arrival he remarked, "Since the formation of the Federal Compact, I doubt if ever the federal & State Governments have ever met at such serious issue. . . . This looks like civil war!!"[75] Virulent anti-Adams statesman Augustin S. Clayton seemed to agree and argued that the federal government had virtually branded Georgians as "seditious people."[76] Well before the state of South Carolina introduced its doctrine of nullification and embarked on the path of secession from the Union, the states of Georgia and Alabama considered just such a course, their dissent based not on tariffs or slavery but on Indian affairs. Of course, slavery was never far out of the picture and both Troup and Clayton implied that if the federal government were willing to send troops to prevent a survey of Indian land, it was a short and slippery slope to interfering with "slave property."[77]

But the ultimate issue was ridding the state of its Indian "inhabitants," and this was accomplished—in part—through the negotiation of the Treaty of the Creek Indian Agency. The government of the state of Georgia, however, believing that the lands ceded in this last treaty had already been purchased by the government, pursuant to the fraudulent Treaty of Indian Springs, tended to see this new treaty as nothing more than a stalling tactic postponing the inevitable—the final removal of all the southern Indians to a territory west of the Mississippi. And, in fact, this train of thought was already being openly debated in the U.S. Congress in early 1827.

In his report on behalf of the Office of Indian Affairs, Thomas L. McKenney suggested that the problem in convincing the southern Indians to remove lay not in the idea of removal itself, but in the mode of convincing them. He recommended that the untenable situation of sovereign Indian nations remaining within the boundaries of hostile southern states be clearly and amply explained to the "enlightened half-breeds" of the four southern nations "from whom the opposition to emigration generally comes."[78] Perhaps McKenney hoped that such elite individuals would be better able to appreciate "the real situation" of their nations. William McIntosh's American-educated son Chilly had apparently reached this grim realization, as one observer said of him: "His mind had been cultivated at the expense of his happiness."[79] McKenney recommended that these "leaders" be singled out to receive generous reservations of lands remaining in the east and that such inducements would be likely to promote a spirit of emigration in the rest of the tribe. In other words, he suggested that they be bribed into signing agreements that would enact the removal of their people while securing valuable lands for themselves.[80] Additionally, McKenney believed that settling this issue with the southern tribes first was of the utmost importance since other Native nations would look to the southern groups and follow in their footsteps.[81]

What is most interesting in McKenney's proposal is his contention that promoting missionary schools within the Indian nations would help, not hinder as was typically believed, the push for wholesale emigration to the west. He further asserted that the teachers at these schools, "who have, and so deservedly, the confidence of the Indians, would exercise the most efficient agency in carrying the plan of removal into effect."[82] It is not surprising, then, that the language of the Treaty of the Creek Agency (1827) contains provisions for the support of Creek children at the Choctaw Academy (Baptist) in Kentucky, as well as subsidies for the Withington Mission (Baptist) and the Asbury Mission (Methodist), both located within the limits of Creek country.[83] These schools could be valuable to the government, not only as a means of subduing and "civilizing" the next generation of Indian children, he argued, but also by convincing them of the propriety of accepting removal as their only viable alternative. But some Creeks also saw these schools as important resources for educating their children in the ways of the white world. Their hope was that they could successfully appropriate skills of reading, writing, and Christian reasoning for the preservation, rather than the dissolution, of their nation.[84] Other southeastern Indian nations, particularly the Cherokees, also saw these missions as a source of moral and epistemological power that could be used to resist efforts to dispossess them. Not surprisingly, as the removal crisis wore on, political leaders in the South began to protest against the missions as bastions of anti-removal and often anti-slavery sentiment.

After the ratification of the Treaty of the Creek Agency, the remainder of Creek people still living on the "Georgia side" of the Chattahoochee River were compelled to retreat to Creek lands along the western edge of the river in what is today southeastern Alabama. Despite the numbers of former McIntosh supporters who had already settled across the Mississippi and pronouncements from state and federal capitals that the rest of the Indians would soon be made to follow, local Creek men and women had other ideas. Their resistance to the most recent treaty and to the continued encroachment of Americans on their lands manifested itself in myriad ways. Increasingly, they communicated their opposition through actions rather than words.

Mansfield Torrance, a state agent in charge of maintaining tolls on the Federal Road in Georgia, reported to Governor Troup that between the location of the old Creek agency (now within Georgia limits) and the new Creek boundary, "the Indians have frequently burnt the fences & houses & cut down the fruit trees."[85] Creeks may have planted many of these fruit trees before their removal across the Chattahoochee River, and destroying them was a direct way of preventing American settlers from benefiting from Creek industry. The destruction of fences is also particularly notable since earlier in the century fences had come to symbolize the adoption of Euro-American philosophies of private property.[86] Burning or otherwise damaging these structures was a direct commentary on such values and necessarily made American settlement of former Creek homesteads more laborious.

Similarly, affidavits from Georgia settlers moving into the area near the new boundary around 1828 describe depredations allegedly committed by

Creeks against their livestock. What is most interesting about these claims is that many of them do not accuse Creeks of outright theft, but instead draw attention to the apparently indiscriminate shooting and mutilation of cattle, with little or no meat taken from the carcasses.[87] Such actions suggest the sort of retributive killings that characterized the Creek War and effectively littered the countryside with the detritus of discontent. Stephen and Benjamin Johnson testified on behalf of their father that they had "frequently found his cattle that had been shot but not killed," adding, "Their father lost more cattle about the time the Indians were removing beyond the Chattahoochee from the lately ceded lands than any other time."[88] Likewise, numerous lower Georgia settlers submitted claims regarding the theft and destruction of crops, believed to have been committed by Creeks removing from or living near the area. John S. Scott similarly reported that "some corn houses had been burned" on the Chattahoochee River and reckoned that the total quantity lost was six or seven hundred bushels.[89]

Such wanton destruction of food supplies implies, like the mutilation of livestock, that the Creeks in the area meant to send the American settlers a message and employed the symbols of American possession and property as their instruments of choice. But it is also important to consider that related acts, if committed as alleged, might have signaled need as much as they signaled vengeance. Burning large stores of corn, for instance, would raise the local price for a bushel of corn, making Indian sales of the same item more lucrative. The same motivation might be attributed to the theft of cattle and hogs; the Johnsons and other deponents claimed that those cattle not killed on the spot were likely driven across the Chattahoochee by the deliberate mixing of American with Creek stock. In addition, the theft of corn and pumpkins, for example, such as that witnessed by William D. Lucas in the "cornfield opposite Broken Arrow in the Creek nation," might have revealed the actual need of Creek people for the means of subsistence. Lucas noted that in addition to seeing where "corn & pumpkins had been carried to their Canoe landings upon the river," he also saw numerous places where the corn had been "shalled by the Indians in the field," which suggests subsistence rather than profit as the motive.[90]

In addition to enacting their resistance on the bodies of animals and the fields of newcomers, Creek people continued to protest American travel through their nation in a variety of other ways. Hiram Chalfinch reported that his trip through the Creek Nation was rudely interrupted by an attack perpetrated "with drawn knives by two Indians." These men allegedly robbed Chalfinch of $12 cash and a wide variety of clothing, including those he was wearing.[91] Such incidents continued over the next several years as evidenced by the arrest of Big Warrior's son and Upper Creek leader Tuskeneah for stopping travelers on the Federal Road, threatening them with harm, and warning them not to travel through Creek country.[92] It is difficult and perhaps counterproductive to try to disaggregate acts of theft from acts of resistance. American travelers on Creek roads were imperiled not merely because of their possessions but also because of what they represented to the Creek people whose territory they traversed.

While some Creeks owned taverns along the Federal Road and other thoroughfares that were reportedly "not much inferior to those in the adjacent country," most were not profiting from the presence of travelers in such an extravagant manner.[93] Like the families that supplied Blount's surveying expedition with corn, watermelons, and beef, the Creek men and women from towns along the roads were occasionally able to sell their surplus produce in small quantities to travelers, both official and unofficial, who passed through their country as well as to soldiers garrisoned at local posts such as Fort Mitchell.[94] Creek women continued to produce baskets and mats of woven cane for sale to travelers and area residents and sometimes earned a handsome profit for their industry.[95] For those Creek people living near important water crossings, such as at the Chattahoochee, Tallapoosa, and Coosa rivers, or even lesser ones in the heart of the nation, operating ferries might also bring profit.[96] And, as we have seen, at some places Creek men and women also charged tolls for travelers to cross bridges over other waterways; whether legitimate or not, these toll stops were another place that they might find revenue as a result of American travel.

The close of the 1820s appeared to many to spell the demise of the Creeks as both the federal government and the states of Georgia and Alabama closed ranks to propel them westward by drawing state boundaries through their territory and opening roads that crossed them. Settlers brought with them the aspirations of a generation, counting on free land and hoping for success in cotton, but they marched headlong into a population of Creek people still determined to outlast their own leaders' admissions of defeat. Despite the treaties of the 1820s that ceded away nearly all their remaining homelands and the active reimagining of Creek places as American spaces, Creek men and women continued to live their lives, raise their children, harvest their small crops, and follow the game when possible. The Creek National Council continued to pursue the most favorable treaty terms they could given the circumstances of their circumscription. The push of southern state sovereignty and the pull of potential westward lands led some to abandon hope of remaining in the South. They may have seen the rise of Andrew Jackson as the final blow to their dreams of keeping their south-eastern homelands. But most preferred to stay, perhaps hoping that the amicable, if ad hoc, trade relationships they had formed with American travelers would keep them all on the straight white path.[97]

Many Creeks made every effort to continue with their lives despite the dramatic worsening of their situation. One sign of such determination is that they still held ball plays between talwas. Ball plays were an inter-town cere-monial sport that had long been central to Creek social and cultural rela-tions for generations. Among southeastern Indians, these events were rau-cous and sometimes violent gatherings, with large numbers of players on both sides, often including both men and women. But they also functioned as important social gatherings where members of allied and rival towns renewed and cemented their relationships with one another. In addition, these ball plays were often preceded by weeks of ceremonies for the purifica-tion and preparation of the players.[98] When travel writer Basil Hall traveled in the Creek Nation in 1828–1829, he observed an inter-town ball play that literally astonished him with its size and vigor. Having heard and believed rumors that the Creeks were "miserable wretches . . . wandering around like bees whose hive had been destroyed," Hall was stunned by the enthusiasm and organization of the ball play.[99] Here was evidence that despite the loss of land, the ascendance of Andrew Jackson, and the ever-louder calls for their removal, Creek people insisted on their right to perform their ceremonies, dances, and games, and, above all, their right to hold themselves together.

Epilogue

In mid-March 1830, a young man named Richardson turned up on the door-step of one Mr. Harris, who lived near the Georgia-Creek border. He was covered in blood. He recounted a journey into the Creek Nation where an elderly Creek man overtook him on the road. To the old man's remarks, young Richardson made no reply, since he did not speak the Creek language. He passed by only to be ambushed later by the same Creek man and two others, who stabbed him in the throat. Rumors suggested that the attack was retaliation for a white traveler's assault of a Creek man several days previous.[1]

In many ways, this brief report, which originally appeared in the *Columbus Enquirer*, encapsulates both the drama and the complexity of crossing the borders of the South in the early nineteenth century. As with the attacks that took place on the roadsides of the Creek Nation during the Creek War, it is difficult and perhaps unwise to reduce such an encounter to a single explanation. The Creek attackers' motivations may have involved blood re-venge, but may also have been rooted in their long and bitter resentment of American travelers in their homelands. It may have been a way to bloody the path that had for so long linked their destiny to that of their American neighbors. Or the report may have been entirely untrue—an example of the misinformation that flowed so easily along the roads that both joined and divided the Creeks and their neighbors. Instead of an innocent victim, per-haps Richardson was a criminal lucky to escape execution by the Creeks, a fugitive who later lied about the reasons he was targeted.

But the most important aspect of this report might not be its content at all. Instead, what should fix our attention is that the incident was first de-scribed in the local newspaper of Columbus, Georgia. This "embryo town," as Basil Hall called it in 1828, was created by the Georgia legislature at the head of navigation on the Chattahoochee River. The city was planted on the eastern shore of the river on land acquired from the Creeks and is now Geor-gia's third-largest city (after Atlanta and Augusta).[2] Almost immediately ad-jacent to the falls of the Chattahoochee, where the river declines precipi-

Figure 4. An 1830s engraving of a newly constructed covered bridge over the Chattahoochee River at Columbus, Georgia. The bridge, the steamboat, the cotton bales, and the town all suggest the rapid transformation of the location from the heart of the Lower Creek world to the commercial jewel of Georgia's Nile. The image appears in Francis de Castelnau, Vues et souvenirs de l'Amérique du Nord, *plate 13, "Pont de Columbus. (Georgie et Alabama)." (Courtesy of Beinecke Rare Book and Manuscript Library, Yale University, New Haven.)*

tously toward the Gulf, Columbus is practically on top of the former center of the Lower Creek World. The Federal Road passed very near the town, as did other trails that linked it to both east and west; now as then it is advertised as a major hub for the interior South.[3] The fact of Richardson's escape is not nearly as significant as the location of its report, once at the heart of the Lower Creeks, by 1830 rapidly becoming the jewel of Georgia's Nile (see figure 4).

While the Creek world had changed dramatically, as the rise of Columbus vividly demonstrates, the U.S. sociopolitical landscape was also undergoing paradigmatic shifts. In many ways, these changes were the culmination of a long series of transformations, foremost among which were the emergence of American political parties, the hardening of racial concepts, and the entrenchment of the market economy. Among the most significant national developments was the election of soldier-hero and land speculator Andrew Jackson to the presidency on a platform that included acting immediately to remedy the "Indian problem."

Casting Indian people as a "few savage hunters" who occupied far more land than was necessary and presented an obstacle to development, Jackson characterized Indian removal as essential for the economic progress of the American nation.[4] In his 1830 address to Congress, he acknowledged the role that Indian affairs had played in conflicts over states' rights and asserted that removal would put "an end to all possible danger of collision between the authorities of the General and State Governments on account of the Indians." For progress and for unity, he claimed, the Indians must go. He asked, "What good man would prefer a country covered with forests and ranged by a few thousand savages to our extensive Republic, studded with cities, towns, and prosperous farms embellished with all the improvements which art can devise or industry execute, occupied by more than 12,000,000 happy people, and filled with all the blessings of liberty, civilization and religion?" Of course, Jackson's vision of "happy people" bringing liberty to the wilderness obscured the fact that the development of the South, and in fact the nation, depended on the continued bondage of thousands of enslaved people of African descent. Their forced migration into the lower South required the absence of Indian peoples in the region, and yet the slaves themselves were rendered invisible in Jackson's plan.

Perhaps most interesting, Jackson depicted the removal of the Creeks and their neighbors in the language of American mobility. He observed that thousands of Americans abandoned their homes every year to seek their fortunes in other places, migrating westward to unfamiliar territories at their own expense and creating new lives there. Why should the removal of the Indians at government expense, for their own benefit, make "humanity weep"? In conclusion, Jackson asked, "Is it supposed that the wandering savage has a stronger attachment to his home than the settled, civilized Christian? Is it more afflicting to him to leave the graves of his fathers than it is to our brothers and children?"[5] Anticipating Frederick Jackson Turner and placing space and mobility squarely at the center of American development, Jackson radically recast the forced migration of Indian peoples from their homelands in the idiom of American opportunity and idealism.[6]

Although the Indian Removal bill was debated and hotly contested by a number of legislators, it was ultimately passed over their objections and over the strenuous protests of the Indian nations it would affect. Particularly demonstrative in opposing the bill was the Cherokee government under the leadership of John Ross. In many ways the fate of the Creeks and other southeastern Indians rested on the success or failure of the Cherokee resistance. After the bill was passed, the states of Georgia and Alabama acted quickly to extend their jurisdiction over the Indians who still lived within their putative limits, declaring them subject to state laws, invalidating their claims to sovereign status, and subjecting them to prejudicial legal procedures. Ross and others led the fight to oppose the extension of state power all the way to the Supreme Court, ultimately resulting in the landmark cases *Cherokee Nation v. Georgia* (1831) and *Worcester v. Georgia* (1832). But the Cherokees and their champions were nevertheless unable to stop the removal process that had been set in motion. Despite the Court's ruling in *Worcester v. Georgia* that the extension of state laws over the Indians was illegal, Jackson and the Congress declined to intervene. In the absence of federal protection, squatters, smugglers, and prospectors swarmed into Indian land.[7]

The situation in Creek country had been deteriorating for quite some time before these cases ever reached the court. One young Tuckabatchee man described the circumstances thus: "The whole [Creek] nation is sinking gradually into destruction every day. Because the chiefs do not listen to the voice of the [U.S.] government and they try to walk in the old way—though they know we have no laws to prevent white people—when they are determined to enjure us."[8] Indeed, after 1829, the state of affairs among the Creeks, living wholly in what is now Alabama, had worsened dramatically. Emigrants and their agents seeking land daily poured over Creek boundaries, flooding the nation with spurious land sale offers and plying hesitant sellers with alcohol and bribes. Others were content to seize Creek lands with no pretense toward sale or purchase. Intruders in Creek country numbered in the thousands and many had "marked out situations they design occupying, by blazing and cutting initials on trees around tract[s]."[9] Thus did the white settlers declare their aspirations by marking yet another line in the landscape.

In addition to the problem of speculators and intruders, soldiers sent routinely from Fort Mitchell (near present-day Phenix City, Alabama) harassed Creeks in neighboring towns to "encourage" them to accept removal. To make matters worse, Jackson had appointed Tennessee crony and staunch anti-Indian politician John Henry Eaton as his secretary of war. Eaton was less than sympathetic when the Creeks petitioned repeatedly for the removal of squatters, protection from state laws, and fulfillment of federal treaty obligations.

But perhaps the most painful development for the Creeks was the emergence of a smallpox epidemic in 1831.[10] The rapid spread of the disease was made worse by the famine that overtook many Creek towns over the course of the year. The combination of these factors was enough to convince

Opothle Yaholo, who had long opposed removal, to sign the 1832 removal treaty.[11] Article One was brief and to the point: "The Creek tribe of Indians cede to the United States all their land, East of the Mississippi river."[12]

For several years after the treaty was signed, most Creeks remained in Alabama. But by 1834, plans for their forced migration were well underway, and by 1836, a majority of the approximately 10,000 remaining members of the Nation had made the forced march. When they arrived, they found that earlier Creek emigrants, largely McIntosh's former supporters, had settled themselves on the choicest lands.[13] Thus they carried with them to the west the political divisions forged in fiery debates back east.

But the Creeks also carried something else. To preserve the logic of social relations between talwas, Creeks appointed special fire carriers to bring embers from each of the ceremonial hearths to the new territory.[14] Most of the Creeks made the journey to Indian Territory along overland routes, making their way to Memphis where they continued by boat for the brief remainder of the trip.[15] Except for the very aged and the very ill, the majority walked. Much like the Cherokee Trail of Tears, the Creeks suffered tremendously on this forced march westward. But the knowledge that their town identities and the linkages that held them together would be preserved must have provided some small solace. Using the embers from fires in the east to create new talwas in Indian Territory was a way of transferring their world, linking their ancestral homelands to their new settlements in the west. Town and village names from the Creek lands in Alabama also began to emerge in the new Creek Nation—as a way of insisting on the survival of their ethnogeography and by extension their survival as a people.[16]

IN MANY WAYS, the issues that emerged from the expansion of the southern states into Creek country would be played out again and again as the nation turned its eyes ever westward. Long before the "iron horse" invaded the Plains, the commercial aspirations of a young America had crashed headlong into Native peoples still living between the Appalachians and the Mississippi River. The refrain of Indians being obstacles to progress would come to dominate American political rhetoric in the era of westward expansion and manifest destiny. The quest for the Oregon Territory or the gold in Dakota and then California sent waves of migrants again into indigenous lands, drawing boundaries, building roads, and demanding rights of way. The debates that emerged from the Creeks' experience with American "improvement" in the first decades of the nineteenth century not only influenced the making of the South, but also the making of a nation. Connecting Washington, D.C., to New Orleans via the Federal Road was only part of a larger expansionist project, one that was continental in scope.

Consider, for example, the first treaty of Fort Laramie (1851). The agreement, signed by U.S. commissioners and members of the Sioux, Cheyenne, Arapaho, Crow, Assiniboin, Gros-Ventre, Mandan, and Arikara nations, was devised in part to ensure the safety of Americans "passing through" the Indians' respective territories. Among other provisions, Article Two of the treaty recognized the United States' right to establish new roads through indigenous lands, while also demanding that the aforementioned nations refrain from harassing or attacking travelers on the two primary travel routes, the Santa Fe and Oregon Trails. While the treaty did not prohibit Native peoples from also traveling in the described territories, within a few short years they would find their mobility and their sovereignty restricted by both the discovery of gold in Montana and elsewhere and by the burgeoning reservation movement.[17]

Not unlike the Creeks, Native peoples of the Plains, the Great Basin, and the Far West had their own ideas about territory, mobility, and sovereignty—ideas they were no more eager to discard than the Creeks had been to shed theirs. And like the Creeks, they made their resistance legible to the rambling American populace in a variety of ways. In 1864, members of several Plains nations burned nearly every Overland Express station for a distance of five hundred miles. And while the second Treaty of Fort Laramie (1868) heralded a new era of dependence for the Sioux and other nations, it also marked the moment that the Americans were forced to abandon the Bozeman Trail that passed from Fort Laramie to the goldfields of Montana. Countless such examples abound in which Native people enacted their resistance to shrinking boundaries and the simultaneously increasing mobility of American migrants. These were not merely battles about territory; they were contests for order in the universe—for the right path and the right to travel it.

Notes

ABBREVIATIONS

ADAH   Alabama Department of Archives and History

AYER   Edward E. Ayer Collection, Newberry Library

BRBL   Beinecke Rare Book and Manuscript Library

CIL   "Creek Indian Letters, Talks & Treaties," Typescript, Louise Caroline Frederick Hays, compiler (1939), Parts I–III, GDAH

DU   Duke University, Special Collections

EKP   Ephraim Kirby Papers, DU

GDAH   Georgia Department of Archives and History

HAR   University of Georgia, Hargrett Rare Book and Manuscript Library, Athens, Georgia

HTL   Harry Toulmin Letters, 1813–1818, ADAH

ICS   Indian Claims and Spoliations 1-1-25, GDAH

LBH   *Letters, Journals and Writings of Benjamin Hawkins*, ed. C. L. Grant, Vol. 1: 1796–1801, Vol. 2: 1802–1816. Savannah: Beehive Press, 1980.

NARA   National Archives and Records Administration

RBP   Richard A. Blount Papers, 1792–1861, ADAH

RG28   Record Group 28, Records of the Office of the Postmaster, Letters Sent, NARA

RG75   Record Group 75, Records of the Bureau of Indian Affairs, including Letters Received by the Office of the Secretary of War Relating to Indian Affairs, 1800–23 and Letters Sent by the Office of the Secretary of War Relating to Indian Affairs, 1800–24, NARA

RG77   Record Group 77, Records of the Office of the Chief of Engineers, Records of the Board on Internal Improvements, including Letters Received, 1824–31, Civil Works Map File, 1800–1947, and Treasure File, NARA

SENADD   Southeastern Native American Documents Database, 1730–1840, Digital Library of Georgia <http://dlg.usg.galileo.edu>

SHC   University of North Carolina, Southern Historical Collection

TCC   Telamon Cuyler Collection, Hargrett Rare Book and Manuscript Library, presented in SENADD

TSLA   Tennessee State Library and Archives, presented in SENADD

ULTB   "Unpublished Letters of Timothy Barnard, 1784–1820," Typescript, Louise Caroline Frederick Hays, compiler (1939), GDAH

1. "Talk from the Upper Creeks to John Stuart," February 4, 1774, quoted in Braund, *Deerskins and Duffels*, 57.

2. Joshua A. Piker contends that internal Creek debates on various trading paths into the Nation should be viewed in the context of community or town-based histories that emphasize the importance of the local in Creek identity and histories. Piker, " 'White & Clean' & Contested."

3. On the Creek policy of neutrality, see Hahn, *Invention of the Creek Nation*. In constructing his argument on the invention of the Creek Nation as characterized by territorially bounded land and a centrally organized political structure devoted to pursuing neutrality with the Spanish, British, and French empires abroad, Hahn draws on Knight, "Formation of the Creeks." Other scholars who have debated the timing and nature of Creek confederation include Braund, *Deerskins and Duffels*; Corkran, *Creek Frontier*; Crane, *Southern Frontier*; Gatschet, *Migration Legend*; Green, *Politics of Indian Removal*.

4. Historians Green and Hahn have most vigorously asserted the role of boundaries in nascent Creek nationalism. Green, *Politics of Indian Removal*; Hahn, *Invention of the Creek Nation*.

5. The terms "middle ground" and "new world" may or may not have had any salience for the peoples who experienced them. I refer here to Richard White's *The Middle Ground: Indians, Empires, and Republics in the Great Lakes Region, 1650–1815* and James Merrell's *The Indians' New World: Catawbas and Their Neighbors from European Contact through the Era of Removal*. Both these works deploy spatial images of social relations across the Indian / European cultural divide—although they do so largely with divergent hypotheses and conclusions—and both of them have rightfully received accolades for their contributions to American Indian historiography. But the spatial terminology they each devised may or may not have had meaning for the Native peoples they studied and yet, as both James T. Carson and Nancy Shoemaker have observed, both concepts became incredibly influential within the field so that "middle grounds" and "new worlds" began appearing all over Native North America. Likewise, the so-called spatial turn in the humanities has resulted in surprisingly few studies that engage geographic categories on the terms that their subjects used them, producing instead a vast array of theoretical devices on the phenomenology of "space and place" without contributing meaningfully to the ethnohistory of spatiality. On White and Merrell, see Shoemaker, *Clearing a Path*, 63, and Carson, "Ethnogeography," 769–88. For examples of the groundless use of geographic language in otherwise valuable recent cultural history, see Faery, *Cartographies of Desire*, and Stoler, *Haunted by Empire*.

6. Indeed, a wide variety of scholars have noted that historic Native North American societies (in contrast to their Western European counterparts) often organize their experiences according to a spatial, not temporal logic. The examples are too numerous to list in full, but for a good beginning, see Deloria, *God Is Red*, 62–77, 122. For a sampling of other literature undoubtedly influenced by Deloria's early work, see Basso, *Wisdom Sits in Places*; Kidwell, Noley, and Tinker, *Native American Theology*, 44–48; Nabokov, *Forest of Time*, 126–49.

7. Carson, "Ethnogeography," 775. Another excellent demonstration of ethnogeographical methods appears in Huber, "Anggor Floods."

8. De Vorsey, "Indian Trails"; Foster, *Archaeology of the Lower Muskogee Creek Indians*, 33–34; Meyer, "Indian Trails of the Southeast," 1.

9. Tanner, "Land and Water Communication Systems," 6–8; Hudson, *Southeastern Indians*, 313–16; Meyer, "Indian Trails of the Southeast," 1.

10. De Vorsey, "Indian Trails"; Foster, *Archaeology of the Lower Muskogee Creek Indians*, 33; Gatschet, *Migration Legend*, 151; Hoffman, "Lucas Vázquez de Allyón's Discovery and Colony," 42; Meyer, "Indian Trails of the Southeast," 4; Truett, *Trade and Travel*, 9.

11. Ethridge, *Creek Country*, 32. Ethridge notes (122), "The most frequently traveled trails within Creek country were the ones connecting the towns. These trails typically ran on both banks of a stream and connected with one another at the fords."

12. Creeks distinguished between talwas and talofas by the fact that a talwa had a commons or square ground with a fire at its center and might encompass several talofas, sometimes many miles apart.

13. Chaudhuri and Chaudhuri, *Sacred Path*, 86–90. Piker notes, "At the town level, the factions and centripetal forces unleashed by individual and clan interests were harnessed to whatever degree possible. Town-based networks, events, and rituals called on towns-people to transcend—although not forsake—personal and familiar agendas and loyalties. In doing so, towns became not only the building blocks of regional and national associations, but also the loci of the discussion, mediation, and reconciliation which made interclan relations, and thus Creek life, possible." Piker, *Okfuskee*, 9–10. On the *talwa* and *talofa* relationship, see Ethridge, *Creek Country*, 28–29, 95–96; Gatschet, "Towns and Villages," 386.

14. Braund, *Deerskins and Duffels*, 141.

15. Important works on the Indian slave trade include Perdue, *Slavery and the Evolution of Cherokee Society*, and Gallay, *Indian Slave Trade*.

16. Corkran, *Creek Frontier*, 5; Ethridge, *Creek Country*, 26–29.

17. Green, *Politics of Indian Removal*, 20–21; Hahn, *Invention of the Creek Nation*, 119.

18. Hitchiti is one of the languages spoken in the Creek confederacy that is not mutually intelligible with Eastern Muskogean dialects such as Alabama, Koasati, Muskogee, and Mikasuki. Other non-Muskogean languages spoken in the Creek country included Yuchi and Shawnee. Western Muskogean includes the Choctaw and Chickasaw dialects. See Braund, *Deerskins and Duffels*, 29–30.

19. Caughey, *McGillivray of the Creeks*, 23, 25.

20. Ethridge, *Creek Country*, 28.

21. Hahn, *Invention of the Creek Nation*, 13. Cowerther Mayit's indication in his complaint that Coweta had been cut off for some time from the British trade at Augusta is thus significant because it reveals the degree to which Coweta had lost luster in the eyes of Georgia officials since founder General James Oglethorpe had attended conventions there in the 1730s. Oglethorpe held a famous treaty meeting there that resulted in a large cession by the Lower Creeks and contributed to the perception among some Upper Creeks that their southeasterly brethren were too amenable to the invaders' wishes. On Coweta's prominence, see, for example, the entry for "Cowetta" in *North-American and West-Indian Gazetteer*, n.p. On Coweta's rise and fall, see Braund, *Deerskins and Duffels*,

139–40. On the importance of Coweta to the emergence of Creek national identity generally, see Hahn, *Invention of the Creek Nation*.

22. Wickham, *Tree That Bends*, 54–56.

23. Ethridge estimates 15,000–20,000 Creeks, while Daniel Usner gives the figure 15,160. Ethridge, *Creek Country*, 30; Usner, "American Indians on the Cotton Frontier," 298.

24. Ethridge, *Creek Country*, 30; Braund, *Deerskins and Duffels*, 27.

25. Chaudhuri and Chaudhuri have suggested that some of the paths linking Creek towns were kept secret as a measure of national security. Chaudhuri and Chaudhuri, *Sacred Path*, 70.

26. Creeks and their Indian neighbors were quick to recognize when surveyors and settlers began to trickle into their territory, using the trade paths for their own purposes. They sometimes reacted by physically obstructing a path or a process that was believed to represent a threat to their security and prosperity. Astute visitors noted the Indians' suspicion. De Vorsey observes, "In 1772 David Taitt, a deputy Indian agent, recounted that when on the trail in the Creek country he placed his servant between himself and his Indian guide, 'thereby preventing him from seeing me take observations of the course of the path and creeks we passed.' At other times Taitt hid his compass on his saddle and surreptitiously took the courses of the trails he was following so as not to offend his Indian hosts." De Vorsey, "Indian Trails."

27. Grantham, *Creation Myths and Legends*, 66; Swanton, *Myths and Tales*, 118–21.

28. Gatschet, *Migration Legend*, 222–24.

29. On Native American creation myths involving emergence as a basic theme, see Kidwell, Noley, and Tinker, *Native American Theology*, 14, 37, 129. A frequently cited example is the Navajo (Diné) creation story. Zolbrod, *Diné Bahané*.

30. Quoted in Swanton, *Religious Beliefs and Medicinal Practices*, 512.

31. Bartram, *Observations on the Creek and Cherokee Indians*, 27; Swanton, *Myths and Tales*, 139–44.

32. Swanton, *Religious Beliefs and Medicinal Practices*, 479, 512–13.

33. Grantham, *Creation Myths and Legends*, 41–43.

34. On the transformation from borderlands to bordered lands, see Adelman and Aron in their seminal essay, "From Borderlands to Borders."

35. Yet much of the literature on the history of early national transportation pays little or no attention to the impact of these projects on the lives of Indian peoples. See for example, Larson, *Internal Improvement*; Malone, *Opening the West*; *Transportation and the Early Nation*; Goodrich, *Government Promotion of American Canals and Railroads*. Two notable exceptions separated by some seventy years are Truett, *Trade and Travel*, and Friend, *Along the Maysville Road*.

36. Southerland and Brown, *Federal Road*, 2, 17–21; Carter, *Territorial Papers*, 5:395–515.

37. Among the first people killed in the conflict was an African American mail carrier. Benjamin Hawkins to William Eustis, August 24, 1812, LBH, 2:615.

38. The implication of this approach is that we need to more carefully consider the importance of Indian affairs within the context of early national southern history. The vast majority of southern history focuses on the genesis and legacy of African slavery and

has not typically contextualized this institution within the fluid racial milieu formed from two hundred years of slavery, intermixture, and revolution among and between Indians, Africans, and Europeans. Blassingame, *Slave Community*; Cooper and Terrill, *American South*; Finkelman, *Slavery and the Founders*; Genovese, *Roll Jordan Roll*; Stampp, *Peculiar Institution*. Notable exceptions include Berlin, *Many Thousands Gone*; Jordan, *White over Black*; Perdue, *Slavery and the Evolution of Cherokee Society*; Morgan, *American Slavery, American Freedom*; Littlefield, *Africans and Creeks*; Rothman, *Slave Country*. Most histories that do focus on American Indians in the South tend to cluster around either the Revolutionary War or the Removal Era. O'Donnell, *Southern Indians in the American Revolution*; Calloway, *American Revolution in Indian Country*; Foreman, *Indian Removal*; Young, *Redskins, Ruffleshirts, and Rednecks*; De Rosier, *Removal of the Choctaw Indians*; Satz, *American Indian Policy*; Wallace, *Long, Bitter Trail*; Green, *Politics of Indian Removal*; Hatley, *Dividing Paths*. This trend is addressed cogently in Merrell, "American Nations."

39. Martin, *Sacred Revolt*, 6–8.

40. Historic Creek political and social identifiers are intensely local in nature—fixing civic and personal identities to specific town sites, landforms, and natural features. Chaudhuri and Chaudhuri, *Sacred Path*, 1; Nabokov, *Forest of Time*, 133–34.

CHAPTER ONE

1. Tallassee King, "A Talk Delivered at Silver Bluff the Third Day of November 1779 to George Galphin Esqr. Commission of Indian Affairs in Southern Departments by the Tallassee King," November 3, 1779, AYER.

2. On red and white moieties among the Creeks, see Chaudhuri and Chaudhuri, *Sacred Path*, 29; Hudson, *Southeastern Indians*, 234–37. On the use of white beads and feathers to signify proper relations, see, for instance, William Hill, Report of the affairs in the Creek agency by William Hill, the asst. in the Upper Creeks, October 9, 1801, NARA, RG75, 75.2; Gatschet, *Migration Legend*, 247.

3. On the "sacred path," see Chaudhuri and Chaudhuri, *Sacred Path*, 1; on *hahagahaga*, the Creek concept of "the paths or laws," see 95–103. See also Swanton, *Religious Beliefs and Medicinal Practices*, 512–13.

4. Braund has also acknowledged the way Creeks used ceremonial relationships to conduct trade and diplomacy on their own terms. *Deerskins and Duffels*, 30. Merrell's *Indians' New World* is another important work detailing the ways in which a southeastern Indian community determined trade and diplomatic relationships according to their own worldviews. For more on the "bright chain of friendship," also known as the "covenant chain," see Jennings, *Ambiguous Iroquois Empire*; Jacobs, "Wampum: The Protocol of Indian Diplomacy"; Richter and Merrell, *Beyond the Covenant Chain*.

5. For further examples, see Timothy Barnard to James Seagrove, June 20, 179[3?], ULTB, 174; Swanton, *Religious Beliefs*, 546–47. Corkran quoting Tese Micco's talk to Governor Wright of Georgia in 1775 and David Taitt's 1775 letter to John Stuart, in Corkran, *Creek Frontier*, 291–92. The Choctaws, another Muskogean-speaking people, also consistently deployed the metaphor of the "path" in their political discourse. See Carson, *Searching for the Bright Path*, 3, 8, 34, 84, 106, 109.

6. "A Talk from the Young Tallassee King from the Up[p]er and lower Towns, of the

Creeks, To George Galphin, Esqr. Continental Commissioner of Indian affairs & [unclear] Hammond and Daniel McMurphy, Esqrs. Commissioners for the States of Carolina and Georgia at Ogechee," December 15, 1778, AYER.

7. See, for example, "Journal of the proceedings of the commissioners appointed to treat with the southern Indians [with accompanying] letter[s], 1785–1786," and "Talk from the White Bird King in answer to [Joseph] Ellicot[t]'s talk," November 8, 1791, TCC, <http://dlg.galileo.usg.edu/> (October 8, 2006); Ellicott, *Journal of Andrew Ellicott*. Corkran also quotes a 1776 talk by the Wolf of Mucclossus to Governor Wright of Georgia in which he said, "Let the talk be made straight"; *Creek Frontier*, 26–27.

8. Danger is not the same thing as evil. Snakes were and are revered in Creek spiritual life and historic Creeks constructed numerous mounds in the shape of serpents to reflect their deep respect for the creatures that abounded in southeastern ecology. Chaudhuri and Chaudhuri, *Sacred Path*, 6, 9. See also naturalist William Bartram's experience upon killing a snake in a Seminole town. Bartram, *Travels of William Bartram*, 164–66.

9. Creek people typically celebrate the Busk, or Green Corn Ceremony, sometime during the month of August with the ripening of the corn; it marks the end of all the past year's strife. Towns and homes are symbolically and literally cleaned and transgressors can return from exile without fear of punishment. See Chaudhuri and Chaudhuri, *Sacred Path*, 52–55; Hudson, *Southeastern Indians*, 365–75; Swann, "Position and State of Manners and Arts," 276. For more on the inter-town ball plays, see Haas, "Creek Inter-Town Relations."

10. Hahn, *Invention of the Creek Nation*, 238.

11. Ibid., 242.

12. Braund notes, however, that the division of Creeks into Upper and Lower coalitions negatively influenced individual town autonomy. *Deerskins and Duffels*, 140. On debates between towns and between Upper and Lower divisions regarding the various trading paths, see Piker, " 'White & Clean' & Contested."

13. "A Talk from the Young Tallassee King from the Up[p]er and lower Towns," December 15, 1778, AYER.

14. Adair, *History of the American Indians*, 274.

15. Foster, *Archaeology of the Lower Muskogee Creek Indians*, 24.

16. Meyer, "Indian Trails of the Southeast," 9.

17. Hudson, *Southeastern Indians*, 315. The "fall line" is "a distinct topographic line . . . [that] demarcates the geological transition from the Piedmont, the Ridge and Valley, the Appalachian Plateau, and the Interior Low Plateaus to the Coastal Plain, the physiographic province that comprises much of the Lower South." Ethridge, *Creek Country*, 33–34.

18. One Lower Creek talofa located on the Chattahoochee River was named for its location at an important crossing place. Its name, *Hu'li taiga*, means "war-ford" or "military river-passage." Gatschet, "Towns and Villages," 397–98.

19. Gatschet, *Migration Legend*, 151.

20. Levy, *Fellow Travelers*, 37, 63.

21. De Vorsey, "Indian Trails," <http://www.georgiaencyclopedia.org/> (April 15, 2006).

22. Romans, *Concise Natural History*, 44.

23. Thicknesse (1790) quoted in De Vorsey, "Indian Trails," <http://www.georgia encyclopedia.org/>. De Vorsey also quotes ethnologist James Mooney's description of a tree known as "Chopped Oak" that bore "tally marks by means of which the Indians kept the record of scalps taken in their forays."

24. Adair, *History of the American Indians*, 183.

25. Levy, *Fellow Travelers*, 64, describes other examples of ways in which "trees were billboards." See also Shoemaker, *Strange Likeness*, 24–28. For more on Native American place-making and concepts of geography, see Basso, *Wisdom Sits in Places*; Galloway, "Storied Land"; Lewis, *Cartographic Encounters*; Lewis, "Indian Delimitations" and "Maps, Mapmaking, and Map Use"; Warhus, *Another America*.

26. Goff, "Some Old Road Names in Georgia," 388–98. Goff also notes that when the Old River Road from Savannah to Augusta was opened, it connected to a trail that the Cherokees had blazed to their country from the same settlements.

27. Goff observes, "This marking was the pioneer equivalent of today's road numbering. A blaze was a smooth-cut gash on the trunk of a tree, while chops or notches were V-shaped indentations that were cut into the trunk." "Some Old Road Names in Georgia," 396. In *New Voyage to Georgia*, the anonymous author narrates a scene in which his company came upon some "vacant" land and one of them "named it after his name, throwing a Bottle of Rum against the largest Pine Tree." *New Voyage to Georgia*, 17. The most convincing study of such customs is found in Seed, *Ceremonies of Possession*.

28. One Creek town, located on the eastern side of the Flint River, was named *Hotali-huyana*, meaning "Hurricane town," for the devastation left by a hurricane. Gatschet, "Towns and Villages," 397.

29. Grantham, *Creation Myths and Legends*, 26; Swanton, *Myths and Tales*, 30–34, 97–98, 154. An interesting reversal of this transformation appears in a Koasati story recorded by Swanton in which "submarine people" leave their watery homes to travel about among earthly people. They are warned by their peers not to eat earthly food lest they remain above water forever. Swanton, *Myths and Tales*, 168–69.

30. Swanton, *Myths and Tales*, 7–9.

31. Ibid., 2–7, 26, 43–44, 88, 108–9, 126–28, 131–33.

32. Grantham, *Creation Myths and Legends*, 28; Swanton, *Myths and Tales*, 17–19, 21–22, 36–37, 98–99, 124, 149, 170–71.

33. Hudson, *Southeastern Indians*, 130, 148, 166.

34. Ethridge, *Creek Country*, 33, 118.

35. Grantham, *Creation Myths and Legends*, 28. See also Swanton, *Myths and Tales*, 147–48, 186–88.

36. Gatschet, *Migration Legend*, 244–51. For an unparalleled analysis of the Cusseta migration legend, see Hahn, "Cussita Migration Legend."

37. In the series of myths describing the origin of the Cussetas and Cowetas, paths are also described as either red or white, according to their orientation for war or peace, and such associations are subsequently attached to the communities themselves. Grantham, *Creations Myths and Legends*, 26–28; Gatschet, *Migration Legend*, 248–49.

38. This is widely discussed in literature on Native American societies. A few brief

examples: Galloway, "Storied Land," 175; Kidwell, Noley, and Tinker, *Native American Theology*, 38–39; Pierotti and Wildcat, "Traditional Ecological Knowledge"; Salmon, "Kincentric Ecology."

39. Baronet, Dedicatory epistle preceding *Discoveries of John Lederer*.

40. Ultimately, British Superintendent of Indian Affairs John Stuart conceived of and surveyed a more realistic and legitimate boundary line between the southeastern Indians and the lower colonies. Known as the Southern Indian Boundary Line, it was in place by 1775 and is the subject of De Vorsey's excellent monograph *The Indian Boundary in the Southern Colonies, 1763–1775*.

41. Green, *Politics of Indian Removal*, xi, 21–35; see generally Hahn, *Invention of the Creek Nation*.

42. Tallassee King, "A Talk Delivered at Silver Bluff," November 3, 1779, AYER.

43. "Talk of the Headmen of Coweta," August 17, 1785, CIL, 1:83–84.

44. Green, *Politics of Indian Removal*, 26.

45. McGillivray to [Arturo] O'Neill, July 24, 1785, in Caughey, *McGillivray of the Creeks*, 93.

46. Journal of the Proceedings of General Andrew Jackson, General David Meriwether, and Jesse Franklin, Esqr. Commissioners appointed by the President of the United States of America "to hold conferences & settle a Treaty or Treaties with the Chickasaw & Cherokee Tribes or Nations of Indians," 1816, Jesse Franklin Indian Treaty Papers, SHC.

47. Braund, *Deerskins and Duffels*, 134; Green, *Politics of Indian Removal*, 3.

48. Braund, *Deerskins and Duffels*, 61; Ethridge, *Creek Country*, 135–37.

49. For an unmatched glimpse of the southeastern Indian discussions of property and territory, see Journal of the Proceedings, 1816, SHC. This journal contains the testimony of Chickasaw and Cherokee leaders, as well as Creek deputies, who describe the relationship of their separate territories, beginning with their origin stories.

50. The Haudenosaunee peoples devised a similar agreement among themselves, known as the "Dish with One Spoon" compact, which allowed various communities to share the hunting grounds between and around them with the understanding that they would never take up arms against one another in competition for the same resources. Hill, "One Village Has Been Made."

51. Citing Swanton, Read claims that the Creek "expressive" term for the dead is "ikán odjálgi," meaning "land owners." Read, "Indian Stream-Names in Georgia," 129.

52. Grantham, *Creation Myths and Legends*, 123–24.

53. In their essay, "Sharing the Land: A Study in American Indian Territoriality," Albers and Kay likewise describe the ways in which various indigenous North American groups articulated a clear sense of territoriality. They argue that such expressions of territoriality are less recognizable if scholars insist on applying definitions based on actual land-use or concepts of ownership; see especially 52–53. Similarly, Shoemaker argues, "How eighteenth-century Indians and Europeans allocated individuals' use of the public domain may have varied, but they conceptualized territorial sovereignty in much the same way. And there is no doubt that Indian communities saw land as sovereign territory." Shoemaker, *Strange Likeness*, 17. An interesting point of divergence in these two discussions is the concept of property. While Albers and Kay maintain that European definitions

of ownership are poorly suited to describe American Indian territoriality, Shoemaker contends that the documentary record overwhelmingly demonstrates that Native and European notions of "land as the property of groups of people" were quite similar.

54. Braund, *Deerskins and Duffels*, 68.

55. Ethridge, *Creek Country*, 135–36. Ethridge notes that William Bartram claimed that only the non-Muskogean speakers of the nation, sometimes called Stinkards, were assigned to specific hunting grounds and that Muskogean speakers had the freedom to range widely, although she doubts his conclusion. *Creek Country*, 290n96 and chap. 10 generally.

56. Braund, *Deerskins and Duffels*, 67–68; Ethridge, *Creek Country*, 135. Those women who remained behind in the towns took care of the small children and the elderly and prepared the fields for spring planting. See also Perdue, *Cherokee Women*.

57. Ronald Takaki has written evocatively about the language of amputation that characterized American officials' discussions of Indian land. Takaki, *Iron Cages*, 59, 92, 200.

58. This was how hunting parties were typically described. See, for instance, Cusetuh King, Little Prince, Little Warrior, "Talk from the Cowetuh, Cusetuh and Old Town Chiefs to the Mad Dog and other Chiefs of the upper towns," September 26, 1801, NARA, RG75, 75.2.

59. Kidwell, Noley, and Tinker, *Native American Theology*, 34, 40–44; see also Martin, *Keepers of the Game*.

60. Ethridge, *Creek Country*, 135.

61. According to Caleb Swann, who traveled in the Creek country in 1791, the Creeks designated the moons according to the planting season, with August being the commencement of a new year. Most Creek hunters were in the woods "a hunting" by late November. Swann, "Position and State of Manners and Arts," 276.

62. Braund, *Deerskins and Duffels*, 136; Green, *Politics of Indian Removal*, 19. Waselkov counter-argues that biased documentary sources have overemphasized the decline of deer populations and that available archaeological evidence suggests no such diminution. He calls for further research, both archival and archaeological, on the matter. Waselkov, "Eighteenth-Century Anglo-Indian trade," 202–5.

63. John Galphin to Henry Osborne, August 1, 1789, CIL, 1:102.

64. Hays notes, "This Uchee Path was supposed to have been used by Oglethorpe when he went to visit the Indian Chiefs at Coweta in 1739, since his Ranger reported he crossed Dallus Creek [Dally's Creek] and this was the only Indian Path shown on the old Maps to have crossed Dallus Creek." CIL, 1:1.

65. Ethridge, *Creek Country*, 122; Piker, *Okfuskee*, 5–6. On north-south paths to the Gulf and debates over individual town preferences for a particular trading path, see generally Piker, " 'White & Clean' & Contested."

66. Tanner, "Land and Water Communication Systems," 12; See also Braund, *Deerskins and Duffels*, 90.

67. Tanner, "Land and Water Communication Systems," 10.

68. Foster, *Archaeology of the Lower Muskogee Creek Indians*, 34.

69. Tanner, "Land and Water Communication Systems," 12. The easternmost portion of this road is clearly visible in Thomas Wright, A Map of Georgia and Florida, 1763, in *Crown Collection*, ser. 3., vol. 1.

70. Capt. George Haigh, "Map showing the Indian Country West of Carolina," 1751, in *Crown Collection*, ser. 3., vol. 1. See also "A New and Accurate Map of the Province of Georgia in North America," 1779, AYER; Justly Watson, "Survey of the Coast from Fort William, near St. Juan's River, to Mosquito River," 1743, in *Crown Collection*, ser. 1., vol. 5; Moore, *Voyage to Georgia*. Louis De Vorsey has also drawn attention to the importance of the town of Ebenezer in colonial Georgia as the place of intersection for several important Indian trails. De Vorsey, "Indian Trails," <http://www.georgiaencyclopedia.org/>.

71. Generally speaking, strategic maps focused primarily on localities, defining the boundaries of a coastal city or depicting a cluster of forts along a particular river. Trade-oriented maps, however, emphasized interregional communication and were much more legible in the context of colonial competition and the transatlantic economy. Emmanuel Bowen, "A New Map of Georgia, with Part of Carolina, Florida and Louisiana," 1748, NARA, RG77, Civil Works Map File.

72. Crane, *Southern Frontier*, 3–18.

73. *North-American and West-Indian Gazetteer*, for example, notes that of all the rivers that empty into the Mississippi on the eastern side, the Cusates, which may refer to the Tennessee River, is "the great road of the traders from thence to the Mississippi and intermediate places" (n.p.).

74. Mid-eighteenth-century maps of the region are notable for their emphasis on these Indian paths and for the breadth of Native-supplied information illuminating territory that was still terra incognita to most colonists. For more examples of Indian collaboration in the creation of colonial maps, see Matthieu Albert Lotter, "Carte Nouvelle de l'Amerique Angloise," n.d., Franco Novacco Map Collection, Newberry Library; M. le baron de Crenay, "Carte de partie de la Louisiane," 1733, Map Collection, Karpinski Photostats, Newberry Library; Arthur Dobbs, *An Account of the Countries Adjoining to Hudson's Bay*; Christophe Dufros, sieur de La Jemeraye, "Carte d'une partie du Lac Superieur," c.1732, AYER; Lederer, *Discoveries of John Lederer*; "Sketch Map of the Rivers Santee, Congaree, Wateree, Saludee, &c., with the road to the Cattauboes," 1750, in *Crown Collection of Photographs of American Maps*, ser. 3., vol. 1.

75. The local Indians, Vanden Bosh observed, avoided placing anything red in or on their canoes, lest the crocodiles become interested and swamp the boat. Vanden Bosh, "A map of the lower Mississippi River, and of the neighboring coast and country to the southwest," 1694, AYER. See also Taitt, *Plan of part of the rivers Tombecbe, Alabama, Tensa, Perdido, & Scambia*, [1771?]. This map shows the Escambia River, called Weeoka or Wewoka by the Creeks, up to a northerly point where Taitt notes, "A boat cannot go any further up the River being blocked with logs. The lower Creeks Indians sometimes cross the River at this place."

76. Littlefield, *Africans and Creeks*, 9–10, 13.

77. T. H. Ball noted, "The common pack-horses were small but hardy, and were accustomed to carry on their peculiar pack-saddles, three bundles of sixty pounds weight each. Two bundles were swung across the saddle so that one was on each side of the horse, and the third bundle was placed upon the saddle. Over the whole was thrown a covering of hide or fur to protect from the rain. . . . On the routes of travel one pack-driver had charge of ten ponies. About twenty-five miles each day was the average rate of travel." Ball, *Glance into the Great South-east*, 58.

78. See, for example: John Barnwell, Report on the building of Fort King George, July 21, 1721, BRBL; Timothy Barnard to David Blackshear, October 14, 1795, ULTB.

79. Hawkins noted two such African American interpreters, both women, during his journey from the Cherokees to the Creeks in 1796; LBH, 1:5, 13. See also Krauthamer, "Kinship and Freedom," 156–57; Littlefield, *Africans and Creeks*, 41; Corkran, *Creek Frontier*, 73.

80. Moore, *Voyage to Georgia*, 97–98.

81. Levy, *Fellow Travelers*, 44; Wight, Journal [of a journey from Pensacola to Tuckabatchee], 1771, ADAH.

82. See *Passports Issued by Governors of Georgia*.

83. Numerous examples of passports issued to Indian people for the purpose of traversing the American states, often to and from the state and national capitals, appear in NARA RG75, 75.2.

84. Tanner notes, "By the mid-eighteenth century, trains of packhorses replaced the Indian burdeners, creating a well-beaten trail pattern." Tanner, "Land and Water Communication Systems," 11.

85. The export of Indian slaves was a primary source of revenue for the colony of South Carolina. Crane, "Tennessee River as the Road to Carolina," 8–9, 15.

86. Ball, *Glance into the Great South-east*, 57; Green, *Politics of Indian Removal*, 19–20. For example, when U.S. Army officer Caleb Swann traveled in the Creek Nation in the late eighteenth century, he noted, "Every town and village has one established white trader in it, and there are several neighborhoods, besides, that have traders. Each trader commonly employs one or two white packhorse men." Swann makes this observation in the context of noting how many whites lived in the Creek Nation; it prefaces his prediction that the number is "sufficient to contaminate all the natives." "Position and State of Manners and Arts," 263.

87. Braund, *Deerskins and Duffels*, 52. While traders were credited with keeping Native and immigrant communities connected, they were simultaneously blamed for inciting the contempt of the Indians with whom they lived. Early in the trade, white traders commonly married into specific communities, more or less conforming to Creek matrilineal society and plying their trade successfully with the help of their wives' clan and family connections. But over the course of the eighteenth century, a new generation of traders emerged. Though still compelled to live among the Indians, they were more defiant of Creek social and familial order. By the mid-eighteenth century, some traders among the Creeks had begun to settle further out from a town's center, revolt against interference of a wife's family in matters of progeny and property, and occasionally engage in small-scale agricultural pursuits apart from the communal subsistence fields and household gardens.

88. Corkran, *Creek Frontier*, 309–11.

89. Braund, *Deerskins and Duffels*, 164–67.

90. For a definition and extended analysis of the term "capitalist vanguard," see Pratt, *Imperial Eyes*, 146–69.

91. Hill, Report of the affairs, October 9, 1801, NARA, RG75, 75.2.

92. "Journal of the proceedings of the commissioners appointed to treat with the southern Indians [with accompanying] letter[s], 1785–1786," TCC, <http://dlg.galileo.usg.edu/>.

93. U.S. Continental Congress, "The committee consisting of Mr. Kearney, Mr. Carrington, Mr. Bingham, Mr. Smith, and Mr. Dane, to whom was referred the report of the secretary at war, and sundry papers relative to Indian affairs in the Southern Department; and also a motion of the delegates from the state of Georgia, report," 1787, BRBL.

94. John Houstoun, "A Talk deld. in Council by the Honble J:H: Esqr. Govr. of the State of Georgia in Answer to One yesterday received from Mingahoopa the Second Chief of the Choctaw Nation," July 17, 1784, CIL, 1:59–60.

95. Carson, *Searching for the Bright Path*, 42.

96. Many Native peoples, such as the Oneidas, Tuscaroras, Penobscots, Passamaquoddys, and Chickasaws, who had allied with the Americans, were also deprived of their lands through fraud and deceit. See Calloway, "Continuing Revolution in Indian Country"; Hine and Faragher, *American West*, 105.

97. Vizente Manuel de Zespedes and Yntipaya Masla, "Talk that Zespedes the Governor of Florida had with Yntipaya Masla, principal warrior of the Lower Creek Indians, called Toclatoche, on the ten articles that were proposed and the answers that he gave to each one of them in order," May 29, 1786, quoted in Caughey, *McGillivray of the Creeks*, 115.

98. George Washington initially opposed the widespread sale of public lands and subsequent discontinuous settlement patterns proposed by the 1785 Land Ordinance, stating in a letter to Richard Henry Lee, "The spirit for emigration is great, people have got impatient, and tho' you cannot stop the road, it is in your power to mark the way; a little while and you will not be able to do either." Quoted in Kain and Baigent, *Cadastral Map*, 290–91.

99. "A Talk from the Young Tallassee King from the Up[p]er and lower Towns," December 15, 1778, AYER. This document represents the only instance I have seen in which the European colonial powers are referred to as "mothers" rather than fathers, brothers, or friends. In the logic of Creek kinship, which is reckoned matrilineally, the invocation of the mother-child relationship invokes a structure of descent, obligation, and social identity that is far more binding than that suggested by "fathers" or "friends."

100. "McGillivray for the Chiefs of the Creek, Chickasaw, and Cherokee Nations, July 10, 1785," quoted in Caughey, *McGillivray of the Creeks*, 91.

101. Hahn, *Invention of the Creek Nation*, 272–73; Braund, *Deerskins and Duffels*, 173.

102. Hahn, *Invention of the Creek Nation*, 269; Piker, " 'White & Clean' & Contested," 339n19.

103. The sectional issues dividing the southern states from their northern counterparts were rooted in larger issues than just Indian affairs. But by far the most ink and vitriol were expended on the problem of Indians on the frontiers and the ways in which the federal policies, often proposed by representatives from northern states, unfairly jeopardized southern commercial and political interests. Interestingly, these debates were also often conducted in extraordinarily gendered terms. See, for instance, the tirades of "MANLIUS" from the *Southern Centinel and Gazette of the State*, September 11, 1794. See also "[Petition of] the citizens of the County of Richmond, [Georgia] to the president and members of the convention of the State of Georgia, 1795 May 1 / by order of the Mechanical Society of Augusta, [Georgia]," TCC, <http://dlg.galileo.usg.edu/> (March 6, 2006); "[Letter] 1788 Aug. 3, Nashville [to] Alexander McGillivray / James Robertson.

Opposition of McGillivray the great chief of the Creeks, 1857 / A. W. Putnam," TSLA, <http://dlg.galileo.usg.edu/> (March 6, 2006).

104. Article Nine of the Articles of Confederation states, "The United States in Congress assembled shall also have the sole and exclusive right and power of . . . regulating the trade and managing all affairs with the Indians, not members of any of the States, provided that the legislative right of any State within its own limits be not infringed or violated." Naturally, this left states like Georgia some interpretive latitude, but the Constitution specifically reserved treaty-making as the exclusive right of the Congress, stating in Article I, Section 10, "No State shall enter into any Treaty, Alliance, or Confederation." See also Littlefield, *Africans and Creeks*, 32–33.

105. For example, in 1770 a group of South Carolina and Georgia traders proposed a cession of land to discharge the debts of Cherokee individuals. Sir James Wright, then governor of Georgia, eventually agreed to allow the cession, though Superintendent of Indian Affairs John Stuart opposed it. The land would be sectioned off and sold and the profits delivered to the traders to absolve the debt. But the Creeks launched a protest in 1773 claiming that the lands the Cherokees had agreed to sell were in fact Creek, not Cherokee, lands. The agreement was then amended so that the benefits of the sale would be applied to debts held by members of both nations. In the end, the cost of surveying and fractioning the ceded lands far exceeded the revenue generated from their sale and the traders were unable to recover much compensation. Thus, the Indians had ceded land to pay for debts that were never discharged; they then had less land and the same debt. See "Case of the Merchants, and other interested in the Lands in the Province of Georgia, ceded by the Cherokee and Creek Indian Nations to His Majesty, for the Purpose of discharging the Debts due from those Nations to the British Traders," AYER.

106. Downes, "Creek-American Relations," 351–52.

107. *Southern Centinel and Gazette of the State*, January 23, 1794. The story reported was dated at Knoxville, December 7, 1793.

108. "Letter, 1786 May 23, [to] Governor [of Georgia, Edward Telfair], [Au]gusta, Georgia / Capt[ain] Joshua Inman," C. Mildred Thompson Collection, SENADD, <http://dlg.galileo.usg.edu/> (April 2, 2006).

109. Ibid. Conversely, in their petition to the Georgia governor, a handful of Greene County citizens presented a more complete picture. They stated that a party of Creeks had entered their settlement, killed two people, and stolen a quantity of goods and that a posse pursued them over the Oconee River. The vigilantes were unable to capture the guilty Indians so when they met with another party of Creeks, who were generally acknowledged to be innocent of the attack, they killed six of them instead. The petitioners observed that the posse's actions "appear'd to alarm our Inhabitants more than the killing of the two white persons knowing that there was a number of the Telasee [Tallassee] Indeans all along in front of us peacibly following their huntings." "[Petition] 1787 July 20, [from] inhabitants of Greene County [Georgia] to [Governor] Geo[rge] Mathews and members of the council," TCC, <http://dlg.galileo.usg.edu/> (November 3, 2006).

110. The limits established by the 1773 treaty were by no means free from dispute. In attempting to run the boundary line according to this agreement, the Georgia surveyor general found that his Indian guides refused to "go above the Tugelo [Tugaloo] Path," five

or six miles short of the corner understood by the commissioners from Georgia to have been the course of the line. "Deposition of Stephen Heard, 1784 May 28 / sworn to [by] Stephen Heard," TCC, <http://dlg.galileo.usg.edu/> (July 8, 2006).

111. LBH, 1:ix.

112. Green, *Politics of Indian Removal*, 28.

113. U.S. Continental Congress, "The committee consisting of Mr. Kearney," 1787, BRBL.

114. "A talk, 1786 Oct. 21, to the Kings, Headmen, and Warriors of the Creek Nation, on Shoulder Bone Creek, near the Oconee River," TCC, <http://dlg.galileo.usg.edu/> (February 8, 2006).

115. "Talk of the Headmen of Coweta," August 17, 1785, CIL, 1:83–84.

116. Ethridge observes that "the Treaty of New York was the model for the next three land cession treaties between the Creeks and the United States." Ethridge, *Creek Country*, 199. See, for example: U.S. Congress, *Creeks*, 1790, <http://infoweb.newsbank.com> (December 12, 2007).

117. U.S. Congress, *Creeks*, 1790, <http://infoweb.newsbank.com>.

118. Their unwillingness to cede lands around Shoulderbone Creek may have also been rooted in historic and spiritual attachments to particular sites within the territory. One observer describing this area noted the presence of "sundry Work[s] of the Antients," including "a Lightwood poste 8 feet high with a head to it which appeard to have been in the ground for Upwards of a hundred years." Samuel Edward Butler, Diary of Samuel Edward Butler, 1784–1786, HAR.

119. Ethridge, *Creek Country*, 199; Braund, *Deerskins and Duffels*, 176; U.S. Congress, *Creeks*, 1790, <http://infoweb.newsbank.com>.

120. "[Letter with deposition] 1790 Nov. 22, State House Augusta, to the President of the Senate and the Speaker of the House of Representatives / Edward Telfair," TCC, <http://dlg.galileo.usg.edu/> (July 14, 2006).

121. *Southern Centinel and Gazette of the State*, September 11, 1794. The biblical reference is to Genesis 49:14–15. On state reactions to the treaty, see also Downes, "Creek-American Relations," 350–73.

122. As Daniel Usner has noted, "The takeoff in cotton production . . . coincided with a decline in the deerskin trade still important to most Indian communities during the early nineteenth century." Usner, "American Indians on the Cotton Frontier," 297. See also Ethridge, *Creek Country*, 12–13; Braund, *Deerskins and Duffels*, 165, 178, 181.

123. Some have argued that Hawkins, by default, filled the leadership vacuum left by the death of Alexander McGillivray. Caughey, *McGillivray of the Creeks*, 54–55. But Green observes that there was a fundamental difference in their purposes: "McGillivray tried to strengthen Creek government in order to preserve the Nation's independence. Hawkins tried to strengthen Creek government in order to control it and thereby destroy the Nation's independence." Green, *Politics of Indian Removal*, 36.

124. Unfortunately, as has been noted by Ethridge, because of the prominence of many of these speculators, the lack of coherent federal management of treaties, and the general will of the federal government to continually expand the national limits, the influence of land speculators continued to "carve away" at Creek country. Ethridge, *Creek Country*, 198.

125. Treaty with the Creeks, 1790, in Kappler, *Indian Affairs: Laws and Treaties*, vol. 2, <http://digital.library.okstate.edu/kappler/Vol2/treaties/cre0025.htm> (February 1, 2007).

126. Jefferson, *Message and Communication*, 1801, 6.

127. See, for example, Treaty with the Creeks, 1805, in Kappler, *Indian Affairs: Laws and Treaties*, vol. 2, <http://digital.library.okstate.edu/kappler/Vol2/treaties/cre0085.htm> (November 20, 2006).

128. In typically biased terms, Hawkins nevertheless noted this transition in his annual communication to the President: "The chiefs, who were apprehensive at first that if their women could clothe and find themselves by their own exertions, would become independent of the degraded state of connection between them." "[Copy of a letter from Benjamin Hawkins, Principal Agent for Indian Affairs, South of the Ohio]," in Jefferson, *Message and Communication*, 1801. See also Braund, *Deerskins and Duffels*, 185.

129. "Copy of a letter from Benjamin Hawkins," in Jefferson, *Message and Communication*, 1801. See also Milfort, *Memoirs or a Quick Glance*, 48.

130. Ethridge, *Creek Country*, 198; Henri, *Southern Indians*, 134, 137–264.

CHAPTER TWO

1. Samuel Elbert, "[Talk] to the Kings, Head Men and Warriors of the Creek Nation," [1785–1786], AYER.

2. The importance of eating and drinking with leaders from other nations was also fundamental to Creek political life. This expectation is rooted in Creek norms of hospitality and reciprocity. See, for example, Bossu, *Travels*, 229; Bartram, *Observations*, 42.

3. At the same time that the Lewis and Clark expedition was underway, several other important surveys focusing on transport and travel were also being undertaken, including a survey of the Mississippi River from the mouth of the Ohio River to the falls of St. Anthony and one from these falls to the source of the Mississippi and to the Lake of the Woods. U.S. Congress, House of Representatives, "Report of the Committee of Commerce and Manufactures," March 8, 1804, BRBL.

4. White Lieutenant of the Oakfuskeys to James Seagrove, August 15, 1792, CIL, 1:254. The phrase is ubiquitous in this era, but the full quote reads, "The great Talk that our beloved men had with your Beloved men at New York we still stand by and shall consent to run the lines and if you are agreed we shall drink out of the same waters."

5. For examples of difficulties proceeding with collaborative surveys due to Creek intransigence and American stubbornness, see Timothy Barnard to William Clarke, April 12, 1785, ULTB, 39; John Carr to William Clark, April 7, 1785, CIL, 1:70; "Journal of the commissioners who attended the running [of] the line between the state of Georgia and the Creek Nation of Indians, 1804 Jan. 20," TCC, <http://dlg.galileo.usg.edu/> (April 5, 2006).

6. As Paul Carter has observed, "The survey, with its triple artillery of map, sketches and journal, was a strategy for translating space into a conceivable object, an object that the mind could possess long before the lowing herds." Carter, *Road to Botany Bay*, 113. See also Goetzmann, *Exploration and Empire*; Kain and Baigent, *Cadastral Map*; Pratt, *Imperial Eyes*; Seed, *Ceremonies of Possession*. In large part, I agree with these approaches,

provided that they are accompanied by a commitment to uncovering the ways in which colonized peoples did (and do) know, name, and possess their land(s).

7. See, for example, Andrew Burns & John Clements to His Excellency Jared Irwin, January 3, 1798, CIL, 2:502–3; Hawkins, "Journal of the Proceedings of the Commissioners Appointed to Ascertain and Mark the Boundary Lines Agreeably to Treaties between the Indian Nations and the United States, 1797," LBH, 1:73–78.

8. "Running the temporary boundary line between [the] state of Georgia and the Creek Indians, 1798 Feb. 22: [survey report]," TCC, <http://dlg.galileo.usg.edu/> (March 5, 2006).

9. Claudio Saunt notes that the earliest recorded use of "Seminole" in English is from 1765. He points out that the word "Seminole" is either derived from the Spanish term "cimmarrones," meaning runaways, or the Muskogee word "ishti semoli," meaning wild men. These groups had split from the larger Creek confederacy in the mid-eighteenth century and moved into lower Georgia and Florida, founding their own tribal towns and governing them somewhat independently of the Lower Towns, although maintaining close ties on many occasions. Saunt, *New Order of Things*, 34–36. On Seminole ethnogenesis, see also Sturtevant, "Creek Into Seminole"; Weisman, "Archaeological Perspectives on Florida Seminole Ethnogenesis."

10. While it is unclear what the name "Methlogee" signifies, "-gee" is often used as a diminutive in Creek names. Read, "Indian Stream-Names," 132.

11. James Seagrove to James Jackson, June 17, 1799 (enclosing "communications with Creek Chief Methlogee"), AYER.

12. Ibid.

13. British land pirate and adventurer William Bowles, who had aspirations for becoming the "supreme leader" of the Creeks, helped to incite some of the nervousness among Lower Creeks and Seminoles about such boundary lines, telling them, "the line is . . . proof positive that your land would have been gone if I had not arrived . . . as far as the line is run It is gone but I will save the little which remains, the line shall goe no further." Report of Emautlau Haujo, December 16, 1799, CIL, 2:584.

14. Seagrove to Jackson, June 17, 1799, AYER.

15. Ibid.

16. Ibid. Seagrove reminded Methlogee of the exact wording of Article 5 of the Coleraine treaty, "The President shall give notice [of the time to run the boundary line] to the Creek Chiefs, who will furnish two principal Chiefs and Twenty Hunters to accompany the persons employed on this business, as hunters and guides, from the Chocktaw Country to the head of St. Mary's. The Chiefs shall each receive half a dollar per day and the hunters one quarter dollar per day, and ammunition and a reasonable value for the Meat delivered by them for the use of the persons in their service."

17. Landers, "Black Community and Culture," 123–25. Landers notes that the Florida slave system "tolerated slave mobility, free market and feast days, and an internal slave economy, and permitted the slaves relatively free cultural expression. . . . More importantly, Florida slaves knew that the power of their owners was limited in key respects by Spanish legal and religious institutions, which were never far away. . . . The proximity of the Seminole nation, trackless forests and swamps, and rivers and oceans provided alternatives for those who would take them," 125. See also Landers, *Black Society in Spanish Florida*.

18. Timothy Barnard to Major Patrick Carr, April 13, 1784, ULTB, 29; [Letter] from Flint River, February 2, 1795, ULTB, 244. One informant told the governor of Georgia that many of these contraband slaves were being sold to Havana, upstream of the established slave trade. Patrick Carr to John Martin, December 12, 1782, CIL, 1:40–41.

19. James T. Carson observes a similar phenomenon among the Choctaws. He notes, "Rather than concede defeat to the new order, Choctaw warriors found two ways to retain their traditions and prerogatives. By drinking rum and by raiding the farms of European and American settlers, they engaged in 'safety valve' behaviors that mitigated internal strife, focused hostilities and tensions beyond the borders of their world, and enabled young men to stake traditional claims to manhood in altogether new ways." Carson, *Searching for the Bright Path*, 62, 64–65. See also Corkran, *Creek Frontier*, 25.

20. Joseph Ellicott, "A Talk to the head king of the Cussetahs [and to] the chiefs and warriors of all the towns in the Creek Nation," TCC, <http://dlg.galileo.usg.edu/> (April 12, 2006).

21. John Carr to William Clark, April 7, 1785, CIL, 1:70. See also Daniel McMurphy to Edward Telfair, July 30, 1786, CIL, 1:129–32.

22. Elbert, "[Talk] to the Kings, Head Men and Warriors of the Creek Nation," [1785–1786], AYER.

23. "Running the temporary boundary line between [the] state of Georgia and the Creek Indians, 1798 Feb. 22: [survey report]," TCC, <http://dlg.galileo.usg.edu/>.

24. James Wright, "Answers to queries sent by the Lords of Trade [in] 1761, 1762," James Wright Collection, HAR, <http://dlg.galileo.usg.edu/> (July 17, 2006).

25. Ellicott, *Journal of Andrew Ellicott*, 233.

26. Alexander McGillivray, [Talk interpreted by James Durouzeaux], 1785, CIL, 1: 87–88.

27. In his official journal, Andrew Ellicott recorded receipt of a 1798 communication from Spanish governor Manuel Luis Gayoso de Lemos indicating "the hostile disposition of the Indians, and their determination to put a stop to the demarcation of the boundary," but Ellicott noted that this was part of a "system of delay" on the part of the Spanish officials, who, like the Indians, were not keen on seeing the line run. Ellicott, *Journal of Andrew Ellicott*, 181.

28. "Talk to Effee Hajo the Mad Dog, & Tustunnegee Thlucco, the Big Warrior, Commissioners of the Creek Nation for reestablishing their Line of Concession East of the Alabama, Oct. 12, 1803," NARA, RG75, 75.2.

29. William Green to William Rabun, May 18, 1819, CIL, 3:909–11; see also Rabun to Edmund P. Gaines, March 18, 1819, Rabun to William S. Mitchell, March 18, 1819, Rabun to Mitchell, April 16, 1819, Georgia, Office of the Governor, Letterbooks, 1786–1897, GDAH.

30. Hawkins to James McHenry, April 11, 1797, LBH, 1:100.

31. Murdock McLeod to James Jackson, October 6, 1799, CIL, 2:582–83.

32. Ellicott, *Journal of Andrew Ellicott*, 206. In a letter to Andrew Pickens, Benjamin Hawkins observed that in settling the date and Indian commissioners for the running of the Creek boundary, "I found this a difficult affair with the young warriors, notwithstanding the repeated stipulations heretofore made with the Chiefs relative to it." Hawkins to Pickens, November 19, 1797, LBH, 1:160.

33. Ellicott, *Journal of Andrew Ellicott*, 220.

34. Micco Thlucco [Big Warrior] to Hawkins, February 2, 1804, ULTB, 287. In an interesting study of cartography in Mexico, Raymond B. Craib notes that inhabitants of rural villages often let disputes between communities stand in the way of surveys to divide their communal lands and he suggests that sometimes they staged "pretended quarrels" as a mode of resistance to state-imposed surveys. The Creeks and their neighbors may also have engaged in this kind of subterfuge. Craib, *Cartographic Mexico*, 59.

35. This was represented to Hawkins by Tustunnuggee Emaultau of Tookaubatche (also known as Jim Boy and High Head Jim), LBH, 1:146. Also quoted in Ethridge, *Creek Country*, 197.

36. John Habersham, "[Letter] 1784 June 19, Augusta, [Georgia to] John Houstoun, [Governor of Georgia]," Keith Read Collection, HAR, <http://dlg.galileo.usg.edu/> (September 21, 2006).

37. Due to the number of investors who were New Englanders, the scheme, once discovered, added to sectional conflicts. See, for example, Clayton, *Vindication of the Recent and Prevailing Policy*; Troup, *Georgia and the General Government*; Troup to John C. Calhoun, Secretary at War, Washington, April 24, 1824, Georgia, Office of the Governor, Letterbooks, 1786–1897, GDAH.

38. See "[citizens] of Liberty County, [Georgia], [Petition] 1793 July 6, Liberty County, [Georgia] to Edward Telfair, Governor [of] Georgia, Augusta / [citizens] of Liberty County, [Georgia]," TCC, <http://dlg.galileo.usg.edu/> (March 14, 2006); Timothy Pickering to Col. David Henley, March 23, 1795, AYER; Pickering to Henley, July 22, 1795, AYER.

39. In fact, James Jackson, the Georgia statesman largely responsible for the repeal of the fraudulent act, had to repel multiple attempts on his life, including one altercation with a Georgia state representative who stabbed him multiple times with a bayonet and attempted to gouge out his eye. Jackson to John Milledge, March 8, 1796, in *Correspondence of John Milledge*, 38–41.

40. Bishop, *Georgia Speculation Unveiled*, 144. For part of the resolution of this unmatched scandal, see *Fletcher v. Peck*, 10 U.S. 87 (1810). Charles Sellers refers to Chief Justice John Marshall's ruling in the case as a "militant assertion of contractual rights and national authority" and calls it a "gratuitous assault on state sovereignty." Sellers, *Market Revolution*, 57. A continuing investigation into Yazoo claims can be found in U.S. Congress, Committee on the Yazoo Claims, *Report of the Committee*, 1814.

41. Hine and Faragher, *American West*, 106–7. The Land Ordinance set the standard for how land would be surveyed—known as the Public Land Survey System—and provided for regular townships subdivided into sections one mile square. U.S. Continental Congress, *An Ordinance for Ascertaining the Mode of Disposing of Lands in the Western Territory*.

42. U.S. Congress, *Georgia Cession*, 1802, <http://infoweb.newsbank.com> (March 25, 2006).

43. U.S. Congress, Commissioners on Georgia Mississippi Territory ceded to the United States, "Message from the President of the United States," 1802, BRBL; Davidson, "Governor John Milledge," 13–14.

44. Cusetuh King, Little Prince, Little Warrior, "A Talk from the Cowetuh, Cusetuh

and Old Town Chiefs to the Mad Dog and other Chiefs of the upper towns," September 26, 1801, NARA, RG75, 75.2.

45. Bridges, "To Establish a Separate and Independent Government," 11–17.

46. Davidson, "Governor John Milledge," 13; Treaty with the Creeks, 1790, in Kappler, *Indian Affairs: Laws and Treaties*, vol. 2, <http://digital.library.okstate.edu/kappler/Vol 2/treaties/creoo25.htm> (February 1, 2007).

47. Hawkins, "Journal of the Occurrences," March 23, 1802, LBH, 2:430.

48. Saunt suggests repeatedly that Creek notions of bounded property are the result of intermixture with whites, asserting that had it not been for the ascendance of what he calls "mestizo elites," Creeks would not have adopted such concepts on a large scale. Saunt, *New Order*, 45–54, 57. I agree with this argument to some extent, particularly where it involved private property, such as the ownership of slaves and the appearance of fences and doorlocks in Creek towns. But the concept of territorial boundaries has an older analog in Creek epistemology.

49. An example is the map drawn by "an Indian Cacique" and presented to Carolina governor Francis Nicholson in 1725, depicting the mapmaker's own community at the center and related communities in circular form, connected by distinct paths. "A Map describing the situation of the several Nations of Indians between South Carolina and the Massisipi River," 1725, in *Crown Collection*. This map has been extensively described and interpreted in Warhus, *Another America*, 77–83.

50. Moore, *Voyage to Georgia*, 97–98.

51. Hahn, *Invention of the Creek Nation*, 8, 189–90, 231.

52. Creeks often referred to themselves as the "older brothers" of the four southeastern Indian nations (Creek, Cherokee, Choctaw, and Chickasaw)—a moniker that resonated in the kin-based political rhetoric that characterized diplomacy between the tribes, since the relationship of elder brother to younger siblings, and by extension uncles to nephews/nieces, was the primary source of familial authority. For example, see Hawkins, [Journal], October 28, 1797, LBH, 1:187.

53. Mucclassee Hopoie, quoted in Hawkins, "Journal of the Occurrences," March 23, 1802, LBH, 2:416–17. Mucclassee Hopoie appears to be paraphrasing a statement made by Chickasaw headman George Colbert in an intertribal discussion about settling lines between the Chickasaws, Choctaws, Creeks, and Americans that took place at the close of the Revolutionary War.

54. U.S. Congress, *Cherokees, Chickasaws, Choctaws, and Creeks*, 1801, <http://infoweb .newsbank.com> (July 20, 2006).

55. Martin echoes Hawkins's opinion, stating, "The United States, through the influence of its agents, opposed any practice or movement that encouraged Native Americans to hold their lands in common. Such a form of land tenure made cessions and sales more difficult to obtain, and above all, the United States wanted more land cessions." Martin, *Sacred Revolt*, 118.

56. The constant reference to "elder brother," *lawa*, and "younger brother," *tcusi*, is a further reflection of southeastern Indian kinship systems in which the relationship between siblings was perhaps the most important of familial relationships, save for the relationship with the mother. In these matrilineal societies, for example, a child's maternal

uncle(s) were often the most significant male figures in his/her life, rather than the child's father, or the father's family. See Hudson, *Southeastern Indians*, 185–91.

57. Hawkins, "Journal of the Occurrences," March 23, 1802, LBH, 2:478.

58. Henry Dearborn to Hawkins, February 19, 1803, NARA, RG75, 75.2.

59. Hawkins, "Journal of the Occurrences," March 23, 1802.

60. Jefferson, "President's Talk to the Creeks," November 2, 1805, NARA, RG75, 75.2.

61. Ibid.

62. William McIntosh, "Talk of McIntosh, a Creek Chief deliver'd to the Presdt. of U.S.," November 4, 1805, NARA, RG75, 75.2.

63. Treaty with the Creeks, 1805, in Kappler, *Indian Affairs: Laws and Treaties*, vol. 2, <http://digital.library.okstate.edu/kappler/Vol2/treaties/cre0085.htm> (November 20, 2006); Saunt, *New Order*, 216–17.

64. Hawkins to John Milledge, August 4, 1805, LBH, 2:496.

65. In agreeing to the treaty, the Creeks reserved a small tract of land known as "Ocmulgee Old Fields," the present-day site of Macon, Georgia.

66. See, for example, the complaint of James Jackson to Georgia governor George Handley in 1788: "Negroes are still going off. Twenty from this County alone . . . went about a fortnight since among which exclusive of my Brothers I have every reason to apprehend are three of my own." Jackson to Handley, October 3, 1788, CIL, 1:187–88; see also, "Affidavit [of] George Spann, 1800 Oct. 3, Jefferson County, Georgia / sworn to before Horatio Marbury," TCC, <http://dlg.galileo.usg.edu/> (August 1, 2006).

67. Passport issued to James Smith, by James Jackson, 1798, 2; Jackson to Col. Gaither, September 16, 1799, 450, both in *Passports Issued by Governors of Georgia*.

68. One aged slave owner in St. Augustine offered $500 to the Seminoles to find thirty-eight slaves allegedly taken by Hitchitis, including, to his great distress, his "dairy maid" and "washer woman." J. P. Fatio to Hawkins, September 4, 1801, NARA, RG75, 75.2. According to Hawkins, it was not the Hitchitis but the Mikasukis who took these slaves and they were "determined not to return them" unless their headman imprisoned in St. Augustine was released.

69. *Southern Centinel and Gazette of the State*, September 15, 1796.

70. James Jackson to Timothy Barnard, March 5, 1799, ULTB, 274b.

71. Moore, *Voyage to Georgia*, 34.

72. John, *Spreading the News*; Larson, *Internal Improvement*. For a military perspective on road networks, see Nelson, "Military Roads," 1–14.

73. The southernmost of these roads led to Port Royal, South Carolina. Nothing further south or west of the Carolinas was recorded. See Colles, *Survey of the Roads*.

74. Morse, *American Geography*, 532–35.

75. The Tombigbee River, alternately spelled Tombigby, Dombigby, Dunbigby, and Dunbigbee, flows generally north-south from present-day northeast Mississippi, until it joins the Black Warrior River to form the Mobile River before emptying into Mobile Bay. In the 1970s, a canal was formed that joined the Tombigbee to the Tennessee River.

76. Butler, "Diary of Samuel Edward Butler, 1784–1786," HAR.

77. "Report of Mr. Hill," January 24, 1802, in Hawkins, "Journal of the Occurrences," March 23, 1802, LBH, 2:406–7. Hawkins curtailed this estimate to 500 in a February 1 letter to Dearborn, 433.

78. See *Passports Issued by Governors of Georgia.* Andrew K. Frank observes that Great Britain, Spain, and the United States all required some species of passport for travel in the Indian nations, but regulation was difficult. See Frank, *Creeks and Southerners*, 32.

79. Waselkov, *Conquering Spirit*, 29.

80. Hawkins, "Journal of the Occurrences," March 23, 1802, LBH, 2:409.

81. "Report of the affairs in the Creek agency by William Hill," October 9, 1801, NARA, RG75, 75.2.

82. Hawkins, "Journal of the Occurrences," March 23, 1802, LBH, 2:409.

83. Ibid.

84. Hawkins to James McHenry, June 24, 1798, LBH, 1:207.

85. U.S. Congress, *Cherokees, Chickasaws, Choctaws, and Creeks*, 1801, <http://infoweb.newsbank.com>.

86. Southerland and Brown, *Federal Road*, 17–21; Carter, *Territorial Papers*, 5:395–515. It is important to note that Jefferson's notion of limited government led him to consider government involvement in road building according to a fairly strict construction of the Constitution. While the Constitution had granted the Congress the power to appropriate funds for military and postal routes, fierce debates accompanied efforts to fund other types of roads in the Early Republic. These debates are addressed most ably in Larson, *Internal Improvement*, 39–69.

87. Postmaster General Gideon Granger to David Thomas, November 30, 1803, quoted in Southerland and Brown, *Federal Road*, 22.

88. Granger to Jefferson, February 6, 1805, NARA, RG28, 28.2. Ulrich Bonnell Phillips noted that when cotton prices were high—as they typically were during the early nineteenth century—slow transport to market on bad roads was acceptable. But when cotton prices were low and planters were pinching every penny, especially after 1817, they began to demand cheaper, more efficient transport. Phillips, *History of Transportation*, 12, 16–17, 56.

89. Phillips observed that internal transportation routes were of paramount importance in the South in this era. Phillips, *History of Transportation*, 1, 45. See also Clark and Guice, *Frontiers in Conflict*, 83–97.

90. Jefferson, "President's Talk to the Creeks, 1805 November 2," NARA, RG75, 75.2.

91. *Orleans Gazette for the Country*, January 29, 1805.

92. "To the honorable the speaker and House of Delegates, for the state of Virginia," 1798, n.p.

93. It should be noted that at various points post office regulations prohibited the carrying of newspapers in the mail. See "Letters from Gideon Granger November 1804," NARA, RG28, 28.2.

94. "Report of the Committee of the Senate of the United States," 1802.

95. For instances of southern editors' obsession with postal information, especially complaints regarding "failures" of the mail, see *Augusta Chronicle*, May 9, 1807; *Georgia Argus*, July 5, 1808, June 24, 1812; *Orleans Gazette for the Country*, May 21, 1805, March 28, 1811; *Louisiana Gazette*, May 28, 1805; *Union*, March 12, 1804, May 29, 1804; *Orleans Gazette; and Commercial Advertiser*, August 10, 1805, April 30, 1806, July 19, 1806, September 18, 1806; *Telegraphe Louisianais and Mercantile Advertiser*, April 7, 1812; *Courier de la Louisiane*, February 1814; *Courier pour la Campagne [Supplement]*, March 29, 1820; *Baton-Rouge Gazette*, July 8, 1820; *Clarion, & Tennessee State Gazette*, November 17, 1818.

96. To "swim your horse" meant that you led the horse through the water by the bridle while you crossed on a bridge alongside. Depending on the horse's experience with water crossings and the depth of the stream or river, this could prove to be a dangerous exercise. Horses might easily lose their footing and occasionally drag their riders and their belongings off the bridge and into the water with them. Additionally, anyone who attempted to swim a laden pack-horse risked the loss of both the horse and the pack because a heavily burdened animal was helpless to right itself in the water should it slip on rocks beneath the surface. Anyone who has attempted to walk through rocky southern streams amid rushing water understands the difficulty of obtaining a secure footing.

97. Granger to Lieut. Pratt, December 9, 1805; "Report of the Postmaster General in compliance with a resolution of the house of representatives of the 17th Instant relative to the post route between Athens in Georgia and New Orleans"; Granger to Harry Toulmin, April 25, 1806, all in NARA, RG28, 28.2.

98. Granger to John B. Wilkinson, February 9, 1802, NARA, RG28, 28.2; Dearborn to Hawkins, July 19, 1803, NARA, RG75, 75.2.

99. See "Letters . . . 1802," NARA, RG28, 28.2. Ethridge has remarked on these problems as well. Ethridge, *Creek Country*, 128.

100. *Southern Centinel and Gazette of the State*, June 30, 1796.

101. Granger to William C. C. Claiborne, July 19, 1805, and "Report of the Postmaster General," 1806, both in NARA, RG28, 28.2.

102. Jefferson, *Message of President Jefferson*, 1805, <http://infoweb.newsbank.com> (March 2, 2006).

103. Ephraim Kirby to Granger, February 5, 1804, EKP.

104. Kirby to Granger, April 7, 1804, EKP.

105. Kirby to Jefferson, April 20, 1804, EKP.

106. Granger to Jefferson, February 6, 1805, NARA, RG28, 28.2.

107. Jefferson, *Message of President Jefferson*, 1805, <http://infoweb.newsbank.com>. On communication and the Southwest, see Clark and Guice, *Frontiers in Conflict*, 83–84.

108. Dearborn to James Wilkinson, June 25, 1801, NARA, RG75, 75.2.

109. U.S. Congress, *Cherokees, Chickasaws, Choctaws, and Creeks*, 1801.

110. Hawkins, "Journal of the Occurrences," March 23, 1802, LBH, 2:415.

111. On the Colberts' stands, see Clark and Guice, *Frontiers in Conflict*, 83–97; Davis, *Way through the Wilderness*, 29–30, 32.

112. Dearborn to Return J. Meigs, February 19, 1803, NARA, RG75, 75.2.

113. John Sevier, "Letter, 1798 July 4 to James Robertson, James Stuart and Lochlen [i.e., Lachlan] McIntosh / John Sevier," Governor Sevier Papers, TSLA <http://dlg.gali leo.usg.edu/> (April 6, 2006).

114. U.S. Congress, *Cherokees, Chickasaws, Choctaws, and Creeks*, 1801.

115. Ibid. Dearborn further advised them to tell the Cherokees that "no white people shall be allowed to travel on the road to Natchez, except such as shall have procured passes from our agents at Tennessee and at Natchez, which passes shall be countersigned by the men who may be stationed at the several houses to be established on the roads, and that gates shall be erected at some of the bridges on that road, and maintained by the United States, to prevent the horses and cattle of the Indians from straying far from home."

116. Dearborn to Meigs, February 19, 1803, NARA, RG75, 75.2.

117. Hawkins, "Journal of the Occurrences," March 23, 1802, LBH, 2:415–17; Hawkins to Dearborn, January 26, 1802, LBH, 2:432.

118. U.S. Congress, *Cherokees, Chickasaws, Choctaws, and Creeks,* 1801. Carson notes that while Americans operated some of the taverns and ferries on the Natchez Trace, quite a number were owned and operated by Choctaw headmen who had agreed to the treaty. Carson, *Searching for the Bright Path,* 72.

119. Clark and Guice, *Old Southwest,* 83–97.

120. U.S. Congress, *Cherokees, Chickasaws, Choctaws, and Creeks,* 1801.

121. Hawkins to Meigs, June 12, 1805, LBH, 2:492. The Chickasaws did indeed manage to cede these disputed lands in an 1805 treaty, primarily in return for forgiveness of their massive debts to traders. See "Articles of arrangement, made and concluded in the Chickasaw country, between James Robertson and Silas Dinsmoor, commissioners of the United States, of the one part; and the Mingo, chiefs, and warriors, of the Chickasaw nation of Indians, of the other part," in U.S. Congress, *Wyandots and others,* 1805.

122. Hawkins, "Journal of the Occurrences," March 23, 1802, LBH, 2:429. The Choctaws' claim included "the lands of the Tuscaloosa (black warrior) [River], the main east fork of the Tombigbee," a line that would be disputed again after the disastrous Treaty of Fort Jackson, in which the Creeks were forced to cede millions of acres of land, including some that actually belonged to the Choctaws and the Cherokees. See Hawkins to John Coffee, February 9, 1816, LBH, 2:772, for an introduction to these problems.

123. Evans, "Highways to Progress," 394–400.

124. McIntosh, "Talk of McIntosh, a Creek Chief deliver'd to the Presdt. of U.S., Nov. 4, 1805," NARA, RG75, 75.2.

125. Treaty with the Creeks, 1805, in Kappler, *Indian Affairs: Laws and Treaties,* vol. 2, <http://digital.library.okstate.edu/kappler/Vol2/treaties/cre0085.htm>.

126. Hawkins to Dearborn, September 11, 1805, LBH, 2:499. Hopoie Micco's caution in this instance was not able to spare his life. He was killed by two Cusseta men in the winter of 1806 and his death caused severe strife because factions could not then agree on who was to be the new speaker. Hawkins to John Forbes, May 29, 1806, LBH, 2:505.

127. Hawkins to Dearborn, January 22, 1807, LBH, 2:511.

128. Frank has persuasively discussed McIntosh's use of patronage as a method for developing his political influence. Frank, *Creeks and Southerners,* 96–113.

129. Hawkins to David Meriwether, October 1, 1807, LBH, 2:516–17.

130. Jefferson to Milledge, November 22, 1802, *Correspondence of John Milledge,* 82.

131. Granger to Jefferson, July 19, 1805, NARA, RG28, 28.2.

CHAPTER THREE

1. "Extract of a letter from a gentleman in Knoxville to his friend in Petersburgh, dated October 24, 1795," in *Southern Centinel and Gazette of the State,* November 26, 1795.

2. Butler, "Diary of Samuel Edward Butler, 1784–1786," HAR.

3. Michaux, *Travels to the Westward.* For an early example of the fervor of cotton fever, see Sibbald, *Notes and Observations.*

4. Hawkins to Joseph Clay, October 13, 1803, LBH, 2:464.

5. Jefferson, "President's Talk to the Creeks," November 2, 1805, NARA, RG75, 75.2.

6. Ibid.

7. Ethridge, *Creek Country*, 137–39.

8. Phelps, *Memoirs and Adventures*, appendix, 7–10.

9. Kirby to Albert Gallatin, July 1, 1804, EKP.

10. Jefferson, *Message from the President*, 1805.

11. Phelps, *Memoirs and Adventures*, appendix, 17.

12. "Recommendation for a passport for Elijah Grande, November 1803," in *Passports Issued by Governors of Georgia*, 6.

13. Phelps, *Memoirs and Adventures*, 31, appendix, 7.

14. So common were passports for men and men only, that we are simply left to wonder what circumstances might have prompted a woman named Sarah Qualls to embark on a journey to the Tombigbee River with two daughters, two small children, and an enslaved African woman. "Minutes Executive Department November 5, 1800–November 1st, 1802 [Record of Passports Issued]," in *Passports Issued by Governors of Georgia*, 249.

15. Hawkins to Timothy Barnard, May 30, 1804, LBH, 2:467.

16. U.S. Congress, House, "Report from the Committee of Claims," 1805.

17. David B. Mitchell to Hawkins, December 18, 1811; John Clark to John Whitehead, February 8, 1820, both in Georgia, Office of the Governor, Letterbooks, 1786–1897, GDAH.

18. Romans, *Concise Natural History*, 29–30.

19. McIntosh, "Talk of McIntosh, a Creek Chief deliver'd to the Presdt of U.S. Nov. 4, 1805," NARA, RG75, 75.2.

20. Bossu, *Travels*, 229.

21. Hawkins, "Journal of the Occurrences," LBH, 2:406–7.

22. William Peters to Governor Josiah Tatnall, February 13, 1802, CIL, 2:642.

23. Jefferson, *Message from the President*, 1805.

24. See "Minutes Executive [Department] November 8, 1799–November 4th, 1800 [Record of Passports Issued]," and "Minutes Executive Department November 5, 1800–November 1st, 1802 [Record of Passports Issued]," in *Passports Issued by Governors of Georgia*, 31–32, 81–244.

25. William Peters to Governor Josiah Tatnall, February 13, 1802, CIL, 2:642.

26. John Cumins to Robert Murdoch, September 8, 1802, BRBL.

27. "Minutes Executive Department November 5, 1800–November 1st, 1802 [Record of Passports Issued]," in *Passports Issued by Governors of Georgia*, 325. Similarly, James Scarlett intended to set out in 1804 with his family, "consisting of Seven white persons and one Negro." "Recommendation for a pass port for James Scarlett, 1804," in *Passports Issued by Governors of Georgia*, 8.

28. Hawkins reported that there was intense conversation among the Creeks when he had "a waggon brought out to my residence at Flint River." Hawkins to Dearborn, March 5, 1805, LBH, 2:489.

29. Littlefield, *Africans and Creeks*, 11–13.

30. Ibid., 39–40, 45–46. The rising number of Africans and African Americans living in the Creek Nation, whether slave or free, is evidenced by the fact that Hawkins and U.S. commissioner David Meriwether felt the need to address the inhabitants of the Creek

Nation as "Every man, red, white or black." "Journal of the conference with the Creeks held late June 1804 between Hawkins and Gen. David Meriwether (U.S. Commrs.) and the Creeks at their annual national council to negotiate for further land cessions," LBH, 2:472.

31. Dubois, *Avengers of the New World*; Wood, *Black Majority*.

32. See, for example, Timothy Barnard to George Mathews, January 21, 1795, ULTB, 242; Barnard to Blackshear, October 14, 1795, ULTB, 248; Barnard to Blackshear, December 18, 1795, ULTB, 256.

33. During his travels in the South, French naturalist François Michaux noted that when Charleston was in the grips of yellow fever, travel of white Americans into and out of the city ceased and "the place is then supplied with provisions only by the negroes, or the native inhabitants." Michaux, *Travels to the Westward*, 7.

34. William Lattimore, [Passport, 1804], in *Passports Issued by Governors of Georgia*, 11.

35. For an overview of free black life in the southern United States and the Caribbean, see Landers, *Against the Odds*.

36. Granger to Jackson, March 23, 1802, NARA, RG28, 28.2.

37. Like the early southern Indian trading paths, the Wilderness Road largely followed large animal traces. Hulbert, *Old National Road*, 16–17.

38. Meyer, *History of Transportation*, 7, 12–18.

39. U.S. Congress, *Cumberland Road*, 1805.

40. Ibid.

41. This was in accordance with Jefferson's initial plan to connect Washington, D.C., to the vital Gulf port, with a road totaling around 1,000 miles in distance. LBH, 2:489n4; Jefferson to Milledge, November 22, 1802, *Correspondence of John Milledge*, 82.

42. Hawkins to Milledge, October 12, 1803; Hawkins to Meigs, September 30, 1803, both in LBH, 2:462–63.

43. "[Communication to the Cherokees?]," October 27, 1805, Penelope Johnson Allen Collection, Hoskins Special Collections Library, University of Tennessee, Knoxville, <http://dlg.galileo.usg.edu/> (March 11, 2006).

44. The best account of these miscarriages of the early road is found in Southerland and Brown, *Federal Road*, 22–32.

45. Granger, "Report of the Postmaster General in compliance with a resolution of the house of representatives of the 17th Instant relative to the post route between Athens in Georgia and New Orleans," 1806, NARA, RG28, 28.2.

46. Ibid. Granger later amended the width of the path to be only four feet wide, asserting, "It would be rather an injury than advantage to clear wider than is necessary for a single horse, as it has been found to encourage a thick growth of brush."

47. Granger to Hawkins, April 24, 1806, in Carter, *Territorial Papers*, 5:459–61, quoted in LBH, 2:509n3, and DeLeon and Southerland, *Federal Road*, 147n2.

48. Granger, "Report of the Postmaster General in compliance with a resolution of the house of representatives of the 17th Instant relative to the post route between Athens in Georgia and New Orleans," 1806, NARA, RG28, 28.2.

49. Creek discontent with the erection of bridges erupted again in early 1810. Hawkins to William Eustis, February 14, 1810, LBH, 2:561.

50. Hawkins to Jefferson, September 13, 1806, LBH, 2:507–8.

51. Ibid., 2:508.

52. Ibid.; see also Waselkov, *Conquering Spirit*, 59, 288n4.

53. Granger to Jackson, March 23, 1802, NARA, RG28, 28.2.

54. According to Robert Sterry [Henry?], who worked on the line, the mail seldom passed to New Orleans in the boat in fewer than twelve or fifteen days. Sterry [Henry?] to Stephen Bradley, November 29, 1806, Joseph Wheaton Papers, HAR.

55. Hawkins to Meriwether, April 18, 1807, LBH, 2:517.

56. Granger to Jefferson, August 4, 1806, NARA, RG28, 28.2.

57. Ibid.

58. Hawkins to Meriwether, April 18, 1807, LBH, 2:517.

59. Joseph Wheaton to Granger, November 28, 1806, Joseph Wheaton Papers, HAR.

60. Ibid. It is probable that this is Captain Thomas Marshall, a white man whose home Wheaton claimed was "the only proper place to exchange the mails," rather than Joseph Marshall or Benjamin Marshall, both of whom were Creeks from Coweta and allies of McIntosh. See also Green, *Politics of Indian Removal*, 98–99, 181.

61. Green, *Politics of Indian Removal*, 98–99, 181.

62. Glass, "[Letter] 1806 Nov. 25, Glass['s] house, Louckout Montin [i.e., Lookout Mountain, Cherokee Nation] to [Colonel] Return J. Meigs," Penelope Johnson Allen Collection <http://dlg.galileo.usg.edu/> (February 28, 2006).

63. Granger to Toulmin, June 27, 1807, NARA, RG28, 28.2.

64. Sevier, "Letter, 1807 Dec. 20, Knoxville, [Tennessee] to the Black Fox, Head Cheif [*sic*] of the Cherokee Nation," Governor Sevier Collection, TSLA, <http://dlg.galileo .usg.edu/> (February 28, 2006). See also the postscript in Glass, "[Letter] 1806 Nov. 25."

65. Hawkins to Dearborn, September 16, 1807, LBH, 2:525.

66. Hawkins to Dearborn, July 9, 1807, LBH, 2:521.

67. Ethridge, *Creek Country*, 154–55.

68. Talk of the Little Prince, October 8, 1807, LBH, 2:528.

69. Quoted in Hawkins to Eustis, December 28, 1809, LBH, 2:559.

70. Sevier, "Letter, 1807 Dec. 20, Knoxville, [Tennessee] to the Black Fox, Head Cheif [*sic*] of the Cherokee Nation," Governor Sevier Collection, TSLA, <http://dlg.galileo .usg.edu/>.

71. In early 1808, Dearborn wrote to Hawkins to inform him of alleged murders of whites by Creeks on the banks of the Tennessee and Duck rivers and to induce Hawkins to "prevent any further act of Hostility." Dearborn to Hawkins, May 30, 1808, NARA, RG75, 75.2.

72. Hawkins to Dearborn, June 28, 1807, LBH, 2:519.

73. Dearborn to Hawkins, August 18, 1807, NARA, RG75, 75.2.

74. Unnamed missionary quoted in McLoughlin, *Cherokees and Christianity*, 22. McLoughlin maintains that this was a "secret mission for the federal government" undertaken by Gideon Blackburn, a Presbyterian minister from Tennessee who operated two mission schools among the Cherokees. McLoughlin asserts that "the government was eager to explore the navigable waterways between Tennessee and the Gulf of Mexico, and he agreed to undertake this. He hired a boat, put his brothers in charge, loaded twenty-two hundred gallons of whiskey on board, and told everyone he was undertaking a business venture to sell whiskey in Mobile" (21–22).

75. Hawkins to Dearborn, December 31, 1810, NARA, RG75, 75.2.

76. Quoted in Hawkins to Eustis, October 10, 1809, LBH, 2:557.

77. Hawkins to Eustis, November 25, 1811, LBH, 2:599.

78. Hawkins to Eustis, June 21, 1810, LBH, 2:564.

79. Hawkins to Eustis, November 19, 1810, LBH, 2:577.

80. Hawkins to Gaines, October 25, 1810, LBH, 2:575.

81. Southerland and Brown, *Federal Road*, 34.

82. James Madison, "Talk to the Chiefs of the Creek Nation," January 14, 1811, NARA, RG75, 75.2.

83. Eustis to Willie Blount, March 28, 1811, NARA, RG75, 75.2.

84. Eustis to Hawkins, January 15, 1811, NARA, RG75, 75.2.

85. Eustis to Willie Blount, March 28, 1811, NARA, RG75, 75.2.

86. Ibid.; Eustis to Hawkins, March 29, 1811, NARA, RG75, 75.2.

87. Hoboheilthlee [Hopoithle] Micco, "Talk to the President of the United States," May 15, 1811, NARA, RG75, 75.2.

88. Ibid.

89. LBH, 2:579.

90. Eustis to Hawkins, July 20, 1811, NARA, RG75, 75.2.

91. Eustis to Hawkins, June 27, 1811, NARA, RG75, 75.2.

92. Ibid.; Southerland and Brown, *Federal Road*, 36.

93. Claudio Saunt has attributed the transformation of the Creeks to the rise of "mestizo elites," those largely self-appointed leaders whose mixed European and Indian ancestry allowed them access to both cultures and afforded them opportunities in both commerce and diplomacy that were typically unavailable to their Indian brethren. He states, "I do not mean to imply that culture and biology are linked. Nevertheless, it appears incontrovertible to me that Creeks who were familiar and comfortable with the market economy, coercive power, and race slavery of colonial settlements were disruptive, and that more often than not these Creeks had acquired that familiarity and comfort from their European forbears." Saunt, *New Order*, 2. Theda Perdue argues, however, that such abundant evidence exists to contradict Saunt's position that we should only with great caution accept the premise that choices about accepting social change were made along biological lines. See Perdue, *'Mixed-Blood' Indians*. Both positions have merit. As Saunt makes clear, there are compelling reasons to consider the opportunities that mixed-ancestry afforded members of the Creek Nation as distinct from those available to those with no European heritage. But this lens does not take into account mixed ancestry from an Indian-Indian perspective. It remains to be seen whether Creek-Cherokee intermixture, or commingling between different members of the ethnic divisions that made up the Creek Nation, say Alabama and Muskogee, had any impact on social relations and governance within the society. More important for this discussion is the lesson drawn from both Saunt and Perdue that we must remain vigilant about simplistic assumptions regarding culture and biology and recognize both those Creeks who fit the "mestizo elite" label and those that didn't and interrogate the reasons that each of them made the choices they did. An interesting and important contribution to this debate is Andrew K. Frank's *Creeks and Southerners*, in which he examines the role of traders and their descendants in the Creek Nation by working outward from Creek epistemological structures such as kinship

and reciprocity. In many ways, his work stakes out an important middle ground between Saunt and Perdue.

94. Ethridge, *Creek Country*, 155; see also Hawkins to Reverend Christian Benzien, October 7, 1810, LBH, 2:569.

95. Ethridge, *Creek Country*, 155, 297n123; Saunt, *New Order*, 213–39.

96. "An Oration Delivered at Twickenham, Madison County, Mississippi Territory, on the 4th of July 1811, by J. W. Walker. Published at the request of the committee of arrangement," *Columbian Centinel*, August 19, 1811.

97. Edmunds, *Shawnee Prophet*, 33–34.

98. This is when the infamous "Battle of Tippecanoe" took place. In a message to the Congress on November 5, President Madison noted the movement of a force of "regulars and militia, embodied in the Indiana territory" toward the northwestern frontier, a move "made requisite by several murders and depredations committed by the Indians, but more especially by the menacing preparations and aspect of a combination of them on the Wabash, under the influence and direction of a fanatic of the Shawnese tribe." Madison, *Message of President Madison*, 1811, <http://infoweb.newsbank.com> (December 3, 2005).

99. Sugden, "Early Pan-Indianism," 284–85; Waselkov, *Conquering Spirit*, 78.

100. *Tustunnuggee Hopoie* is a title meaning "far-off warrior" rather than a personal name. It would have been common for Creek talwas to each have their own Tustunnuggee Hopoie, identifiable by an additional geographic referent. However, most references to Tustunnuggee Hopoie in early nineteenth-century sources refer specifically to a man known more commonly to outsiders as Little Prince. Whereas the Tustunnuggee Hopoie mentioned in this instance was from the Upper Creek talwa of Tuckabatchee, Little Prince was from the Lower Creek talwa of Broken Arrow. Similarly, nearly every Creek talwa would have so-called big warriors, one of the three common grades of warriors, but most references to "Big Warrior" during this era indicate Big Warrior of Tuckabatchee, an Upper Creek leader who died in 1824. On Creek military titles, see Hudson, *Southeastern Indians*, 225–26.

101. Hawkins to Eustis, January 13, 1812, LBH, 2:601. See also Hawkins to Eustis, September 21, 1811, LBH, 2:591. Woodward claimed, "The Indians that originally inhabited from the middle parts of the Carolinas (particularly South Carolina,) and Georgia to the seaboard, were known as Yamacraws or Yamasees, Oconees, Ogeeches, and Sowanokees or People of the Glades. The Sowanokees are known as the Shawnees—the other Indians know them by no other name to this day but Sowanokee; and the Savannah river was known as Sowanokee Hatchee Thlocka, which signifies the Big River of the Glades, or what we call Savannah. And these Indians the Creeks found to be their equals as warriors; but when the whites began to approach them from the east, and the Creeks already very close on the west, the Sowanokees or Shawnees fell back on the north and northwest. Tecumseh was of that stock." Woodward, *Woodward's Reminiscences*, 18. See also Frank, *Creeks and Southerners*, 21; Grantham, *Creation Myths and Legends*, 17–18; Martin, *Sacred Revolt*, 116. Waselkov further asserts that one or both of the brothers' parents may have been Creek as well as Shawnee and expands on the potential kin connections. Waselkov, *Conquering Spirit*, 77.

102. Waselkov, *Conquering Spirit*, 82.

103. Sugden explains that various versions of this visit exist and there are some doubts

as to whether Tecumseh actually uttered this oft-quoted threat. But whether or not he actually threatened to shake the ground, Sugden notes, "the significance of these earthquakes, occurring just after Tecumseh had left the south and while he toured the west, cannot be overstated. The idea that Tecumseh foretold them, as McKenney and Stiggins said, need not be accepted, but he may have promised the Creeks that he would give them a sign of some kind, and left them to fulfill his prophecy with the first unusual occurrence. The ensuing shocks greatly advanced the cause of Tecumseh among the Creeks and elsewhere." Sugden, "Early Pan-Indianism," 288–90.

104. Haywood, *Natural and Aboriginal History*, 30. For additional accounts of the earthquake, see "Earthquake on the Mississippi," *New-York Commercial Advertiser*, March 19, 1812, 2, "Earthquake," *Poulson's American Daily Advertiser*, January 11, 1812, 2, "New-York, Feb. 11. Earthquake," *Hampshire Federalist*, February 20, 1812, 2, all in *Early American Newspapers, Series I, 1690–1876*, <http://infoweb.newsbank.com> (March 14, 2006); Burckhard and Petersen, *Partners in the Lord's Work*, 67–68.

CHAPTER FOUR

1. *Georgia Journal*, March 25, 1812, quoted in LBH, 2:602n1.
2. Austill, "Memories of Journeying," 93.
3. Champagne, *Social Order and Political Change*, 117–20.
4. Hawkins to Eustis, November 25, 1811, LBH, 2:599.
5. Hawkins to Eustis, October 3, 1811, LBH, 2:593–94.
6. LBH, 2:594.
7. Hawkins to Eustis, October 3, 1811, LBH, 2:593–94. This despite their repeated pronouncements that they did not possess the coercive authority to compel their young warriors to do or not do anything.
8. Hawkins to Eustis, February 3, 1812; Hawkins to Eustis, February 26, 1812; Hawkins to Eustis, March 30, 1812, LBH, 2:602–4.
9. See Eustis's replies to Hawkins's queries, Eustis to Hawkins, February 18, 1812; Eustis to Hawkins, April 6, 1812; Eustis to Hawkins, June 16, 1812, all in NARA, RG75, 75.2; Hawkins to Mitchell, April 6, 1812, LBH, 2:606.
10. Saunt recounts a fascinating endeavor on the part of Francis to solicit help from the Spanish using his newfound literacy, given to him in a dream by the Master of Breath. The paper he sent, however, apparently contained only "crooked marks" and was wholly unintelligible to the Spanish commandant at Pensacola. Saunt, *New Order*, 253–54. On other local prophets, see Waselkov, *Conquering Spirit*, 82–88.
11. Waselkov has astutely observed that the Native revitalization movements roughly coincided with the Second Great Awakening, a spiritual revival that swept the United States beginning in the 1790s. Black and white Americans in the western territories were particularly moved by the revelatory messages they heard at camp meetings across the region. The New Madrid earthquakes had an equally stunning impact on their religious awakening. Waselkov, *Conquering Spirit*, 80–82.
12. Martin makes a strong case that African American eschatological traditions influenced the development and execution of Red Stick prophecies. Martin, *Sacred Revolt*, 73–75.
13. Dowd, *Spirited Resistance*, 123–47.

14. Ibid., 139.

15. As John Sugden has noted, in many ways this movement left open the possibility of future Indian activism across tribal and geographic boundaries. Sugden, "Early Pan-Indianism," 273–304.

16. Hawkins to Eustis, September 21, 1811, LBH, 2:591.

17. Tustunnuggee Hopoie, quoted in Hawkins to Eustis, January 13, 1812, LBH, 2:601. See also Hawkins to Eustis, March 30, 1812, LBH, 2:604.

18. Drawing on J. D. Dreisbach, a descendant of Weatherford's, Benjamin W. Griffith asserts that Weatherford openly opposed Tecumseh when he visited the Creeks. Griffith, *McIntosh and Weatherford*, 77–78.

19. Waselkov, *Conquering Spirit*, 91–95; Woodward, *Woodward's Reminiscences*, 37.

20. Davis, " 'Much of the Indian Appears,' " 77–79.

21. Hawkins to Eustis, November 5, 1810, LBH, 2:576.

22. See, for example, U.S. Congress, *Captures of American Vessels*, 1812.

23. One such incident was the attack of the H.M.S. *Leopard* on the U.S.S. *Chesapeake* in the summer of 1807. An embargo on trade with Britain was passed in 1807 as a result of these aggressions and was not lifted until 1809. Meanwhile, Napoleon Bonaparte's imperial machinations kept European affairs in the forefront of U.S. political and economic concerns. William H. Crawford, "[Letter] 1809 Feb. 4, Washington, [D.C.] to Jared Irwin, Governor [of Georgia], Milledgeville, Georgia," TCC, <http://dlg.galileo.usg.edu> (April 12, 2006).

24. Madison, *Message from the President of the United States*, 1813, 6–7.

25. "Extract of a letter from J. Rhea, captain thirteenth regiment of infantry, dated Fort Wayne, March 14, 1812," in U.S. Congress, *Hostile Movements*, 1812.

26. George M. Troup to Mitchell, March 17, 1810, AYER.

27. Hickey observes, "The vote on the war bill—79–49 in the House and 19–13 in the Senate—was the closest vote on any declaration of war in American history. . . . Most representatives and senators from Pennsylvania and the South and West voted for the war, while most from the North and East voted against it. But the sectional breakdown was really a reflection of party strength, for the vote on the war bill was essentially a party vote. About 81 percent of the Republicans in both houses of Congress voted for the measure, while all the Federalists voted against it." Hickey, *War of 1812*, 46.

28. George M. Troup to Mitchell, March 17, 1810.

29. Hickey, *War of 1812*, 1–28. On the maritime difficulties in particular, Hickey notes, "Between 1807 and 1812 the two belligerents [Great Britain and France] and their allies seized about 900 American ships." Ibid., 19.

30. Hickey, *War of 1812*, 30. For a general survey of the causes of the War of 1812, see Goodman, "Origins of the War of 1812"; for a view into economic forces at work in the call to war, see Latimer, "South Carolina—A Protagonist of the War of 1812"; Horsman, "Western War Aims, 1811–1812"; for an alternate view of the causes of the war that focuses on "national honor" and the "War Hawks," see Risjord, "1812: Conservatives, War Hawks and the Nation's Honor."

31. Hickey, *War of 1812*, 42–43.

32. Lucy Thornton to Sarah A. R. Cobb, July 23, 1812, Cobb/Lamar/Erwin Collection, HAR.

33. Two important books on the topic of Indians in the War of 1812 are Benn, *Iroquois in the War of 1812*; Sugden, *Tecumseh's Last Stand*.

34. See the documents contained in U.S. Congress, *Hostile Movements*, 1812.

35. Eustis to Hawkins, June 19, 1812, NARA, RG75, 75.2. This letter appears to be a circular that was sent to all Indian agents—further underscoring the importance of the Indian frontiers, north and south, to the war.

36. The woman is referred to in the letter simply as "Mrs. Crawley." Eustis to Hawkins, June 22, 1812, NARA, RG75, 75.2. For more details on this incident, see Griffith, *McIntosh and Weatherford*, 80–82.

37. Griffith, *McIntosh and Weatherford*, 81; Woodward, *Woodward's Reminiscences*, 35–36.

38. John Floyd, "Extract from a letter of John Floyd to Gov. David B. Mitchell, Dated Head Quarters, Capt Hope, September 15, 1813," CIL, 3:818. Woodward claimed, "Ask an Indian that is acquainted with the original names and customs, what a Red Stick Warrior, is, and he will tell you it is an Autisee or Otisee." Woodward, *Woodward's Reminiscences*, 24–25; Waselkov, *Conquering Spirit*, 86.

39. Hawkins to Eustis, March 9, 1812, LBH, 2:603.

40. The man killed was named Thomas Meredith. Griffith, *McIntosh and Weatherford*, 80; Hawkins to Eustis, April 6, 1812; Hawkins to Mitchell, April 6, 1812, both in *LBH*, 2:605–6; Waselkov, *Conquering Spirit*, 88.

41. Hawkins to Eustis, August 24, 1812, LBH, 2:615; Hawkins to Toulmin, August 26, 1812, AYER. See also Mitchell to Hawkins, August 31, 1812, Georgia, Office of the Governor, Letterbooks, 1786–1897, GDAH.

42. Mitchell to Brigadier General John Floyd, April 12, 1813, Georgia, Office of the Governor, Letterbooks, 1786–1897, GDAH.

43. Hawkins to Mitchell, April 6, 1812, LBH, 2:606.

44. Hickey, *War of 1812*, 82.

45. Hawkins to Eustis, August 24, 1812, LBH, 2:615.

46. Hawkins to Eustis, March 9, 1812, LBH, 2:603.

47. Hawkins to Toulmin, August 26, 1812, AYER.

48. Saunt, *New Order*, 206–7. See also Mitchell to Floyd, September 12, 1812; Mitchell to Hawkins, February 8, 1813, Georgia, Office of the Governor, Letterbooks, 1786–1897, GDAH.

49. Hawkins to Toulmin, September 16, 1812, AYER.

50. Waselkov notes that Hawkins was also trying to protect the authority of the Creek National Council which he had labored to reorganize during his tenure among the Creeks. Waselkov, *Conquering Spirit*, 88.

51. Green, *Politics of Indian Removal*, 41; Griffith, *McIntosh and Weatherford*, 79, 83; Saunt, *New Order*, 242; Waselkov, *Conquering Spirit*, 88–89.

52. Woodward, *Woodward's Reminiscences*, 35–36.

53. Hawkins to Eustis, November 2, 1812, LBH, 2:621.

54. Gatschet, "Towns and Villages," 411.

55. Woodward, *Woodward's Reminiscences*, 37–38. The civil division within the Creek Nation is often described as a division between Upper and Lower towns, but as Waselkov has observed, "Although most Red Sticks inhabited Upper Creek talwas, some support for the

prophets also appeared among the Lower Creeks and more than a few Yuchis (in the Lower Creek country) took up arms against the Americans." Waselkov, *Conquering Spirit*, 90.

56. Waselkov, *Conquering Spirit*, 89.

57. Hawkins, "Talk to the Creek Chiefs," enclosed in Hawkins to Alexander Cornells, March 25, 1813, LBH, 2:631.

58. Hawkins to John Armstrong, April 6, 1813, LBH, 2:633.

59. Big Warrior and Alexander Cornells to Toulmin, April 18, 1813, *Frontier Claims in the Lower South*; Griffith, *McIntosh and Weatherford*, 83.

60. Hawkins to Mitchell, April 26, 1813, LBH, 2:634. Three more supporters of Little Warrior were later captured and killed and the Shawnee sympathizer himself was executed near Coosa River. Saunt, *New Order*, 251–52. Martin notes that it was as this moment that Captain Isaacs, once a leading prophet, was branded a traitor by his fellow Red Sticks, since he participated in the punishment of these murderers. Martin, *Sacred Revolt*, 125–26.

61. Saunt, *New Order*, 216–18. Saunt details the ways in which the annuities were converted from general payments divided among local leaders and then passed onto the needs of individual towns to what were essentially bribes paid to those chiefs willing to adhere to the agent's policies and adopt the plan of civilization. See also Frank, *Creeks and Southerners*, chap. 6, on this system of patronage.

62. Armstrong to General John Mason, April 23, 1813, NARA, RG75, 75.2.

63. Armstrong to Hawkins, May 1, 1813, NARA, RG75, 75.2.

64. Griffith, *McIntosh and Weatherford*, 86.

65. Hawkins to Armstrong, March 1, 1813, LBH, 2:629.

66. Quoted in Hawkins to James Monroe, January 18, 1813, LBH, 2:628. See also Mitchell to Floyd, April 12, 1813, Georgia, Office of the Governor, Letterbooks, 1786–1897, GDAH.

67. "Report of Mr. James C. Warren to his Excellency D. B. Mitchell on his mission to Jasper County and the Creek Agency," April 13, 1813, CIL, 3:775–77. See also Allen Tooke to Mitchell, April 9, 1813, CIL, 3:770–72.

68. Hawkins to Armstrong, May 3, 1813, LBH, 2:638. See also Hawkins to Armstrong, June 7, 1813, LBH, 2:640.

69. Hawkins to Eustis, November 9, 1812, LBH, 2:621.

70. Thomas Flournoy to Mitchell, April 15, 1813, CIL, 3:780. For additional evidence of the "friendly disposition" of many Creeks despite the rumors to the contrary, see also "Report of Mr. James C. Warren," CIL, 3:775–77.

71. Martin asserts that Big Warrior and Alexander Cornells were related. Martin, *Sacred Revolt*, 94.

72. Big Warrior and Alexander Cornells to Toulmin, April 18, 1813, *Frontier Claims in the Lower South*.

73. Ibid.

74. John Hanes, et al. to Major General James Wilkinson, April 17, 1813, Creek War Military Records, 1813–ca. 1820, ADAH.

75. Robert J. Walton to Mitchell, July 26, 1813, CIL, 3:787; Big Warrior, et al., to Walton, July 24, 1813, CIL, 3:788.

76. Hawkins to Armstrong, July 28, 1813, LBH, 2:651.

77. As Martin observes, some Creek people "performed pastoralist innovations without sacrificing their culture's bedrock principles of reciprocity and redistribution of wealth. Just because they raised stock, they did not necessarily become market-oriented, money-mongering individuals." Martin, *Sacred Revolt*, 104.

78. Saunt, *New Order*, 254–57. Waselkov claims that "burning and pillaging" was "standard punishment meted out for decades by Creek talwas to enforce order and encourage obedience among recalcitrants." Waselkov, *Conquering Spirit*, 98.

79. Hawkins to Armstrong, April 26, 1813, LBH, 2:636.

80. Ibid., 2:636–37.

81. "Extract from Executive Minutes 1812–1814, [containing] a letter from Colo. Benjamin Hawkins, 6th April 1813," CIL, 3:773–74. See also "Report of Mr. James C. Warren," CIL, 3:775–77. Interestingly, some of this commerce may have been related to the need for military stores in the absence of the quartermaster and commissary departments that had been abolished in 1802. The army had resorted to private contracts for the supply of rations, including flour, pork, rum, brandy or whiskey, and other necessaries. These contractors were not overseen by the government and sometimes charged exorbitant prices for their goods, thereby shoring up the frontier economy and bolstering support for the war in the West. Hickey, *War of 1812*, 78–79.

82. For a study of British traders in Pensacola, see Coker and Watson, *Indian Traders*.

83. William Pierce and J. Pierce to Toulmin, July 18, 1813, *Frontier Claims*.

84. High Head Jim quoted in "Deposition of Samuel Manac," August 2, 1813, ADAH.

85. Big Warrior to Hawkins, August 4, 1813, CIL, 3:808. This was later known as the Battle of Burnt Corn because it took place near the head of Burnt Corn Creek or Spring. See also Toulmin to Brigadier General Ferdinand L. Claiborne, July 23, 1813, HTL; Joseph Carson to Claiborne, July 30, 1813, Joseph Carson Letter, 1813, ADAH; Waselkov, *Conquering Spirit*, 98–102.

86. "View of the Valley of the Mississippi: or the Emigrant's and Traveller's Guide to the West," 1832, Graff Collection, Newberry Library. See also Gilbert C. Russell to Governor William W. Bibb, n.d., Alabama Territory Records, ADAH; "Deposition of Samuel Manac," August 2, 1813, ADAH.

87. Another brother-in-law was Red Stick leader William Weatherford. Waselkov, *Conquering Spirit*, 93.

88. "Deposition of Samuel Manac," August 2, 1813, ADAH; see also Waselkov, *Conquering Spirit*, 83, 97–98.

89. Austill, "Memories of Journeying," 93.

90. Elijah Gordy to Mitchell, May 17, 1813, CIL, 3:781–82.

91. According to the Consumer Price Index method of calculating relative values of monetary sums, $7.50 in 1813 would purchase about $105.00 of goods in 2007, the most recent year for which data is available. Williamson, "Six Ways to Compute the Relative Value," <http://www.measuringworth.com/uscompare/> (June 20, 2008).

92. In another more clearly defined "right of way" incident, James Wilkinson, heading the militia stationed at Mobile, was stopped on the Federal Road in the company of James Cornells, who testified that the "enemies of the Big Warrior, who declared themselves enemies of the U.S. Requested the General to know when he would be ready to fight them," using the road as a stage to enact their hostile intentions. See "Deposition of James

Cornells, 3d August, 1813," Mississippi (Territory): Correspondence (Judge Toulmin's Letters, ca. 1810–1816), ADAH.

93. Martin, *Sacred Revolt*, 124, 126. Martin also observes that some popular narratives about Tecumseh credited him with releasing power contained in the Lower World to destroy the old order and remake the Indians' world. Martin, *Sacred Revolt*, 115, 124.

94. Toulmin to Governor David Holmes, August 10, 1813, Mississippi (Territory): Correspondence (Judge Toulmin's Letters, ca. 1810–1816), ADAH.

95. William Pierce and J. Pierce to Toulmin, July 18, 1813, *Frontier Claims*.

96. Toulmin to Claiborne, July 23, 1813, HTL. See also Carson to Claiborne, July 30, 1813, Joseph Carson Letter, 1813, ADAH.

97. Toulmin to Claiborne, July 23, 1813, HTL; "Extract of a letter from Judge Toulmin to a gentleman in high office, at the seat of government," August 13, 1813, *Frontier Claims*.

98. Hawkins to Mitchell, June 24, 1813, LBH, 2:642.

99. Mitchell to Armstrong, July 29, 1813, Georgia, Office of the Governor, Letterbooks, 1786–1897, GDAH.

100. Walton to Mitchell, July 26, 1813, CIL, 3:788.

101. Both Martin and Griffith note that Big Warrior had considered joining the Red Sticks but was denounced by them and forced to take the opposite course. Griffith, *McIntosh and Weatherford*, 73; Martin, *Sacred Revolt*, 136.

102. Big Warrior to Hawkins, July 26, 1813, CIL, 3:796–97.

103. Martin estimates that at its height, the Red Stick movement involved 7,000 to 9,000 men, women, and children, but he does not explain how he arrived at this number. Martin, *Sacred Revolt*, 133.

104. Toulmin to Claiborne, July 23, 1813, HTL. Similarly, Hopoithle Micco reportedly said, "I am not at war with any nation of people, I am settling an affair with my own Chiefs." Hawkins to John Armstrong, July 20, 1813, LBH, 2:648.

105. Toulmin to Claiborne, July 23, 1813, HTL.

106. "Extract of a letter from Judge Toulmin," August 13, 1813, *Frontier Claims*.

107. Toulmin to Claiborne, July 23, 1813, HTL.

108. "Deposition of James Cornel[l]s, 3d August 1813," Mississippi (Territory): Correspondence (Judge Toulmin's Letters, ca. 1810–1816), ADAH.

109. "A demand on the Fanatical Chiefs and associates of an explanation of their conduct. To Creek Chiefs who have taken the talks of the prophets," enclosed in Hawkins to Armstrong, July 13, 1813, LBH, 2:647.

110. Hawkins to Armstrong, July 28, 1813, LBH, 2:651.

111. Hawkins to Tustunnuggee Thlucco [Big Warrior], July 26, 1813, LBH, 2:650.

112. Big Warrior and Tustunnuggee Hopoie, "Head Chiefs of the Upper & Lower Creeks—their talks to Colo. Benjamin Hawkins Agent for I.A., Coweta, 4th August 1813," CIL, 3:806–7.

113. Armstrong to Hawkins, July 22, 1813, NARA, RG75, 75.2. See also Mitchell to Armstrong, July 29, 1813; Mitchell to Willie Blount, July 29, 1813, Georgia, Office of the Governor, Letterbooks, 1786–1897, GDAH.

114. Ball, *Glance into the Great South-east*, 64.

115. "Extract of a letter from Judge Toulmon [Toulmin] to the Governor, received yesterday by Express," in *Monitor*, October 9, 1813.

116. The quintessential account of the Battle of Fort Mims is in Waselkov, *Conquering Spirit*. The estimates of those killed and kidnapped appear on 137 and 151.

117. "A demand on the Fanatical Chiefs," July 13, 1813, LBH, 2:647.

118. Elijah Clark to Daniel Clark, Louisiana Collection, Papers, 1779–1937, American Antiquarian Society.

119. Ibid.

120. Royall, *Letters from Alabama*, 17.

121. "Extract of a letter from Judge Toulmon [Toulmin]," *Monitor*, October 9, 1813. One Tennessee newspaper printed the letter of a soldier stationed near Fort Stoddert, who asked, "Will not this tale of horror excite emotions of sorrow & vows of revenge from every part of our territory? If scenes like that of Tensaw be looked on with unconcern—if the young of our country do not rise in arms and revenge their lost countrymen they are unworthy of the names of Americans." "Letter of George Dougherty to a Mr. Isler, Cantonment, Mt. Vernon, near Fort Stoddert, September 4, 1813," in *Nashville Examiner*, September 29, 1813.

122. *Wilson's Knoxville Gazette*, September 20, 1813.

123. See, for example, *Georgia Argus*, September 15, 1813; "An Address, Delivered by the Rev. Mr. Craighead, at a meeting of the officers &c. in Nashville on the 11th ult.," in *Madison Gazette*, October 19, 1813.

124. Andrew Jackson, "General Orders," in *Louisiana Gazette for the Country*, October 23, 1813.

125. Jackson to Mitchell, October 10, 1813, CIL, 3:831–32.

126. Nelson, "Military Roads for War and Peace," gives an excellent overview of the importance of roads and road building to military efforts in the Early Republic, particularly during the War of 1812.

127. *Madison Gazette*, October 19, 1813. For later road building during the end of the war and the War of 1812, see entry titled "David Blackshear" in Northen, *Men of Mark in Georgia*, 170.

128. "General Jackson's Campaign Against the Creek Indians, 1813 & 1814," NARA, RG77, Treasure File; Nelson, "Military Roads for War and Peace—1791–1836," 5–6.

129. Mitchell to Floyd, September 26, 1812; Mitchell to Blackshear, October 6, 1813, both in Georgia, Office of the Governor, Letterbooks, 1786–1897, GDAH.

130. Edmund Bryan, "Account of the March of the 7th Reg. of No. Carolina Detached Militia, in the Service of the United States, from Salisbury to Fort Hawkins, thence to Fort Jackson near the Confluence of the Coosa & Tallapoosa Rivers—also a part of the same down the Allabama to Camp Pearson. Fort Decatur," July 10, 1814, Bryan & Leventhorpe Family Papers, SHC; Mitchell to Armstrong, July 29, 1813; Mitchell to Blount, July 29, 1813, both in Georgia, Office of the Governor, Letterbooks, 1786–1897, GDAH.

131. Hugh Montgomery to [Peter Early?], January 10, 1814, CIL, 3:850–51.

132. Samuel Bains to Christiana Bains, November 25, 1813, Creek War Military Records, 1813–ca. 1820, ADAH. Georgia governor Mitchell predicted the problem of troop movements from Tennessee south into Creek country, despite Jackson's efforts to create new paths. Mitchell to Armstrong, July 29, 1813, Georgia, Office of the Governor, Letterbooks, 1786–1897, GDAH.

133. Thomas Crawford to Eleaner Crawford, March 24, 1814, Thomas Crawford Papers, SHC.

134. William McCauley to Doctor John McCauley, April 15, 1814, Andrew McCauley Papers, SHC. For more on the difficulties of transporting troops and supplies during the War of 1812 in both the northwestern and southwestern theaters, see Nelson, "Military Roads for War and Peace," 1–7.

135. Thomas Pinckney, "Circular, Head Quarters, Sixth & Seventh Districts, Fort Hawkins," December 27, 1813, Thomas Pinckney Papers, 1771–1818, DU.

136. Ball, *Glance into the Great South-east*, 131–32, 167–68.

137. Toulmin noted, "Boats indeed loaded with provisions for the troops, did descend the river [Coosa] . . . but the hazard was very considerable, and some of them were destroyed." Toulmin, "A Geographical Sketch, of the Country bordering on the Alabama, and included in the treaty made by General Jackson and the Creek Indians," in *Knoxville Register*, September 21, 1816.

138. *Narrative of the Life and Death of Lieut. Joseph Morgan Willcox*, n.p. For more on river transport of military supplies, see Hawkins, "Letter with information of hostile appearances among the Simenolies [i.e., Seminoles] and hostile Creeks, 1814 No. 15, Creek Agency [to Peter] Early, Governor [of Georgia], Milledgeville, Georgia," TCC, <http://dlg.galileo.usg.edu> (April 4, 2006); William McCauley to John McCauley, April 15, 1814, Andrew McCauley Papers, SHC; Edmund Bryan to [?], June 1, 1814, Bryan & Leventhorpe Family Papers, SHC; Bryan, "Account of the March of the 7th Reg. of No. Carolina Detached Militia, in the Service of the United States, from Salisbury to Fort Hawkins, thence to Fort Jackson near the Confluence of the Coosa & Tallapoosa Rivers— also a part of the same down the Allabama to Camp Pearson. Fort Decatur 10th July 1814," Bryan & Leventhorpe Family Papers, SHC; William B. Lenoir to General William Lenoir, December 13, 1813, Lenoir Family Papers, SHC. In general, see also Eaton, *Life of Andrew Jackson*.

139. William B. Lenoir to General William Lenoir, December 13, 1813, Lenoir Family Papers, SHC; *Louisiana Gazette and New Orleans Advertiser [Weekly Edition]*, February 19, 1814; *Monitor*, August 6, 1814.

140. Thomas Crawford to Eleaner Crawford, March 24, 1814, Thomas Crawford Papers, SHC.

141. *Georgia Argus*, June 1, 1814. A report of "Red Clubs" assembling at Pensacola to receive "munitions of war" from Havana is dated "Creek Agency, May 24." See also *Nashville Examiner*, May 4, 1814; *Monitor*, August 6, 1814; *Georgia Argus*, August 10, 1814.

142. *Georgia Argus*, June 1, 1814. These peace terms are quoted from those "communicated by General Pickney [sic] to Col. Hawkins."

143. Treaty with the Creeks, 1814, in Kappler, *Indian Affairs: Laws and Treaties*, vol. 2, <http://digital.library.okstate.edu/kappler/Vol2/treaties/cre0107.htm> (March 14, 2006).

144. Hawkins to Armstrong, August 16, 1814, LBH, 2:693.

145. Hawkins to Monroe, October 12, 1814, LBH, 2:696; Hawkins to Little Prince and Big Warrior, November 3, 1814, LBH, 2:700.

146. Madison, *Message from the President*, December 5, 1815, 5.

147. LBH, 2:712, 720n2.

148. George Graham to Hawkins, July 12, 1815, NARA, RG75, 75.2.

149. Hawkins to Alexander Cornells, June 24, 1815, LBH, 2:737.

150. Hawkins to Early, April 21, 1815, LBH, 2:724.

151. Hawkins to Jackson, May 5, 1815, LBH, 2:725–26.

152. Graham to Sevier and Mr. William Barnett, September 2, 1815, NARA, RG75, 75.2.

153. Journal of the Proceedings, 1816, Jesse Franklin Indian Treaty Papers, SHC.

154. Hawkins to Monroe, October 5, 1814, LBH, 2:696. See also Hawkins to Peter Lequex, November 5, 1814, LBH, 2:702; Hawkins to Monroe, January 23, 1815, LBH, 2:716.

155. Hawkins to Early, District of Ft. Hawkins, April 21, 1815, LBH, 2:724. This letter also states the following: "I have heard for certainty an Indian woman ate her own child."

156. Big Warrior to Jackson, October 3, 1815, AYER.

157. "Journal of the Occurrences at the Convention of the Creeks at Tookaubatche commencing on September 9, 1815," LBH, 2:754–59.

158. Ibid. Big Warrior continued, "I told him [Jackson] he was taking all my land from me, he was going to leave us to suffer. The General's answer was if you will not sign the treaty I will give you provisions, ammunition and you must go down to Pensacola and join your friends, Red Sticks and British. He told me by the time I got to Pensacola he would be on my tracks and whip me and the British into the sea."

CHAPTER FIVE

1. Paulding, *Letters from the South*, 204–5. Paulding later became famous (and infamous) for his novel *Westward Ho!* (1832) and his defense of slavery, *Slavery in the United States* (1836). For a critique of Paulding's impact on American letters, see Drinnon, *Facing West*, 119–30.

2. Paulding, *Letters from the South*, 205.

3. William H. Crawford to Hawkins, October 16, 1815, NARA, RG75, 75.2.

4. Augustin Harris Hansell, "Memoirs, 1817–1906," Augustin Harris Hansell Memoirs, SHC.

5. William H. Crawford to Hawkins, October 16, 1815, NARA, RG75, 75.2.

6. In fact, as late as 1827, the state of Georgia was still endeavoring to secure military land bounties for militia claims dating as far back as the 1790s, based on the assertion that such lands were "justly due to those individuals who defended the frontier of this State against the invasions of the Indians, at a time when the emergency would not admit of delay." U.S. Congress, *Application of Georgia*, 1827.

7. Samuel Bains to Christiana Bains, November 25, 1813, Creek War Military Records, 1813–ca. 1820, ADAH.

8. William B. Lenoir to General William Lenoir, December 13, 1813, Lenoir Family Papers, SHC.

9. Paulding, *Letters from the South*, 140.

10. See, for example, selections from 1817 from John Coffee Papers, 1796–1887, ADAH.

11. Brown, *Western Gazetteer*, 16.

12. Goff, "Cow Punching in Old Georgia," 16.

13. Ethridge, *Creek Country*, 241.

14. Big Warrior, Tustunnuggee Hopoie, "Talk from the Creek Chiefs, to [David B.] Mitchell, Fort Hawkins," July 8, 1817, David Henley Papers, 1791–1800, DU.

15. Ibid.

16. Green, *Politics of Indian Removal*, 52–53.

17. The interventions of British merchant Alexander Arbuthnot, arguably a friend to the Creeks in Florida, as well as the intrigues of former British officers George Woodbine and Robert C. Armbrister, complicated the situation between Creeks and Americans over 1817–1818. Andrew Jackson ultimately executed Arbuthnot and Armbrister, while Woodbine managed to escape capture. Owsley, *Struggle for the Gulf Borderlands*, 184–85.

18. Edmund P. Gaines to Governor William Rabun, July 20, 1817, CIL, 3:895–96.

19. Gaines to Rabun, December 14, 1817, CIL, 3:902. See also *Reflector*, December 9, 1817. Gaines was ultimately prevented from carrying a new war into the Spanish territory by order of the War Department, but he continued to pursue those "hostile" Indians remaining in and around the lands ceded in the Fort Jackson treaty. See George Graham to Mitchell, November 3, 1817, AYER.

20. Mitchell to William Bibb, December 15, 1817, Alabama Territory Records, ADAH. It is also important to remember that American criminals sometimes plied these trails robbing and harassing travelers, occasionally in the guise of local Indians. For instance, Joseph Hare, a notorious mail robber who terrorized the interior South for years, recounted in his gallows confession an incident in which he and fellow criminals spoke to a group of travelers "in the Creek tongue . . . told them we were Indians, that did not think it any harm to take money from white people." Hare, *Confession of One of the Mail Robbers*, 6.

21. For instance, $5,000 was appropriated and transmitted to Mitchell in late 1817 to repair portions of the Federal Road, a continuation of the work General Gaines had already begun with his troops. Graham to Mitchell, November 3, 1817, AYER.

22. Ibid.

23. "Creek deputation to Graham," March 8, 1817, quoted in Griffith, *McIntosh and Weatherford*, 181.

24. Graham to Mitchell, November 3, 1817, AYER.

25. Big Warrior, Tustunnuggee Hopoie, "Talk from the Creek Chiefs, to [D.B.?] Mitchell, Fort Hawkins," July 8, 1817, David Henley Papers, 1791–1800, DU. The Treaty of Washington (1805) stipulated that the Creeks would allow Americans to use the Ocmulgee for navigation and fisheries, provided no fish traps were used and nets were pulled to the eastern shore only. There were no provisions for the construction of mills because such structures interfered with the natural flow of the river and thus had a negative impact on Creek ability to fish there.

26. Hansell, "Memoirs, 1817–1906," 6.

27. Israel Pickens to Major Thomas Lenoir, May 1, 1817, Pickens Family Papers, 1799–1855, ADAH.

28. Blowe, *Geographical, Historical, Commercial and Agricultural View*, 652.

29. [Jefferson?] M. Goode to James A. Tait, December 27, 1817, Tait Family Papers, ADAH.

30. Flint, *Condensed Geography and History*, 1:482.

31. Pickens to Martha Pickens, January 7, 1817, Chiliab Smith Howe Papers, SHC.

32. Pickens to General William Lenoir, January 18 and 21, 1818, Pickens Family Papers, 1799–1855, ADAH.

33. Thomas Ritchie to Albert G. Ruffin, April 3, 1817, Francis G. Ruffin Papers, SHC.

34. Paulding noted further, "The prospect of exchanging a little exhausted farm, for

one ten times as large, where the labours and privations of a few years are repaid by the sweets of independence to themselves and their children, will allure many of the young ones of the East." Paulding, *Letters from the South*, 83.

35. Goode to Tait, December 27, 1817, Tait Family Papers, ADAH.

36. Pickens to William Lenoir, January 18 and 21, 1818, Pickens Family Papers, 1799–1855, ADAH.

37. Pickens to William Lenoir, December 27, 1818, Pickens Family Papers, 1799–1855, ADAH.

38. Owen, *John Owen's Journal*, n.p.

39. *Reflector*, February 24, 1818.

40. *Georgia Journal*, August 20, 1822.

41. For another example from the region, see *Clarion, & Tennessee State Gazette*, November 17, 1818.

42. See, for instance, this lengthy argument: "On the Subject of Internal Improvement," [n.p., 1818].

43. U.S. Congress, House, *Message from the President*, 1818.

44. John C. Calhoun suggested the expediency of utilizing military labor on commercial roads as both beneficial to "the commerce, the manufactures, the agriculture, and political prosperity of the country" as well as a check on the "deleterious effects" of idle garrison life, noting that "among the leading inducements to enlist, is the exemption from labor." Quoted from a report Calhoun submitted as secretary of war to Henry Clay, Speaker of the House of Representatives, in *New Orleans Chronicle*, March 3, 1819.

45. Georgia, *Acts of the General Assembly*, 134–42.

46. *Knoxville Register*, April 13, 1819.

47. See also the advertisement of the formation of the Milledgeville Turnpike Company, *Georgia Patriot*, February 11, 1823.

48. Caroline Howard to Harriet Jay, March 19, 1819, Gilman Family Papers, 1809–1888, American Antiquarian Society; for another effort to improve river navigation, see John Clark to Governor John Geddes, June 30, 1820, Georgia, Office of the Governor, Letterbooks, 1786–1897, GDAH. In 1817, the first transatlantic steamer, owned by Georgia citizens, departed from Savannah. Phillips, *Georgia and State Rights*, 141.

49. McAdam, *Practical Essay*, 5.

50. Ira Berlin has described the transformation of the interior South as such: "The seaboard planters' westward migration soon connected with the northward expansion of plantation culture in the lower Mississippi Valley to create what would soon become the heartland of the plantation South." Berlin, *Many Thousands Gone*, 357.

51. On the east-west and north-south division over the extension of slavery and the Missouri Controversy more specifically, see Hammond, *Slavery, Freedom, and Expansion*, 6–7, 55–75.

52. Pickens to William Lenoir, June 5, 1819, Pickens Family Papers, 1799–1855, ADAH. As Andrew Rothman has noted, "Cotton planters assumed they needed slave labor just as they needed soil and rain." Rothman, *Slave Country*, 49. Similarly, James David Miller asserts, "Slaveholding emigrant families . . . proved incapable of thinking about western land without reference to the human property they knew would transform it for them." Miller, *South by Southwest*, 5.

53. Brown, *Western Gazetteer*, 235. See also Blowe, *Geographical, Historical, Commercial, and Agricultural View.*

54. Pickens to Thomas Lenoir, October 6, 1816, Pickens Family Papers, 1799–1855, ADAH.

55. Pickens to William Lenoir, December 8, 1816, Chiliab Smith Howe Papers, SHC. Almost twenty years later, the practice of sending slaves ahead was still apparent. In 1824, Lukas Vischer observed "a caravan . . . consist[ing] of a planter from South Carolina who was moving his home to Alabama, whither he had already brought thirty Negroes the previous year, and now had his family and domestics follow him in two carriages, three wagons, and on horseback." Collins, "Notes and Documents," 254–55. On slaves brought into the southwest by planters or in advance of them, see also Libby, *Slavery and Frontier Mississippi*, 37–38, 61, 67–68, 70, 75.

56. Owen, *John Owen's Journal*, preface 3–4.

57. Harris, *Remarks Made during a Tour*, 21. See also Mary Burney, "Petition, to the Legislature of the Alabama Territory," February 17, 1817, Alabama Territory Records, ADAH.

58. Hine and Faragher, *American West*, 165.

59. John Owen repeatedly remarked on the presence of "negro drivers" along their route. Owen, *John Owen's Journal*, n.p. See also Libby, *Slavery and Frontier Mississippi*, 62–63.

60. Johnson, *Soul by Soul*, 45–77, 214–15.

61. Buttrick, *Buttrick's Voyages*, 214. Walter Johnson has argued that rather than dehumanizing slaves, traders used their humanity—treating property as people, rather than people as property. He uses the example of traders raping enslaved women as an extreme instance of traders' "brutal recognition of their slaves' humanity." Johnson, *Soul by Soul*, 63. While such examples are certainly compelling and it is clear that traders had a fundamental interest in understanding slave behavior, at least in order to better surveil and control them, my point here is that slaves were transported in ways that closely resembled the transportation of other chattel to and from markets along the southern roads.

62. Ingraham, *South-West*, 233–34, 238; Libby, *Slavery and Frontier Mississippi*, 64. See generally Johnson, *Soul by Soul*.

63. Ingraham, *South-West*, 243–44.

64. See, for example, Hall, *Travels in North America*, 126–29.

65. Ball, *Fifty Years in Chains*, 19, 29. Although some doubt has been cast on a number of the most readily accessible fugitive slave narratives, largely as a result of the involvement of white abolitionists as transcribers and/or editors, George M. Fredrickson and Christopher Lasch maintain that Ball's account rings true. Fredrickson and Lasch, "Resistance to Slavery," 324n19. See also Roper, *Narrative of the Adventures*. On the reliability of slave narratives as a form of evidence, see Blassingame, "Using the Testimony of Ex-Slaves," 473–92.

66. Ball, *Glance into the Great South-east*, 179, 193–94; Brown, *Western Gazetteer*, 16; Libby, *Slavery and Frontier Mississippi*, 75.

67. See generally Rothman, *Slave Country*.

68. Libby, *Slavery and Frontier Mississippi*, 60. The rapid movement of slaves into the interior South only increased as the antebellum period wore on. Herbert G. Gutman has

suggested that the speed with which large numbers of enslaved people were relocated from the Upper South to the Lower South permitted a significant level of cultural continuity between communities in the two locales. Gutman, *Black Family*, 154.

69. Ball, *Fifty Years in Chains*, 11–12.

70. Grimes, *Life of William Grimes*, 22.

71. Ball, *Slavery in the United States*, 69, 72.

72. As Libby has noted, planter migrations were perhaps the preferable form of slave relocation since such migrants "tended to preserve some families because their slaves often were married to one another," and they did not "experience the sense of loss, rejection, and insecurity that accompanied being sold." Libby, *Slavery and Frontier Mississippi*, 67.

73. Harris, *Remarks Made during a Tour*, 21.

74. Pickens to William Lenoir, May 17, 1822, Pickens Family Papers, 1799–1855, ADAH; Pickens to William B. Lenoir, June 2, 1823, Chiliab Smith Howe Papers, SHC.

75. See, for example, runaway slave ads in *Alabama Journal*, June 27, 1827, and August 22, 1828. See also J. M. Calhoun to Samuel Pickens, March 9, 1831, Pickens Family Papers, 1799–1855, ADAH.

76. Roper, *Narrative of the Adventures*, 69–70. Larry Gara notes that the use of such false passes or papers was fairly common among fugitives. Gara, *Liberty Line*, 46–47.

77. Ball, *Slavery in the United States*, 49; Franklin and Schweninger, *Runaway Slaves*, 109, 110, 114.

78. Parks, "Follow the Drinking Gourd," 81–84. Parks recorded this song from a man of African descent he met in College Station, Texas, in 1918. The man recalled the song as having been sung by slaves he knew as a child. While local geographical knowledge, particularly among slaves recently relocated to the Lower South from other regions, was uncommon, knowledge of the importance of the Big Dipper and the North Star and their use in navigating was not. Gara, *Liberty Line*, 46.

79. The Tombigbee River region occasionally provided refuge for small maroon communities, confirming its importance as a landmark for the use of runaways. For example, the following report appeared in the *Alabama Journal* in the summer of 1827: "A nest of runaway negroes was discovered last week in the fork of the Alabama and Tombeckbe Rivers. . . . They had two cabins, and were about to build a fort. . . . Some of these negroes have been run away several years." *Alabama Journal*, June 27, 1827. Such swampy areas were known to be favorite hiding places for fugitives throughout the South. Gara, *Liberty Line*, 28; Vlach, "Above Ground on the Underground Railroad," 100–102. Jane Landers also describes several autonomous villages established by fugitives in present-day Florida, including Pilaklikaha, Mulatto Girl's Town, King Heijah's Town, Bucker Woman's Town, Boggy Island, and Big Swamp. Landers, "Southern Passage," 130. Despite the Herculean efforts of some fugitives to find freedom from slavery by traveling to the North, as Franklin and Schweninger note, the dream of freedom "went unfulfilled for the vast majority of runaways." Although a tremendous folk history of runaways and underground railroads has flourished since the nineteenth century, their actual chances of success were quite slim. Franklin and Schweninger, *Runaway Slaves*, 116–17.

80. Roper, *Narrative of the Adventures*, 59; William J. W. Wellborn, "Letter, 1836 June 19, Milledgeville, G[eorgi]a [to] W[illia]m Schley, [Governor of Georgia], Columbus,

G[eorgi]a," TCC, <http://dlg.galileo.usg.edu> (March 20, 2006); Wood, *Black Majority*, 114–15, 123–24. Barbara Krauthamer has described the process by which skilled slave men, hired out as boatmen, blacksmiths, and wagoners, brought extensive information back to their slave communities upon each return, thereby equalizing the apparent gender disparity in local geographical knowledge that resulted from enslaved women's relative immobility compared to enslaved men. Krauthamer, "Kinship and Freedom," 150.

81. Pickens to William B. Lenoir, December 6, 1823, Chiliab Smith Howe Papers, SHC.

82. Ball, *Slavery in the United States*, 358.

83. Peter F. Jaillet to Joel Crawford, 1825, Farish Carter Papers, SHC.

84. The continued "combination" of former Red Sticks, escaped slaves, and "Florida Indians" against the lower American settlements and local travelers ensured that protracted military engagements and the efforts toward "reducing the Indians" would dominate the public mind. Edward F. Tattnall, "Letter, 1817 Mar. 20, Savannah, [Georgia] to W[illia]m Rabun, [Governor of Georgia], Milledgeville, Geo[rgi]a," TCC, <http://dlg.galileo.usg.edu> (April 2, 2006). For an example of increasingly hostile public opinion regarding the southern Indians, see Barber, *Narrative of the Tragical Death of Mr. Darius Barber*.

85. *Reflector*, April 7, 1818; *Georgia Journal*, November 14, 1826; *Halcyon, and Tombeckbe Public Advertiser*, February 8, 1819; *Savannah Daily Republican*, June 13, 1821.

86. *Montgomery Republican*, January 24, 1824.

87. *Georgia Journal*, Milledgeville, September 24, 1822.

88. "Deposition of Isaac Bush, Richmond County, Georgia, October 16, 1824," CIL, 3:976; *Georgia Journal*, March 17, 1828.

89. Franklin and Schweninger, *Runaway Slaves*, 115; Krauthamer, "Kinship and Freedom," 159.

90. Franklin and Schweninger, *Runaway Slaves*, 112.

91. Wright, *Creeks and Seminoles*, 218–19.

92. A. B. Shehee to Clark, November 24, 1819, CIL, 3:926–27.

93. Gaines, "[Letter], 1817 Dec. 2, Headquarters, Fort Scott [Decatur County, Georgia to] D[avid] B. Mitchell, Creek Agency," TCC, <http://dlg.galileo.usg.edu> (April 5, 2006). See also Gaines to Rabun, July 20, 1817, CIL, 3:895–96; Gaines to Rabun, December 14, 1817, CIL, 3:902.

94. Green suggests that William McIntosh's prominence in Creek national politics grew tremendously in the postwar years in part because both Big Warrior and Little Prince had become aged and largely ineffective. Green, *Politics of Indian Removal*, 59.

95. Mitchell, "Letter, 1817 Dec. 15, Creek Agency [to] William Rabun, Governor of Georgia," TCC, <http://dlg.galileo.usg.edu> (April 2, 2006). Gaines apparently relied on a Lower Creek leader known as Otis or Onis Harjo, along with McIntosh. See Gaines to Rabun, July 20, 1817, CIL, 3:895–96; Gaines to Rabun, December 14, 1817, CIL, 3:902.

96. "Copy of a letter from David B. Mitchell, Esquire, Agent for Indian Affairs, to Governor Rabun, dated 'Creek Agency, January 8, 1818,'" in *Reflector*, January 13, 1818; Mitchell to Gaines, February 23, 1818, AYER.

97. Similar attacks were reported throughout 1818. See, for example, *Clarion, & Tennessee State Gazette*, October 27, 1818; *Reflector*, March 10, 1818.

98. *Louisiana Rambler*, March 28, 1818.

99. Michael Green asserts that the division between Big Warrior and McIntosh was a longstanding one, exacerbated by the arrival of the new Creek agent John Crowell, who challenged McIntosh's control of Creek annuities and quickly allied with Big Warrior to offset the Coweta headman's influence in the National Council, particularly where the issue of Christian missions was concerned. Green, *Politics of Indian Removal*, 59–67.

100. William Green to Rabun, June 30, 1819, CIL, 3:921–25.

101. William Green to Rabun, May 13, 1819, CIL, 3:906–7.

102. William Green to Rabun, May 18, 1819, CIL, 3:909–11.

103. Ibid.

104. Robert Jackson to Rabun, May 18, 1819, CIL, 3:911–12. See also Robert Jackson to [Rabun?], May 22, 1819, CIL, 3:913; Robert Jackson to Rabun, May 29, 1819, CIL, 3:914–15; Robert Jackson to Rabun, June 24, 1819, CIL, 3:919–20.

105. William Green to [Rabun?], June 3, 1819, CIL, 3:916–18.

106. William Green to Rabun, June 30, 1819, CIL, 3:921–25.

107. Shehee to Clark, November 24, 1819, CIL, 3:926–27.

108. It may have also represented the anxiety of American inhabitants who feared that their farms would be found to sit on the wrong side of the line once the survey was completed. Elsewhere in the United States, frontier Americans took myriad opportunities to defy official attempts to demarcate lands they had already settled. For an entertaining fictional account of settler hostility toward colonial surveyors, see Pynchon, *Mason & Dixon.*

109. McIntosh was not unique among elite Indian leaders. Major Ridge, a pro-American Cherokee leader who fought alongside Jackson in the Creek War, owned a lucrative ferry landing on the Coosa River, and George Colbert, pro-American headman of the Chickasaws, owned several profitable businesses, including a ferry where the Natchez Trace crossed the Tennessee River. John R. Smith to Postmaster General John McLean, October 18, 1824, NARA, RG77, Letters Received, 1824–1831. According to one guidebook, Colbert's ferry netted $2,000 each year, largely owing to the travel of boatmen who had descended on the Mississippi River to New Orleans and returned to their homes in the Ohio Valley by land. The income from such an establishment was sturdily connected to both the booming flat-boat trade that made New Orleans the "Alexandria of America" and the influx of settlers who crowded the West. Brown, *Western Gazetteer*, 116, 123.

110. Green, *Politics of Indian Removal*, 45–68; Griffith, *McIntosh and Weatherford*, 195–211.

111. Thomas Stocks, "Memorandums taken on my Tour to Pensecola Commencing the 15 April 1819," Thomas Stocks Journal 1819, ADAH.

112. "Testimony of Hugh W. Ector, Sworn to and Subscribed before William H. Torrance, & William N. Williamson, Union County, Georgia, August 16, 1821," CIL, 3:952. Green has suggested that the Creeks who signed the treaty may have taken a calculated risk designed to preserve their place in the South. As he notes, the parcel ceded was nearly useless to the Creeks since squatters and American hunters trespassed there constantly and they may have relinquished it knowing that their most precious holdings were in the interior of the nation further west. Green asserts that agreeing to cede this dispensable land in 1821 must have sharpened the Creeks' resolve to cede nothing more, as evidenced in the passage of a law immediately following the treaty making further cessions punishable by death. Green, *Indian Removal*, 74–75.

113. Clark to John Quincy Adams, January 19, 1820; Clark to Adams, February 2, 1820; Clark to Generals John McIntosh, David Adams, Daniel Newnan, January 17, 1821; Clark to John C. Calhoun, February 8, 1821, all in Georgia, Office of the Governor, Letterbooks, 1786–1897, GDAH.

114. The chief complaint seems to have involved the location of the western treaty limits. Clark to Wilson Lumpkin, March 21, 1821, Georgia, Office of the Governor, Letterbooks, 1786–1897, GDAH.

115. Collins, "Notes and Documents," 266; Green, *Politics of Indian Removal*, 57–59; Griffith, *McIntosh and Weatherford*, 209.

116. For more on the McIntosh tavern, see Boatright, "McIntosh Inn."

117. Green, *Politics of Indian Removal*, 60–62.

118. Collins, "Notes and Documents," 269–70.

119. *Georgia Journal*, September 24, 1822; for word of improvements on the Federal Road, see *Montgomery Republican*, January 24, 1824.

120. For the price of provisions, see Israel Pickens to Mrs. Martha Pickens, January 7, 1817, Chiliab Smith Howe Papers, SHC; Darby, *Emigrant's Guide*, 38.

121. *Montgomery Republican*, March 20, 1824.

122. For instance, surveyor John Coffee recorded almost daily purchases of all sorts of supplies from local Indians while he was engaged in running the boundary lines of the upper tract of the Fort Jackson cession. Among other necessaries, he purchased sugar and coffee from "Honey's wife," whiskey from "the Bears Nest," and Pork from ."the Night Killer." Journal, January 10–16, 1817, John Coffee Papers, 1796–1887, ADAH. It is possible that these were Cherokee rather than Creek individuals since Coffee's surveys bordered disputed lands. The names certainly resemble other identifiable Cherokee names from the period.

123. Collins, "Notes and Documents," 253, 257, 262.

124. Andrew Jackson claimed that Mitchell had seized all the ferries in the Creek Nation prior to his dismissal as Creek agent and charged exorbitant fees. If true, Mitchell's departure may have occasioned a sort of free-for-all as ferries and perhaps bridges as well returned to Creek hands. Jackson quoted in Griffith, *McIntosh and Weatherford*, 199.

125. Clark to Calhoun, November 26, 1821; Troup to Calhoun, April 24, 1824, both in Georgia, Office of the Governor, Letterbooks, 1786–1897, GDAH.

126. *Cahawba Press and Alabama State Intelligencer*, November 22, 1824.

127. Little Prince, et al., "[Letter] 1824 Dec. 8 to the Commissioners," TCC, <http://dlg.galileo.usg.edu> (February 28, 2006).

128. Green, *Politics of Indian Removal*, 86–93.

129. McIntosh et al., "Memorial of the Creek Indians to be laid before the extra session Comd. to the Legislature, 23 May 1825," CIL, 3:1002–6.

130. Indeed, the treaty indicated that "the Chiefs of the Creek Towns have . . . expressed a willingness to emigrate beyond the Mississippi, *those of Tokaubatchee excepted*," (emphasis in original). Treaty with the Creeks, 1825, Kappler, *Indian Affairs: Laws and Treaties*, vol. 2, <http://digital.library.okstate.edu/kappler/Vol2/treaties/cre0214.htm> (January 10, 2009).

131. Wright, *Creeks and Seminoles*, 239.

132. Etomme Tustunnuggee, "Letter, 1825 Feb. 17, Milledgeville, [Georgia to] G[eorge]

M. Troup, Governor [of Georgia]," TCC, <http://dlg.galileo.usg.edu> (February 28, 2006).

133. Green, *Politics of Indian Removal*, 88.

134. Creek Delegation, "[Talk] 1825 Dec. 16, Washington [D.C., to the] Secretary of War," TCC, <http://dlg.galileo.usg.edu> (February 28, 2006).

135. Ibid. For a similar statement, see also Extract from Hopoithloyoholo in Gaines to Pickens, July 4, 1825, AYER.

136. Richard A. Blount, Journal, Georgia-Alabama Boundary Commission, July 9–17, 1826, 86, RBP.

137. Jane Hawkins, "Letter, 1825 May 3, Fayett[e] County, [Georgia to] Colo[nel] Duncan G. Campbell and Major James Meriwether, United States Commissioners, Watkinsville, Clarke C[oun]ty, G[eorgi]a," TCC, <http://dlg.galileo.usg.edu> (March 12, 2006).

138. Peggy and Susannah McIntosh, "Letter, 1825 May 3, Line Creek, Fayett[e] County, Georgia [to] Colo[nel] Duncan G. Campbell and Major James Meriwether, United States Commissioners, Watkinsville, Clarke C[oun]ty, G[eorgi]a," TCC, <http://dlg.galileo .usg.edu> (February 26, 2006); *Cahawba Press and Alabama State Intelligencer*, May 4, 1825.

139. William McIntosh, "Letter, 1825 Apr. 12, Lock,chau Talo-fau or Acre Town [to] Geo[rge] M. Troup, [Governor of Georgia], Milledgeville, Georgia," TCC, <http://dlg .galileo.usg.edu> (February 28, 2006). In the same collection, see also Etomme Tustun-nuggee, "Letter, 1825 Feb. 17."

140. *Cahawba Press and Alabama State Intelligencer*, May 4, 1825. Wright disagrees with the analysis common in American accounts of the execution that the Creeks were simply enacting a law. He writes, "Menawa and the angry warriors accompanying him were mad because McIntosh had sold their lands and they feared that diverse Muscogulges might soon lose virtually all of their eastern domain." Wright, *Creeks and Seminoles*, 240. It seems probable that both factors motivated McIntosh's executioners.

141. Green, *Politics of Indian Removal*, 150.

CHAPTER SIX

1. Troup, *Georgia and the General Government*, 9–10. See also *Southern Recorder*, September 13, 1828. An observer of Alabama development proclaimed, "In this age of canalling, Alabama has caught the spirit." Flint, *Condensed Geography*, 495.

2. *Georgia Journal*, November 14, 1826.

3. "Map of Reconnaissance Exhibiting the Country Between Washington and New Orleans with the Routes Examined in Reference to a Contemplated National Road Between These Two Cities, annexed to the reports of 1826 and 1828," 1828, NARA, RG77, Civil Works Map File.

4. Etheldred Williams to Postmaster General John McLean, n.d., NARA, RG77, Letters Received; "Memorial to the President of the United States [on the] National Road from the City of Washington to New-Orleans," February 3, 1825, NARA, RG77, Letters Received.

5. A. Rawlings to McLean, October 1, 1824; Vincent Bennet to [McLean?], October 2,

1824; David McNair to Major General Samuel Houston, November 29, 1824, all in NARA, RG77, Letters Received.

6. "Memorial to the President," February 3, 1825, and John Falconer to William Tell Poussin, December 21, 1825, in NARA, RG77, Letters Received.

7. Ball, *Slavery in the United States*, 52.

8. Crawford to Mitchell, August 24, 1817, AYER.

9. Treaty with the Creeks, 1827, Kappler, *Indian Affairs: Laws and Treaties*, vol. 2, <http://digital.library.okstate.edu/kappler/Vol2/treaties/cre0284.htm> (January 10, 2008). See also Blount, Journal, June 26–July 6, 1826, 13–15, and Journal, August 9–14, 1826, 135–40, both in RBP.

10. Montgomery, *Discourse*, 6–7.

11. Hutchins, *Historical Narrative*, 93–94.

12. *Alabama Republican*, April 18, 1818.

13. *Blakeley Sun, and Alabama Advertiser*, December 15, 1818.

14. *L'Ami de Lois et Journal du Soir*, March 17, 1818; *Clarion, & Tennessee State Gazette*, November 3, 1818; *Alabama Courier*, March 19, 1819; *Halcyon, and Tombeckbe Public Advertiser*, May 3, 1819. See also Blowe, *Geographical, Historical, Commercial and Agricultural View*, 113; Brown, *Western Gazetteer*, 223–24; Dana, *Geographical Sketches*, 26, 197; Miller, *New States and Territories*, 27–30.

15. Treaty with the Creeks, 1826, Kappler, *Indian Affairs: Laws and Treaties*, vol. 2, <http://digital.library.okstate.edu/kappler/Vol2/treaties/cre0264.htm> (April 23, 2006).

16. Ibid.

17. James Meriwether, "[Letter] 1826 Feb. 23, Washington, [D.C. to] G[eorge] M. Troup, [Governor of Georgia," TCC, <http://dlg.galileo.usg.edu> (March 15, 2006).

18. As Green has noted, Opothle Yaholo rose to prominence after Big Warrior's death in 1825, and with his political leadership the Creek National Council was strengthened and empowered again to act as the voice of the Nation. Green, *Politics of Indian Removal*, 108–9.

19. Along with Opothle Yaholo and a handful of other authorized Creek representatives, the delegation in Washington included the National Council's secretary, Cherokee John Ridge. The involvement of Cherokee delegates in the negotiation of this and the subsequent treaty (Treaty of Creek Agency, 1827) is discussed cogently in Green, *Politics of Indian Removal*, 111, 120, 124–25, 129–30, 132–39.

20. *Columbian Centinel*, May 5, 1826.

21. Troup, *Georgia and the General Government*, 16.

22. Ibid., 5.

23. Green particularly notes the role of General Edmund P. Gaines's involvement in the federal versus state wrangling over the Creek treaties. Gaines was sent by Adams to investigate Creek opposition to the original treaty, determine Crowell's role in the affair, and try to effect an understanding between the state and the federal government. Gaines was anything but welcome in Troup's eyes and soon came under attack, as did Crowell and other "meddlers" for standing in Georgia's way. Green, *Politics of Indian Removal*, 113–14.

24. Troup, *Georgia and the General Government*, 22.

25. John Murphy, "[Letter] 1826 May 29, Claiborne, [Alabama to] George M. Troup,

Governor of Georgia, Milledgeville, Georgia," TCC, <http://dlg.galileo.usg.edu> (April 12, 2006).

26. *Georgia Statesman*, May 2, 1826.

27. *Georgia Journal*, November 14, 1826.

28. For the precise treaty language, see Treaty with the Creeks, 1826, Kappler, *Indian Affairs: Laws and Treaties*, vol. 2, <http://digital.library.okstate.edu/kappler/Vol2/treaties/creo264.htm>.

29. Troup, *Georgia and the General Government*, 29.

30. Ibid., 23.

31. Eliza Goffe to Joseph Goffe, March 25, 1828, Joseph Goffe Papers, 1721–1846, American Antiquarian Society. The same year, British traveler Basil Hall remarked of his route in Georgia, "Our road . . . if road it ought to be called—lay through the heart of the forest, our course being pointed out solely by blazes, or slices, cut as guiding marks on the sides of the trees. It was really like navigating by means of the stars over the trackless ocean!" Hall, *Travels in North America*, 3:252.

32. John Rogers Vinton, "Journal of my Excursion to Georgia, & the Creek Nation—Also of my tour with Genl Brown through the Southern & Western borders," January 29–July 30, 1827, John Rogers Vinton Papers, 1814–1861, DU.

33. *Southern Recorder*, September 13, 1828.

34. See, for example, Sellers, *Market Revolution*, 60–68, 71–79.

35. Clayton, *Vindication of the Recent and Prevailing Policy*, 18. See also Troup to Calhoun, April 24, 1824, Georgia, Office of the Governor, Letterbooks, 1786–1897, GDAH.

36. *Columbian Centinel*, May 5, 1826. Clayton called Adams "a short lived and maddened freak of power." Clayton, *Vindication of the Recent and Prevailing Policy*, x.

37. Troup, *Georgia and the General Government*, 23.

38. An excerpt from a Fayetteville, North Carolina, newspaper reprinted in *Columbian Centinel*, June 30, 1826.

39. John Forsyth, "[Letter] 1826 June 15, Sand Hills, [Georgia]," TCC, <http://dlg.galileo.usg.edu> (April 1, 2006); See also Clayton, *Vindication of the Recent and Prevailing Policy*.

40. Blount, Journal, June 26–July 1826, 12, RBP.

41. See Georgia, House of Representatives, "Resolution, [regarding the running of the boundary line between Alabama and Georgia]," December 7, 1826, RBP.

42. Blount, Journal, July 9–17, 1826, 38, RBP.

43. Ibid.

44. General Alexander Ware, "Letter, 1825 July 11, Fort Troup, Fayette County, [Georgia] to George M. Troup, [Governor of Georgia], Milledgeville, G[eorgi]a," TCC, <http://dlg.galileo.usg.edu> (April 1, 2006); Blount, Journal, July 26–August 7, 1826, 90, RBP.

45. James Barbour, "[Letter] 1826 Sept. 16, Department of War, [Washington, D.C. to] George M. Troup, Gov[erno]r of Georgia," TCC, <http://dlg.galileo.usg.edu> (April 14, 2006).

46. For stoppages in Cherokee country, see "Extract of a letter from Hamilton Fulton, Esq. (State Engineer) to Governor Troup, dated Rossville, (Tenn.) 12 June, 1826," reprinted in *Augusta Chronicle and Georgia Gazette*, July 4, 1826; *Georgia Journal*, November 14, 1826.

47. Blount, Journal, July 9–17, 1826, 42, 49, RBP.

48. Blount reported with more than a little trepidation, "Altho' we had seen no human being, except one party, for a week the Indians had seen us frequently & cou'd tell him [Major Lewis] where we camp'd & had seen us on Sunday & knew our movements daily." Blount, Journal, July 26–August 7, 1826, 88, RBP.

49. Troup to the Georgia Commissioners, July 12, 1826, enclosed in Blount, Journal, July 26–August 7, 1826, 91, RBP.

50. Clayton, *Vindication of the Recent and Prevailing Policy*, 35.

51. See Essays No. 4 and No. 5 in Clayton, *Vindication*.

52. Blount, Journal, July 26–August 7, 1826, 115, RBP. It is unclear from Blount's journal whether this statement is his opinion or that of the old woman.

53. Ibid., 114.

54. See, for instance, Thomas Spalding, "[Letter] 1827 Mar. 12, Florida Line, to George M. Troup, Gov[ernor of Georgia], Milledgeville, G[eorgi]a"; Spalding, "[Letter] 1827 May 8, Milledgeville, [Georgia], to Ge[orge] M. Troup, Governor [of Georgia], Milledgeville, Georgia," both in TCC, <http://dlg.galileo.usg.edu> (March 18, 2006).

55. Blount, Journal, 1826, 32, 36, 40, 55, RBP.

56. Blount, Journal, July 9–17, 1826, 40–42, RBP.

57. Ibid.

58. Blount, Journal, September 14, 1826, 1, RBP.

59. Blount, Journal, July 9–17, 1826, 49, RBP. Such a strategy was typical in Cherokee Country as well. See entries for August 9–14, 1826, 129.

60. Blount, Journal, 1826, 41, 59, 101, 109, RBP.

61. Blount, Journal, July 26–August 7, 1826, 120, RBP. See also entries for August 7–9, 1826, 121.

62. Blount, Journal, July 9–17, 1826, 43, RBP.

63. Blount, "A Sketch of the Cherokee disposition towards running the boundary line of Georgia, thro' their Country," August 31, 1826, RBP.

64. Ibid.

65. Latour, *Historical Memoir of the War*, 9.

66. Flint, *Condensed Geography and History*, 1:491.

67. Howell Tatum, "Topographical notes and observations on the Alabama River," 1814–1815, BRBL.

68. *Georgia Journal*, July 14, 1828. Although ludicrous in its claims, this sort of promotional literature would be echoed again and again as American settlers pushed ever westward. In the midst of 1830s "Texas fever," for example, Mary Austin Holley wrote that the soil there "yields the fruit of nearly all latitudes, almost spontaneously, with a climate of perpetual summer." In the 1840s, claims about the great wealth available in the California Gold Rush would set a new bar for exaggeration in booster literature. Holley quoted in Hine and Faragher, *American West*, 168–69; for examples of the Gold Rush language, see 238.

69. Sellers, *Market Revolution*, 16.

70. Hall, *Travels in North America*, 197–98.

71. Ingraham, *South-West*, 233–34. See also Sellers, *Market Revolution*, 66. It is worth noting that at least some southerners were conflicted about the reliance on the slave system. See, for example, Nathan Hopkins to Aaron B. Olmstead, March 24, 1837, BRBL.

72. Treaty with the Creeks, 1827, Kappler, *Indian Affairs: Laws and Treaties*, vol. 2, <http://digital.library.okstate.edu/kappler/Vol2/treaties/cre0284.htm>.

73. For a detailed view of the controversy, from the perspective of the Georgia legislature, see U.S. Congress, House, *Proceedings of the Legislature of Georgia*, 1827, 727–862.

74. Green, *Politics of Indian Removal*, 101–3.

75. Vinton, "Journal of My Excursion to Georgia," January 29–July 30, 1827, John Rogers Vinton Papers, 1814–1861, DU.

76. Clayton, *Vindication of the Recent and Prevailing Policy*, 12.

77. Ibid., 13, 17. In an 1829 response to congressional rejection of Alabama's extension of state laws over the Creeks, Alabama state representative Dixon Lewis similarly argued, "If Congress can invade the jurisdiction of a State, and in any way extend or abridge the rights of individuals, what is to prevent its interference with the slave population of the southern states? If it can say to the state of Alabama, that Indians cannot be citizens, it can by a similar exercise of municipal power within its limits, say that Negroes shall not be slaves." Lewis, quoted in Green, *Politics of Indian Removal*, 147.

78. U.S. Congress, House, "Emigration of the Indians West of the Mississippi," 1827, 700.

79. Auguste Levasseur, *Lafayette in America in 1824 and 1825; or a Journal of a Voyage to the United States*, 1829, quoted in Benton, *Very Worst Road*, 19.

80. He distilled the philosophy further, adding, "There is enough of the love of property in most of the Indians in the States to induce them to prefer a government suited to their condition, as to the simple elements of which it would be composed; and to hold lands in severalty, in preference to the present, and, as many of them believe, very uncertain tenure by which they hold them at all." U.S. Congress, House, "Emigration of the Indians West of the Mississippi," 1827, 700.

81. Ibid.

82. Ibid.

83. Treaty with the Creeks, 1827, Kappler, *Indian Affairs: Laws and Treaties*, vol. 2, <http://digital.library.okstate.edu/kappler/Vol2/treaties/cre0284.htm>.

84. Thomas L. McKenney, "[Letter] 1826 Apr. 3, Department of War, Off[ice of] Indian Affairs, to Opothle Yoholo and other members of the Creek Delegation," "[Letter] of correspondence [promoting the] education of the Creek Indian Children," n.d., both in Keith Read Collection, HAR, <http://dlg.galileo.usg.edu> (March 15, 2006).

85. Mansfield Torrance, "[Letter], 1827 Jan. 7, Flint River [to] George M. Troup, [Governor of Georgia], Milledgeville, Georgia," TCC, <http://dlg.galileo.usg.edu> (March 16, 2006).

86. For an extended discussion of the importance of fences in the Creek Nation, see Saunt, *New Order*, 171–74.

87. See, for instance, Georgia Governor's Office, Executive Department, "A List of Persons who have lost property by the Creek Indians in [various counties, with sworn affidavits]," ICS.

88. Affidavit of Stephen Johnson and Benjamin Johnson, Baker County, Georgia, July 30, 1828, ICS.

89. Affidavit of John S. Scott, Baldwin County, Georgia, November 10, 1828, ICS.

90. Affidavit of William D. Lucas, Muscogee County, Georgia, August 18, 1828, ICS.

See also Affidavit of Slady Warren, Lee County, Georgia, July 9, 1828, and Affidavit of Stephen Johnson, Baker County, Georgia, July 29, 1828, both in ICS.

91. Affidavit of Hiram Chalfinch, Randolph County, Georgia, April 24, 1829, ICS.

92. Green, *Politics of Indian Removal*, 164, 166.

93. Flint, *Condensed Geography and History*, 1:157; Hamilton, *Men and Manners in America*, vol. 2, 1833, quoted in Benton, *Very Worst Road*, 71.

94. Royall, *Mrs. Royall's Southern Tour, or Second Series of the Black Book*, vol. 3, 1831, quoted in Benton, *Very Worst Road*, 64.

95. Levasseur, *Lafayette in America*, quoted in Benton, *Very Worst Road*, 21.

96. Bernard, Duke of Saxe-Weimar-Eisenach, *Travels through North America during the Years 1825 and 1826*, vol. 2, 1828, quoted in Benton, *Very Worst Road*, 27.

97. This was especially true among the Lower Creeks, who had always been physically closer to American settlements and had accepted the new economy more readily than their brethren in the Upper towns. See Green, *Politics of Indian Removal*, 150–51.

98. Haas, "Creek Inter-Town Relations," 479–89; Hewitt, "Notes on the Creek Indians," 153; Mooney, "Cherokee Ball Play"; Swanton, *Social Organization and Social Usages*, 461–63.

99. Hall, *Travels in North America*, 289–91.

EPILOGUE

1. *Augusta Chronicle and Georgia Advertiser*, March 27, 1830.

2. Hall, *Forty Etchings*, unnumbered page facing Plates nos. XXV and XXVI.

3. The Columbus, Georgia, Convention and Visitors Bureau describes the city thus: "Columbus is ideally located where five major highways intersect." "Columbus at a Glance," <http://www.visitcolumbusga.com/about.aspx?id=664> (December 17, 2008).

4. As evidence of how radically Jackson understated American Indian populations east of the Mississippi, the Creeks in Alabama alone numbered approximately 15,000. Green, *Politics of Indian Removal*, 181.

5. Jackson, *On Indian Removal*, December 6, 1830; see also Robert H. Adams, *Speech of Mr. Adams, of Mississippi: On the Bill to Remove the Indians West of the Mississippi*, 1830, SENADD, HAR, <http://dlg.galileo.usg.edu> (December 16, 2006).

6. On Turner and his frontier thesis, see Billington, *Frederick Jackson Turner*; Bogue, *Frederick Jackson Turner*; Frederick Jackson Turner, *Frontier in American History*; Turner, *Rereading Frederick Jackson Turner*.

7. On Indian Removal as a movement, its supporters and opponents, and the Cherokee cases in particular, see Conser, "John Ross and the Cherokee Resistance Campaign, 1833–1838"; Everett, *Conduct of the Administration*; Foreman, *Indian Removal*; Hershberger, "Mobilizing Women, Anticipating Abolition"; McLoughlin, *Cherokee Renascence in the New Republic*; Rogin, *Fathers and Children*; Satz, *American Indian Policy in the Jacksonian Era*; Wallace, *Long, Bitter Trail*; Young, "Indian Removal and Land Allotment."

8. John Davis to William Walker, February 14, 1828, quoted in Green, *Politics of Indian Removal*, 151.

9. William Moor to Eneah Micco and others, December 6, 1831, quoted in Green, *Politics of Indian Removal*, 169; "Memorial of the Creek Nation of Indians, January 17,

1832," 22nd Cong., 1st Sess., SENADD, HAR <http://dlg.usg.galileo.edu> (January 5, 2007). The situation was much the same in Cherokee country. See, for example, N. L. Hutchins to George R. Gilmer, February 1, 1831, in *Passports Issued by Governors of Georgia*, 30. For more on the frauds following Creek allotment, see Young, *Redskins, Ruffle-shirts, and Rednecks*.

10. Green, *Politics of Indian Removal* 169.

11. Chaudhuri and Chaudhuri, *Sacred Path*, 148; Green, *Politics of Indian Removal*, 170–73.

12. Treaty with the Creeks, 1832, Kappler, *Indian Affairs: Laws and Treaties*, vol. 2, <http://digital.library.okstate.edu/kappler/vol2/treaties/cre0341.htm> (January 10, 2009).

13. Chaudhuri and Chaudhuri, *Sacred Path*, 148.

14. Hurt, "Defining American Homelands," 25.

15. Litton, "Journal of a Party of Emigrating Creek Indians, 1835–1836," 228, 229n13–14.

16. Hurt, "Defining American Homelands," 25–26.

17. Treaty of Fort Laramie with the Sioux, Etc., 1851, Kappler, *Indian Affairs: Laws and Treaties*, vol. 2, <http://digital.library.okstate.edu/KAPPLER/VOL2/treaties/sio0594.htm> (December 16, 2008); Hine and Faragher, *American West*, 251; Utley and Washburn, *Indian Wars*, 167, 171. The 1868 Treaty of Fort Laramie, long seen as marking the beginning of the reservation era, contained even more explicit language about the importance of American mobility. Among the many transformative provisions codified in the document was Article 11: "They [the Sioux and Arapaho] withdraw all pretence of opposition to the construction of the railroad now being built . . . and they will not in future object to the construction of railroads, wagon-roads, mail-stations, or other works of utility or necessity, which may be ordered or permitted by the laws of the United States." While the situation in Sioux country was clearly distinct from that of Creek country some sixty years earlier, the similarity of American concerns for the safety of travelers, the economic progress of the nation, and the expansion of interstate and inter-territorial communication is certainly worthy of note. Treaty with the Sioux—Brulé, Oglala, Miniconjou, Yanktonai, Hunkpapa, Blackfeet, Cuthead, Two Kettle, Sans Arc, and Santee—and Arapaho, 1868, Kappler, *Indian Affairs: Laws and Treaties*, vol. 2, <http://digital.library.okstate.edu/Kappler/Vol2/treaties/sio0998.htm> (December 16, 2008).

Bibliography

MANUSCRIPT AND MAP COLLECTIONS

Athens, Ga.
  Hargrett Rare Book and Manuscript Library, University of Georgia
      Diary of Samuel Edward Butler, 1784–1786
      Cobb / Lamar / Erwin Collection
      Telamon Cuyler Collection
      Keith Read Collection
      C. Mildred Thompson Collection
      James Wright Collection
      Joseph Wheaton Papers
Chapel Hill, N.C.
  Southern Historical Collection, University of North Carolina
      Bryan and Leventhorpe Family Papers
      Farish Carter Papers
      Thomas Crawford Papers
      Jesse Franklin Treaty Papers
      Augustin Harris Hansell Memoirs
      Chiliab Smith Howe Papers
      Lenoir Family Papers
      Andrew McCauley Papers
      Francis G. Ruffin Papers
Chicago, Ill.
  Newberry Library
      Edward E. Ayer Collection
      Franco Novacco Map Collection
      Graff Collection
      Karpinski Photostats
College Park, Md.
  National Archives and Records Administration
      Records of the Office of the Chief of Engineers, Records of the Board on Internal
        Improvements, Record Group 77, Letters Received, 1824–31, Entry 216, 217,
        Civil Works Map File, 1800–1947, and Treasure File
Durham, N.C.
  Duke University, Special Collections Library

David Henley Papers, 1791–1800
Ephraim Kirby Papers, 1763–1879
Thomas Pinckney Papers, 1771–1818
John Rogers Vinton Papers, 1814–1861
Knoxville, Tenn.
Tennessee State Library and Archives
Governor Sevier Papers
Tennessee Historical Society Collection
Hoskins Special Collections Library, University of Tennessee
Penelope Johnson Allen Collection
Montgomery, Ala.
Alabama Department of Archives and History
Alabama Territory Records
Richard A. Blount Papers, 1792–1861
Joseph Carson Letter, 1813
John Coffee Papers, 1796–1887
Creek War Military Records, 1813–ca. 1820
The Deposition of Samuel Manac, August 2, 1813
Mississippi (Territory): Correspondence (Judge Toulmin's Letters, ca. 1810–1816)
Pickens Family Papers, 1799–1855
Thomas Stocks Journal, 1819
Tait Family Papers
Harry Toulmin Letters, 1813–1818
Morrow, Ga.
Georgia Department of Archives and History
"Creek Indian Letters, Talks & Treaties," 1705–1829, Parts 1–3, Typescript,
Louise Caroline Frederick Hays, compiler
Georgia Surveyor General Department, Maps
Georgia, Office of the Governor, Letterbooks, 1786–1897
Indian Claims & Spoliations, 1-1-25
Thomas Stocks Surveying Diary, 1818.
"Unpublished Letters of Timothy Barnard, 1784–1820," Typescript,
Louise Caroline Frederick Hays, compiler
New Haven, Conn.
Beinecke Rare Book and Manuscript Library, Yale University
General Manuscript Collection
Yale Collection of Western Americana
Washington, D.C.
National Archives and Records Administration
Records of the Bureau of Indian Affairs, Letters Received by the Office of the
Secretary of War Relating to Indian Affairs, 1800–23, Record Group 75,
Microcopy 271
Records of the Bureau of Indian Affairs, Letters Sent by the Office of the
Secretary of War Relating to Indian Affairs, 1800–24, Record Group 75,
Microcopy 15

Records of the Office of the Postmaster, Letters Sent, Record Group 28,
    Microcopy 601
Worcester, Mass.
  American Antiquarian Society
    Gilman Family Papers, 1809–1888
    Joseph Goffe Papers, 1721–1846
    Louisiana Collection Papers, 1779–1937

NEWSPAPERS

All of the following newspapers were consulted at the American Antiquarian Society,
    Worcester, Mass.

Alabama Courier (Claiborne, Ala.)
Alabama Journal (Montgomery, Ala.)
Alabama Republican (Huntsville, Ala.)
Augusta Chronicle (Augusta, Ga.)
Augusta Chronicle and Georgia Gazette (Augusta, Ga.)
Baton-Rouge Gazette (Baton Rouge, La.)
Blakeley Sun, and Alabama Advertiser (Blakeley, Ala.)
Cahawba Press and Alabama State Intelligencer (Cahawba, Ala.)
Clarion, & Tennessee State Gazette (Nashville, Tenn.)
Columbian Centinel (Athens, Ga.)
Columbian Centinel (Augusta, Ga.)
Courier de la Louisiane (New Orleans, La.)
Courier pour la Campagne (New Orleans, La.)
Georgia Argus (Milledgeville, Ga.)
Georgia Journal (Milledgeville, Ga.)
Georgia Patriot (Milledgeville, Ga.)
Georgia Statesman (Milledgeville, Ga.)
Halcyon, and Tombeckbe Public Advertiser (St. Stephens, Ala.)
Hampshire Federalist (Springfield, Mass.)
Knoxville Register (Knoxville, Tenn.)
L'Ami de Lois et Journal du Soir (New Orleans, La.)
Louisiana Gazette (New Orleans, La.)
Louisiana Gazette and New Orleans Advertiser [Weekly Edition] (New Orleans, La.)
Louisiana Gazette for the Country (New Orleans, La.)
Louisiana Rambler (Alexandria, La.)
Madison Gazette (Huntsville, Ala.)
Monitor (Washington, Ga.)
Montgomery Republican (Montgomery, Ala.)
Nashville Examiner (Nashville, Tenn.)
New Orleans Chronicle (New Orleans, La.)
New-York Commercial Advertiser (New York, N.Y.)
Orleans Gazette for the Country (New Orleans, La.)
The Orleans Gazette; and Commercial Advertiser (New Orleans, La.)

Poulson's American Daily Advertiser (Philadelphia, Pa.)
Reflector (Milledgeville, Ga.)
Savannah Daily Republican (Savannah, Ga.)
Southern Centinel and Gazette of the State (Augusta, Ga.)
Southern Recorder (Milledgeville, Ga.)
Telegraphe Louisianais and Mercantile Advertiser (New Orleans, La.)
Union (New Orleans, La.)
Wilson's Knoxville Gazette (Knoxville, Tenn.)

PUBLISHED BOOKS AND ARTICLES

Acts of the General Assembly of the State of Georgia, passed at Milledgeville, at an annual session in November and December, 1818. Milledgeville, Ga.: S. and F. Grantland, 1818.

Adair, James. *The History of the American Indians.* 1775. Ed. Kathryn E. Holland Braund. Tuscaloosa: University of Alabama Press, 2005.

Adelman, Jeremy, and Stephen Aron. "From Borderlands to Borders: Empires, Nation-State, and the Peoples in between in North American History." *American Historical Review* 104:3 (1999): 814–41.

Albers, Patricia, and Jeanne Kay. "Sharing the Land: A Study in American Indian Territoriality." In *A Cultural Geography of North American Indians,* ed. Thomas E. Ross and Tyrel G. Moore, 47–91. Boulder, Colo.: Westview Press, 1987.

Austill, Margaret Ervin. "Memories of Journeying through Creek County and Childhood in Clarke County, 1811–1814." *Alabama Historical Quarterly* 6:1 (1944): 92–93.

Ball, Charles. *Fifty Years in Chains; or, The Life of an American Slave.* New York: H. Dayton, Publisher, 1859. <http://docsouth.unc.edu/fpn/ball/menu.html>. March 15, 2006.

———. *Slavery in the United States.* New York: John S. Taylor, 1837. <http://docsouth.unc.edu/neh/ballslavery/menu.html>. March 15, 2006.

Ball, T. H. *A Glance into the Great South-east, or Clarke County, Alabama and Its Surroundings, from 1540–1877.* Chicago: Knight and Leonard, 1882.

Barber, Eunice. *Narrative of the Tragical Death of Mr. Darius Barber, and His Seven Children, Who Were Inhumanely Butchered by the Indians, in Camden County, Georgia, January 26, 1818.* Boston: David Hazen, 1818.

Baronet, Sir William Talbot. Dedicatory epistle preceding *The Discoveries of John Lederer, in Three Several Marches from Virginia, to the West of Carolina, and Other Parts of the Continent: Begun in March 1669, and Ended in September 1670.* London: J. C. for Samuel Heyrick, 1672.

Bartram, William. *Observations on the Creek and Cherokee Indians.* 1789. In *A Creek Source Book,* ed. William C. Sturtevant, 386–415. New York: Garland Publishing, 1987.

———. *The Travels of William Bartram: Naturalist's Edition.* Ed. Francis Harper. 1958. Reprint, Athens: University of Georgia Press, 1998.

Basso, Keith. *Wisdom Sits in Places: Landscape and Language among the Western Apache.* Albuquerque: University of New Mexico Press, 1996.

Benn, Carl. *The Iroquois in the War of 1812*. Toronto: University of Toronto Press, 1998.

Benton, Jeffrey C., ed. *The Very Worst Road: Travellers' Accounts of Crossing Alabama's Old Creek Indian Territory, 1820–1847*. Eufaula, Ala.: Historic Chattahoochee Commission, 1998.

Berlin, Ira. *Many Thousands Gone: The First Two Centuries of Slavery in North America*. Cambridge, Mass.: Harvard University Press, 1998.

Billington, Ray Allen. *Frederick Jackson Turner: Historian, Scholar, Teacher*. New York: Oxford University Press, 1973.

Bishop, Abraham. *Georgia Speculation Unveiled: In Two Numbers*. Hartford: Elisha Babcock, 1797.

Blassingame, John. *The Slave Community: Plantation Life in the Antebellum South*. New York: Oxford University Press, 1972.

——. "Using the Testimony of Ex-Slaves: Approaches and Problems." *Journal of Southern History* 41:4 (1975): 473–92.

Blowe, Daniel. *A Geographical, Historical, Commercial and Agricultural View of the United States of America; Forming a Complete Emigrant's Directory Through Every Part of the Republic*. London: Edwards and Knibb; Liverpool: W. Grapel, 1820.

Boatright, Sherry L. "The McIntosh Inn and Its Place in Creek Indian History." Atlanta: State of Georgia, Department of Natural Resources, Office of Planning and Research, Historic Preservation Section, 1976.

Bogue, Allan G. *Frederick Jackson Turner: Strange Roads Going Down*. Norman: University of Oklahoma Press, 1998.

Bossu, M. *Travels through That Part of North America Formerly Called Louisiana. By Mr. Bossu, Captain in the French Marines*. London: T. Davies, 1771.

Braund, Kathryn E. Holland. *Deerskins and Duffels: The Creek Indian Trade with Anglo-America*. Lincoln: University of Nebraska Press, 1993.

Bridges, Edwin. "To Establish a Separate and Independent Government." *Furman Review* 5 (1974): 11–17.

Brown, Samuel. *The Western Gazetteer; or Emigrant's Directory, Containing a Geographical Description of the Western States and Territories*. Auburn, N.Y.: H. C. Southwick, 1817.

Buckingham, James. *The Slave States of America*. 2 vols. London: Fisher, Son and Company, 1842.

Burckhard, Johann Christian, and Karsten Petersen. *Partners in the Lord's Work: The Diary of Two Moravian Missionaries in the Creek Indian Country, 1807–1813*. Trans. and ed. Carl Maulshagen and Gerald H. Davis. Research Paper Number 21. Atlanta: School of Arts and Sciences Research Papers, Georgia State College, 1969.

Buttrick, Tilly. *Buttrick's Voyages, Travels, and Discoveries, 1812–1819*. In *Early Western Travels, 1748–1846*, Vol. 8, ed. Reuben Gold Thwaites, 19–95. Cleveland: The A. H. Clark Company, 1904.

Calloway, Colin G. *The American Revolution in Indian Country: Crisis and Diversity in Native American Communities*. New York: Cambridge University Press, 1995.

——. "The Continuing Revolution in Indian Country." In *Native Americans and the Early Republic*, ed. Frederick E. Hoxie, Ronald Hoffman, and Peter J. Albert, 3–33. Charlottesville: University Press of Virginia, 1999.

Carson, James Taylor. "Ethnogeography and the Native American Past." *Ethnohistory* 49:4 (2002): 769–88.

———. *Searching for the Bright Path: The Mississippi Choctaws from Prehistory to Removal.* Lincoln: University of Nebraska Press, 1999.

Carter, Clarence, ed. *The Territorial Papers of the United States.* 28 vols. Washington, D.C.: Government Printing Office, 1934.

Carter, Paul. *The Road to Botany Bay: An Exploration of Landscape and History.* Chicago: University of Chicago Press, 1989.

Casey, Edward S. "How to Get from Space to Place in a Fairly Short Stretch of Time: Phenomenological Prolegomena." In *Senses of Place,* ed. Steven Feld and Keith Basso, 13–52. Santa Fe: School of American Research, 1996.

Castelnau, Francis de. *Vues et souvenirs de l'Amérique du Nord.* Paris: A. Bertrand, 1842.

Caughey, John Walton. *McGillivray of the Creeks.* Norman: University of Oklahoma Press, 1938.

Champagne, Duane. *Social Order and Political Change: Constitutional Governments among the Cherokee, the Choctaw, the Chickasaw, and the Creek.* Stanford: Stanford University Press, 1992.

Chaudhuri, Jean, and Joyotpaul Chaudhuri. *A Sacred Path: The Way of the Muscogee Creeks.* Los Angeles: UCLA American Indian Studies Center, 2001.

Clark, Thomas D., and John D. W. Guice. *Frontiers in Conflict: The Old Southwest, 1795–1830.* Albuquerque: University of New Mexico Press, 1989.

Clayton, Augustin S. *A Vindication of the Recent and Prevailing Policy of the State of Georgia, Both in Reference to Its Internal Affairs, and Its Relation with the General Government.* Athens, Ga.: O. P. Shaw, 1827.

Coker, William S., and Thomas D. Watson. *Indian Traders of the Southeastern Spanish Borderlands: Panton, Leslie & Company and John Forbes & Company, 1783–1847.* Pensacola: University of West Florida Press, 1986.

Colles, Christopher. *A Survey of the Roads of the United States of America.* New York: s.n., 1789.

Collins, Robert P. "Notes and Documents: A Swiss Traveler in the Creek Nation: The Diary of Lukas Vischer, March 1824." *Alabama Review* 59 (2006): 243–84.

"Columbus at a Glance." <http://www.visitcolumbusga.com/about.aspx?id=664>. December 17, 2008.

Conser, Walter H., Jr. "John Ross and the Cherokee Resistance Campaign, 1833–1838." *Journal of Southern History* 44:2 (1978): 191–212.

Cooper, William J., Jr., and Thomas E. Terrill. *The American South: A History.* Vol. 1. 2nd ed. New York: McGraw-Hill, 1996.

Corkran, David. *The Creek Frontier, 1540–1783.* Norman: University of Oklahoma Press, 1967.

Craib, Raymond B. *Cartographic Mexico: A History of State Fixations and Fugitive Landscapes.* Durham, N.C.: Duke University Press, 2004.

Crane, Verner. *The Southern Frontier, 1670–1732.* 1928. Reprint, New York: W. W. Norton, 1981.

———. "The Tennessee River as the Road to Carolina: The Beginnings of Exploration and Trade." *Mississippi Valley Historical Review* 3:1 (1916): 3–18.

Dana, Edmund P. *Geographical Sketches on the Western Country*. Cincinnati: Looker, Reynolds and Company Printers, 1819.

Darby, William. *The Emigrant's Guide to the Western and Southwestern States and Territories*. New York: Kirk and Mercein, 1818.

Davidson, Victor. "Governor John Milledge." In *Correspondence of John Milledge, Governor of Georgia, 1802–1806*, ed. Harriet Milledge Salley, 7–18. Columbia, S.C.: State Commercial Printing Company, 1949.

Davis, Karl. "'Much of the Indian Appears': Adaptation and Persistence in a Creek Community, 1783–1854." Ph.D. diss., University of North Carolina, 2003.

Davis, William C. *A Way through the Wilderness: The Natchez Trace and the Civilization of the Southern Frontier*. New York: HarperCollins, 1995.

Deloria, Vine, Jr. *God Is Red: A Native View of Religion*. 1973. Reprint, Golden, Colo.: Fulcrum Publishing, 1994.

De Rosier, Arthur H., Jr. *The Removal of the Choctaw Indians*. Knoxville: University of Tennessee Press, 1970.

De Vorsey, Louis. *The Indian Boundary in the Southern Colonies, 1763–1775*. Chapel Hill: University of North Carolina Press, 1961.

———. "Indian Trails." *New Georgia Encyclopedia*. <http://www.georgiaencyclopedia .org/>. March 15, 2006.

Dobbs, Arthur. *An Account of the Countries Adjoining to Hudson's Bay, in the North-West Part of America*. London: J. Robinson, 1744.

Dowd, Gregory. *A Spirited Resistance: The North American Indian Struggle for Unity, 1745–1815*. Baltimore: Johns Hopkins University Press, 1992.

Downes, Randolph C. "Creek-American Relations, 1790–1795." *Journal of Southern History* 8:3 (1942): 350–73.

Drinnon, Richard. *Facing West: The Metaphysics of Indian-Hating and Empire-Building*. Minneapolis: University of Minnesota Press, 1980.

Dubois, Laurent. *Avengers of the New World: The Story of the Haitian Revolution*. Cambridge, Mass.: Harvard University Press, 2004.

Eaton, John Henry. *The Life of Andrew Jackson*. Philadelphia: M. Carey and Son, 1817.

Edmunds, R. David. *The Shawnee Prophet*. Lincoln: University of Nebraska Press, 1983.

Ellicott, Andrew. *The Journal of Andrew Ellicott*. Philadelphia: Budd and Bartram, 1803.

Ethridge, Robbie. *Creek Country: The Creek Indians and Their World*. Chapel Hill: University of North Carolina Press, 2003.

Evans, E. Raymond. "Highways to Progress: Nineteenth Century Roads in the Cherokee Nation." *Journal of Cherokee Studies* (Fall 1977): 394–400.

Everett, Alexander H. *The Conduct of the Administration*. Boston: Stimpson and Class, 1832.

Faery, Rebecca Blevins. *Cartographies of Desire: Captivity, Race, and Sex in the Shaping of an American Nation*. Norman: University of Oklahoma Press, 1999.

Finkelman, Paul. *Slavery and the Founders: Race and Liberty in the Age of Jefferson*. Armonk, N.Y.: M. E. Sharpe, 1996.

Flint, Timothy. *A Condensed Geography and History of the Western States, or the Mississippi Valley*. Vol. 1. Cincinnati: E. H. Flint, 1828.

Foreman, Grant. *Indian Removal: The Emigration of the Five Civilized Tribes of Indians*. Norman: University of Oklahoma Press, 1972.

Foster, H. Thomas, II. *Archaeology of the Lower Muskogee Creek Indians, 1715–1836.* Tuscaloosa: University of Alabama Press, 2007.

——, ed. *The Collected Works of Benjamin Hawkins, 1796–1810.* Tuscaloosa: University of Alabama Press, 2003.

Frank, Andrew K. *Creeks and Southerners: Biculturalism on the Early American Frontier.* Lincoln: University of Nebraska Press, 2005.

Franklin, John Hope, and Loren Schweninger. *Runaway Slaves: Rebels on the Plantation.* New York: Oxford University Press, 1999.

Fredrickson, George M., and Christopher Lasch. "Resistance to Slavery." *Civil War History* 13 (1967): 315–29.

Friend, Craig Thompson. *Along the Maysville Road: The Early American Republic in the Trans-Appalachian West.* Knoxville: University of Tennessee Press, 2005.

Frontier Claims in the Lower South: Records of Claims Filed by Citizens of the Alabama and Tombigbee River Settlements in the Mississippi Territory for Depredations by the Creek Indians during the War of 1812. Ed. Richard S. Lackey. New Orleans: Polyanthos, 1977.

Gallay, Allan. *The Indian Slave Trade: The Rise of the English Empire in the American South, 1670–1717.* New Haven, Conn.: Yale University Press, 2002.

Galloway, Patricia. "A Storied Land: Choctaw Place-Names and the Emplotment of Land Use." In *Practicing Ethnohistory: Mining Archives, Hearing Testimony, Constructing Narrative.* Lincoln: University of Nebraska Press, 2006.

Gara, Larry. *The Liberty Line: The Legend of the Underground Railroad.* Lexington: University Press of Kentucky, 1967.

Gatschet, Albert S. *A Migration Legend of the Creek Indians.* 1884. Reprint, New York: AMS Press, 1969.

——. "Towns and Villages of the Creek Confederacy in the XVIII and XIX Centuries." 1901. In *A Creek Source Book,* ed. William C. Sturtevant. New York: Garland Publishing, 1987.

Genovese, Eugene. *Roll Jordan Roll: The World the Slaves Made.* New York: Pantheon Books, 1974.

Goetzmann, William H. *Exploration and Empire: The Explorer and the Scientist in the Winning of the American West.* Austin: Texas State Historical Association, 1993.

Goff, John H. "Cow Punching in Old Georgia." *Two Articles Relating to the Economic History of Georgia.* Studies in Business and Economics, 5. Atlanta: Emory University, School of Business Administration, 1950. 16–23.

——. "Retracing the Old Federal Road." *Two Articles Relating to the Economic History of Georgia.* Studies in Business and Economics, 5. Atlanta: Emory University, School of Business Administration, 1950. 3–15.

——. "Some Old Road Names in Georgia." In *Placenames of Georgia: Essays of John H. Goff,* ed. Francis Lee Utley and Marion R. Hemperley, 388–98. Athens: University of Georgia Press, 1975.

Goodman, Warren H. "The Origins of the War of 1812: A Survey of Changing Interpretations." *Mississippi Valley Historical Review* 27 (1941): 171–86.

Goodrich, Carter. *Government Promotion of American Canals and Railroads, 1800–1890.* New York: Columbia University Press, 1960.

Grantham, Bill. *Creation Myths and Legends of the Creek Indians*. Gainesville: University Press of Florida, 2002.

Green, Michael D. *The Politics of Indian Removal: Creek Government and Society in Crisis*. Lincoln: University of Nebraska Press, 1982.

Griffith, Benjamin W., Jr. *McIntosh and Weatherford, Creek Indian Leaders*. Tuscaloosa: University of Alabama Press, 1988.

Grimes, William. *Life of William Grimes, the Runaway Slave*. New York: s.n., 1825. Documenting the American South. <http://docsouth.unc.edu/neh/grimes25/grimes25.html>. March 16, 2006.

Gutman, Herbert S. *The Black Family in Slavery and Freedom, 1750–1925*. New York: Vintage Books, 1976.

Haas, Mary R. "Creek Inter-Town Relations." *American Anthropologist* New Series 42:3.1 (1940): 479–89.

Hahn, Steven C. "The Cussita Migration Legend: History, Ideology, & the Politics of Mythmaking." In *Light on the Path: The Anthropology and History of the Southeastern Indians*, ed. Thomas J. Pluckhahn and Robbie Ethridge, 57–93. Tuscaloosa: University of Alabama Press, 2006.

——. *The Invention of the Creek Nation: 1670–1763*. Lincoln: University of Nebraska Press, 2004.

Halbert, H. S., and T. H. Ball. *The Creek War of 1813 and 1814*. Chicago: Donohue and Henneberry, 1895.

Hall, Basil. *Forty Etchings, from Sketches Made with the Camera Lucida, in North America, in 1827 and 1828*. 4th ed. Edinburgh: Cadell and Company, 1830.

——. *Travels in North America, in the Years 1827 and 1828*. Vol. 3. Edinburgh: Cadell and Company; London: Simpkin and Marshall, 1829.

Hammond, John Craig. *Slavery, Freedom, and Expansion in the Early American West*. Charlottesville: University Press of Virginia, 2007.

Hare, Joseph. *Confession of One of the Mail Robbers, Joseph Hare, Alias Joseph Thompson Hare, and According to His Own Narrative the Greatest Robber That Ever Lived*. Philadelphia: Printed for the Publisher, 1818.

Harris, William Tell. *Remarks Made during a Tour through the United States of America, in the Years 1817, 1818 and 1819*. Liverpool: Henry Fisher, 1819.

Hatley, M. Thomas. *The Dividing Paths: Cherokees and South Carolinians through the Era of Revolution*. New York: Oxford University Press, 1993.

Hawkins, Benjamin. *Letters, Journals and Writings of Benjamin Hawkins*. 2 vols. Ed. C. L. Grant. Savannah: Beehive Press, 1980.

Haywood, John. *The Natural and Aboriginal History of Tennessee*. Nashville: George Wilson, 1823.

Henri, Florette. *The Southern Indians and Benjamin Hawkins, 1796–1816*. Norman: University of Oklahoma Press, 1986.

Hershberger, Mary. "Mobilizing Women, Anticipating Abolition: The Struggle against Indian Removal in the 1830s." *Journal of American History* 86:1 (1999): 15–40.

Hewitt, J. N. B. "Notes on the Creek Indians." Ed. John R. Swanton, Bureau of American Ethnology Bulletin, no. 123, 119–59. Washington, D.C.: Government Printing Office, 1939. Reprinted in *A Creek Source Book*, ed. William C. Sturtevant. New York: Garland Publishing, 1987.

Hickey, Donald. *The War of 1812: A Forgotten Conflict*. Urbana: University of Illinois Press, 1989.

Hill, Susan. "One Village Has Been Made: The 19th Century Consolidation of the Grand River Community." Lecture delivered at Yale University, October 11, 2006.

Hine, Robert V., and John M. Faragher. *The American West: A New Interpretive History*. New Haven, Conn.: Yale University Press, 2000.

Hoffman, Paul E. "Lucas Vázquez de Allyón's Discovery and Colony." In *The Forgotten Centuries: Indians and Europeans in the American South, 1521–1704*, ed. Charles Hudson and Carmen Chaves Tesser, 36–49. Athens: University of Georgia Press, 1994.

Horsman, Reginald. "Western War Aims, 1811–1812." *Indiana Magazine of History* 52 (1957): 1–16.

Huber, Peter B. "Anggor Floods: Reflections on Ethnogeography and Mental Maps." *Geographical Review* 69:2 (1979): 127–39.

Hudson, Charles. *The Southeastern Indians*. Knoxville: University of Tennessee Press, 1976.

——, and Carmen Chaves Tesser, eds. *The Forgotten Centuries: Indians and Europeans in the American South, 1521–1704*. Athens: University of Georgia Press, 1994.

Hulbert, Archer B., ed. *The Crown Collection of Photographs of American Maps*. Series 1. Vol. 5. London: Colonial Office Library, 1907.

——. *The Crown Collection of Photographs of American Maps*. Series 3. Vol. 1. London: Colonial Office Library, 1914.

——. *The Old National Road: A Chapter of American Expansion*. Columbus, Oh.: F. J. Heer, 1901.

Hurt, Douglas A. "Defining American Homelands: A Creek Nation Example, 1828–1907." *Journal of Cultural Geography* 21:1 (2003): 19–43.

Hutchins, Thomas. *An Historical Narrative and Topographical Description of Louisiana and West-Florida*. Philadelphia: privately printed, 1784.

Ingraham, J. H. *The South-West. By a Yankee*. No. 1. New York: Harper and Brothers, 1835.

Jackson, Andrew. *On Indian Removal*. December 6, 1830. Records of the United States Senate, 1789–1990. <http://www.ourdocuments.gov/doc.php?flash=true&doc=25&page=transcript>. December 15, 2006.

Jacobs, Wilbur R. "Wampum: The Protocol of Indian Diplomacy." *William and Mary Quarterly*, 3rd Ser., 6:4 (1949): 596–604.

Jefferson, Thomas. *Message and Communication from the President of the United States to the Senate and House of Representatives; Delivered on the Commencement of the First Session of the Seventh Congress. The 8th of December, 1801. With Accompanying Documents*. Washington, D.C.: Samuel Harrison Smith, 1801.

——. *Message from the President Communicating Information in Part, on the Subject of a Post Road, from the City of Washington to New Orleans. In Pursuance of a Resolution of the House of the 31st of December Last*. Washington, D.C.: William Duane and Son, 1805.

——. *Message of President Jefferson, communicated on Tuesday, December 3, 1805*. 9th Cong., 1st sess., 1805. In *American State Papers, 1789–1838*. <http://infoweb.newsbank.com>. March 2, 2006.

Jennings, Francis. *The Ambiguous Iroquois Empire: The Covenant Chain Confederation of Indian Tribes with English Colonies from Its Beginnings to the Lancaster Treaty of 1744.* New York: W. W. Norton, 1984.

John, Richard. *Spreading the News: The American Postal System from Franklin to Morse.* Cambridge, Mass.: Harvard University Press, 1995.

Johnson, Walter. *Soul by Soul: Life in the Antebellum Slave Market.* Cambridge, Mass.: Harvard University Press, 1999.

Jordan, Winthrop. *White over Black: American Attitudes toward the Negro, 1550–1812.* Chapel Hill: University of North Carolina Press, 1968.

Kain, Roger J. P., and Elizabeth Baigent. *The Cadastral Map in the Service of the State.* Chicago: University of Chicago Press, 1992.

Kappler, J., ed. *Indian Affairs: Laws and Treaties.* Vol. 2. Washington, D.C.: Government Printing Office, 1904. <http://digital.library.okstate.edu/kappler/>. January 10, 2009.

Kidwell, Clara Sue, Homer Noley, and George E. Tinker. *A Native American Theology.* Maryknoll, N.Y.: Orbis Books, 2001.

Knight, Henry C. *Letters from the South and West; by Arthur Singleton.* Boston: Richardson and Lord, 1824.

Knight, Vernon J. "The Formation of the Creeks." In *The Forgotten Centuries: Indians and Europeans in the American South, 1521–1704,* ed. Charles Hudson and Carmen Chaves Tesser, 373–92. Athens: University of Georgia Press, 1994.

Krauthamer, Barbara. "Kinship and Freedom: Fugitive Slave Women's Incorporation into Creek Society." In *New Studies in the History of American Slavery,* ed. Edward E. Baptist and Stephanie M. H. Camp, 148–65. Athens: University of Georgia Press, 2006.

Landers, Jane, ed. *Against the Odds: Free Blacks in the Slave Societies of the Americas.* London and Portland, Ore.: Frank Cass, 1996.

——. "Black Community and Culture in the Southeastern Borderlands." *Journal of the Early Republic* 18:1 (1998): 117–34.

——. *Black Society in Spanish Florida.* Urbana: University of Illinois Press, 1999.

——. "Southern Passage: The Forgotten Route to Freedom in Florida." In *Passages to Freedom: The Underground Railroad in History and Memory,* ed. David W. Blight, 117–32. Washington, D.C.: Smithsonian Books, 2004.

Larson, John Lauritz. " 'Bind the Republic Together': The National Union and the Struggle for a System of Internal Improvements." *Journal of American History* 74:2 (1987): 363–87.

——. *Internal Improvement: National Public Works and the Promise of Popular Government in the Early United States.* Chapel Hill: University of North Carolina Press, 2001.

Latimer, Margaret Kinard. "South Carolina—A Protagonist of the War of 1812." *American Historical Review* 61 (1955–1956): 914–29.

Latour, Arsene L. *Historical Memoir of the War in West Florida and Louisiana in 1814–1815.* Philadelphia: John Conrad and Company, 1816.

Lederer, John. *The Discoveries of John Lederer.* London: J. C. for Samuel Heyrick, 1672.

Levy, Philip. *Fellow Travelers: Indians and Europeans Contesting the Early American Trail.* Gainesville: University Press of Florida, 2007.

Lewis, Malcolm G., ed. *Cartographic Encounters: Perspectives on Native American Mapmaking and Map Use*. Chicago: University of Chicago Press, 1998.

——. "Indian Delimitations of Primary Biogeographic Regions." In *A Cultural Geography of North American Indians*, ed. Thomas E. Ross and Tyrel G. Moore, 93–104. Boulder, Colo.: Westview Press, 1987.

——. "Maps, Mapmaking, and Map Use by Native North Americans." In *History of Cartography*, Vol. 2, book 3, *Cartography in the Traditional African, American, Australian, and Pacific Societies*, ed. David Woodward and G. Malcolm Lewis, 51–182. Chicago: University of Chicago Press, 1998.

Libby, David J. *Slavery and Frontier Mississippi, 1720–1835*. Jackson: University Press of Mississippi, 2004.

Littlefield, Daniel F., Jr. *Africans and Creeks: From the Colonial Period to the Civil War*. Westport, Conn.: Greenwood Press, 1979.

——. *Africans and Seminoles: From Removal to Emancipation*. Westport, Conn.: Greenwood Press, 1977.

Litton, Gaston. "The Journal of a Party of Emigrating Creek Indians, 1835–1836." *Journal of Southern History* 7:2 (1941): 225–42.

Madison, James. *Message from the President of the United States, to Both Houses of Congress, at the Commencement of the Second Session of the Thirteenth Congress, December 7, 1813*. Washington, D.C.: Roger C. Weightman, 1813.

——. *Message from the President of the United States, to the Congress, at the Commencement of the First Session of the Fourteenth Congress, December 5, 1815*. Washington, D.C: William A. Davis, 1815.

——. *Message of President Madison, Communicated on Tuesday, November 5, 1811*. 12th Cong., 1st sess., 1811. In *American State Papers, 1789–1838*. <http://infoweb.news bank.com>. December 3, 2005.

Malone, Laurence J. *Opening the West: Federal Internal Improvements before 1860*. Westport, Conn.: Greenwood Press, 1998.

Martin, Calvin. *Keepers of the Game: Indian-Animal Relationships and the Fur Trade*. Berkeley: University of California Press, 1978.

Martin, Joel. *Sacred Revolt: The Muskogees' Struggle for a New World*. Boston: Beacon Press, 1991.

McAdam, John L. *A Practical Essay on the Scientific Repair and Preservation of Public Roads*. London: B. McMillan, 1819.

McLoughlin, William G. *The Cherokees and Christianity, 1794–1870: Essays on Acculturation and Cultural Persistence*. Ed. Walter H. Conser Jr. Athens: University of Georgia Press, 1994.

——. *Cherokee Renascence in the New Republic*. Princeton, N.J.: Princeton University Press, 1986.

Merrell, James. "American Nations, Old and New." In *Native Americans and the Early Republic*, ed. Frederick E. Hoxie, Ronald Hoffman, and Peter J. Albert, 333–53. Charlottesville: University Press of Virginia, 1999.

——. *The Indians' New World: Catawbas and Their Neighbors from European Contact through the Era of Removal*. New York: W. W. Norton, 1991.

Meyer, Balthasar Henry. *History of Transportation in the United States before 1860*.

Prepared by Caroline E. MacGill. Washington, D.C.: Carnegie Institution of Washington, 1917.

Meyer, William E. "Indian Trails of the Southeast." *Forty-second Annual Report of the Bureau of American Ethnology to the Secretary of the Smithsonian Institution, 1924–25.* 1928. Reprint, Nashville: Blue and Gray Press, 1971.

Michaux, François André. *Travels to the Westward of the Allegany Mountains.* London: Barnard and Sultzer, 1805.

Milfort, Louis. *Memoirs or a Quick Glance at My Various Travels and My Sojourn in the Creek Nation.* 1802. Trans. and ed. Ben C. McCary. Reprint, Kennesaw, Ga.: Continental Book Company, 1959.

Miller, Andrew. *New States and Territories, or The Ohio, Indiana, Illinois, Michigan, North-Western, Missouri, Louisiana, Mississippi, and Alabama, in Their Real Characters, in 1818.* Keene, N.H.: s.n., 1819.

Miller, James David. *South by Southwest: Planter Emigration and Identity in the Slave South.* Charlottesville: University Press of Virginia, 2002.

Montgomery, Sir Robert. *A Discourse Concerning the Design'd Establishment of a New Colony to the South of Carolina, in the Most Delightful Country of the Universe.* London: s.n., 1717.

Mooney, James. "The Cherokee Ball Play." *American Anthropologist* 3:2 (1890): 105–32.

Moore, Francis. *A Voyage to Georgia. Begun in the Year 1735.* London: Jacob Robinson, 1744.

Morgan, Edmund S. *American Slavery, American Freedom: The Ordeal of Colonial Virginia.* New York: W. W. Norton, 1975.

Morse, Jedidiah. *The American Geography: or, a View of the Present Situation of the United States of America.* London: John Stockdale, 1794.

Nabokov, Peter. *A Forest of Time: American Indian Ways of History.* New York: Cambridge University Press, 2002.

A Narrative of the Life and Death of Lieut. Joseph Morgan Willcox, Who Was Massacred by the Creek Indians, on the Alabama River, (Miss. Ter.) on the 15th of January, 1814. Marietta, Oh.: R. Prentiss, 1816.

Nelson, Harold L. "Military Roads for War and Peace—1791–1836." *Military Affairs* 19:1 (1955): 1–14.

A New Voyage to Georgia. By a Young Gentleman: Giving an Account of His Travels to South Carolina, and Part of North Carolina. London: J. Wilford, 1735.

The North-American and West-Indian Gazetteer. London: G. Robinson, 1776.

Northen, William J., ed. *Men of Mark in Georgia: A Complete and Elaborate History of the State from Its Settlement to the Present Time.* Vol. 2. 1907. Reprint, Spartanburg, S.C.: Reprint Company, Publishers, 1974.

O'Donnell, James, III. *Southern Indians in the American Revolution.* Knoxville: University of Tennessee Press, 1973.

"On the Subject of Internal Improvement." 1818. *Early American Imprints, 1801–1819.* Ser. 2, B2803, no. 45163.

Owen, John. *John Owen's Journal of His Removal from Virginia to Alabama in 1818.* Ed. Thomas McAdory Owen. Baltimore: Friedenwald Company, 1897.

Owsley, Frank Lawrence, Jr. *Struggle for the Gulf Borderlands: The Creek War and the Battle of New Orleans, 1812–1815.* Gainesville: University Press of Florida, 1981.

Parks, H. B. "Follow the Drinking Gourd." In *Follow de Drinkin' Gou'd*, ed. J. Frank
Dobie, 81–84. Austin: Texas Folklore Society, 1928.

Passports Issued by Governors of Georgia 1785 to 1820. Compiled by Mary G. Bryan.
Reprinted from the National Genealogical Society Quarterly. Arlington, Va.: 1959.

Paulding, James K. *Letters from the South, Written during an Excursion in the Summer of
1816*. Vol. 1. New York: James Eastburn and Company, 1817.

Perdue, Theda. *Cherokee Women: Gender and Culture Change, 1700–1835*. Lincoln:
University of Nebraska Press, 1998.

——. *'Mixed Blood' Indians: Racial Construction in the Early South*. Athens: University of
Georgia Press, 2003.

——. *Slavery and the Evolution of Cherokee Society, 1540–1866*. Knoxville: University of
Tennessee Press, 1979.

Phelps, Matthew. *Memoirs and Adventures of Captain Matthew Phelps*. Bennington, Vt.:
Anthony Haswell, 1802.

Phillips, Ulrich Bonnell. *Georgia and State Rights*. 1902. Reprint, Macon, Ga.: Mercer
University Press, 1984.

——. *A History of Transportation in the Eastern Cotton Belt to 1860*. 1908. Reprint, New
York: Octagon Books, 1968.

Pierotti, Raymond, and Daniel Wildcat. "Traditional Ecological Knowledge." *Ecological
Applications* 10:5 (2000): 1333–40.

Piker, Joshua. *Okfuskee: A Creek Indian Town in Colonial America*. Cambridge, Mass.:
Harvard University Press, 2004.

——. " 'White & Clean' & Contested: Creek Towns and Trading Paths in the Aftermath
of the Seven Years' War." *Ethnohistory* 50:2 (2003): 315–47.

Pratt, Mary Louise. *Imperial Eyes: Travel Writing and Transculturation*. New York:
Routledge, 1992.

Pynchon, Thomas. *Mason & Dixon*. New York: Henry Holt, 1997.

Read, William A. "Indian Stream-Names in Georgia." *International Journal of American
Linguistics* 15:2 (1949): 128–32.

Richter, Daniel K., and James H. Merrell, eds. *Beyond the Covenant Chain: The Iroquois
and Their Neighbors in Indian North America, 1600–1800*. Syracuse: Syracuse
University Press, 1987.

Risjord, Norman K. "1812: Conservatives, War Hawks and the Nation's Honor." *William
and Mary Quarterly*, 3rd Ser., 18:2 (1961): 196–210.

Rogin, Michael. *Fathers and Children: Andrew Jackson and the Subjugation of the
American Indian*. New York: Knopf, 1975.

Romans, Bernard. *A Concise Natural History of East and West Florida*. 1775. Reprint,
New Orleans: Pelican Publishing Company, 1961.

Roper, Moses. *A Narrative of the Adventures and Escape of Moses Roper, from American
Slavery*. Philadelphia: Merrihew & Gunn, 1838. Documenting the American South.
<http://docsouth.unc.edu/roper/roper.html>. March 15, 2006.

Rothman, Andrew. *Slave Country: American Expansion and the Origins of the Deep
South*. Cambridge, Mass.: Harvard University Press, 2005.

Royall, Anne Newport. *Letters from Alabama on Various Subjects*. Washington, D.C.:
s.n., 1830.

Salley, Harriet Milledge, ed. *Correspondence of John Milledge, Governor of Georgia, 1802–1806*. Columbia, S.C.: State Commercial Printing Company, 1949.

Salmon, Enrique. "Kincentric Ecology: Indigenous Perceptions of the Human-Nature Relationship." *Ecological Applications* 10:5 (2000): 1327–32.

Satz, Ronald N. *American Indian Policy in the Jacksonian Era*. Lincoln: University of Nebraska Press, 1974.

Saunt, Claudio. *A New Order of Things: Property, Power, and the Transformation of the Creek Indians, 1733–1816*. New York: Cambridge University Press, 1999.

Seed, Patricia. *Ceremonies of Possession in Europe's Conquest of the New World, 1492–1640*. New York: Cambridge University Press, 1995.

Sellers, Charles. *The Market Revolution: Jacksonian America 1815–1846*. New York: Oxford University Press, 1991.

Shoemaker, Nancy, ed. *Clearing a Path: Theorizing the Past in Native American Studies*. New York: Routledge, 2002.

———. *A Strange Likeness: Becoming Red and White in Eighteenth-Century North America*. Oxford: Oxford University Press, 2004.

Sibbald, George. *Notes and Observations on the Pine Lands in Georgia, Shewing the Advantages they Possess, Particularly in the Culture of Cotton*. Augusta, Ga.: William J. Bunce, 1801.

Southerland, Henry DeLeon, Jr., and Jerry Elijah Brown. *The Federal Road through Georgia, the Creek Nation, and Alabama, 1806–1836*. Tuscaloosa: University of Alabama Press, 1989.

Stampp, Kenneth M. *The Peculiar Institution: Slavery in the Antebellum South*. New York: Knopf, 1956.

Stoler, Ann Laura, ed. *Haunted by Empire: Geographies of Intimacy in North American History*. Durham, N.C.: Duke University Press, 2006.

Sturtevant, C. William. "Creek Into Seminole." In *North American Indians in Historical Perspective*, ed. Eleanor B. Leacock, 92–128. New York: Random House, 1971.

Sugden, John. "Early Pan-Indianism; Tecumseh's Tour of the Indian Country, 1811–1812." *American Indian Quarterly* 10:4 (1986): 273–304.

———. *Tecumseh's Last Stand*. Norman: University of Oklahoma Press, 1985.

Swann, Caleb. "Position and State of Manners and Arts in the Creek, or Muscogee Nation in 1791." In *Information Respecting the History, Condition, and Prospects of the Indian Tribes of the United States*, ed. Henry R. Schoolcraft. Part 5. Philadelphia: J. B. Lippincott and Company, 1855.

Swanton, John R. *The Indians of the Southeastern United States*. Bureau of American Ethnology Bulletin, no. 137. Washington, D.C.: Government Printing Office, 1946.

———. *Myths and Tales of the Southeastern Indians*. Norman: University of Oklahoma Press, 1995. Originally published by Bureau of American Ethnology Bulletin, no. 88. Washington, D.C.: Government Printing Office, 1928.

———. *Religious Beliefs and Medicinal Practices of the Creek Indians*. Forty-second Annual Report of the Bureau of American Ethnology. Washington, D.C.: Government Printing Office, 1928.

———. *Social Organization and Social Usages of the Indians of the Creek Confederacy*. Forty-second Annual Report of the Bureau of American Ethnology. Washington, D.C.: Government Printing Office, 1911.

Taitt, David. *A Plan of Part of the Rivers Tombecbe, Alabama, Tensa, Perdido, & Scambia in the Province of West Florida; with a Sketch of the Boundary between the Nation of Upper Creek Indians and That Part of the Province Which Is Contiguous Thereto, as Settled at the Congresses at Pensacola in the Years 1765 & 1771.* [1771?] Library of Congress Geography and Map Division, Washington, D.C. <http://hdl.loc.gov/loc.gmd/g3971p.ar164900>. August 13, 2006.

Takaki, Ronald. *Iron Cages: Race and Culture in 19th-Century America.* 2nd ed. New York: Oxford University Press, 2000.

Tanner, Helen Hornbeck. "The Land and Water Communication Systems of the Southeastern Indians." In *Powhatan's Mantle: Indians in the Colonial Southeast,* ed. Peter H. Wood, Gregory A. Waselkov, and M. Thomas Hatley, 6–20. Lincoln: University of Nebraska Press, 1989.

"To the Honorable the Speaker and House of Delegates, for the State of Virginia, [microform]: The Petition of Sundry Inhabitants of the Federal District, and of the State of Virginia." Alexandria, Va.: s.n., 1798. *Early American Imprints, 1639–1800.* Ser. 1, B1130, no. 48638.

Transportation and the Early Nation. Indianapolis: Indiana Historical Society, 1982.

Troup, George M. *Georgia and the General Government.* Milledgeville, Ga.: Camak and Ragland, 1826.

Truett, Randall Bond. *Trade and Travel around the Southern Appalachians before 1830.* Chapel Hill: University of North Carolina Press, 1935.

Turner, Frederick Jackson. *The Frontier in American History.* New York: H. Holt, 1920.

———. *Rereading Frederick Jackson Turner: "The Significance of the Frontier in American History," and Other Essays.* New York: H. Holt, 1994.

U.S. Congress. *Application of Georgia for the Remuneration of Citizens of That State for Military Services. Communicated to the House of Representatives, January 8, 1827.* 19th Cong., 2nd sess., 1827. In *American State Papers, 1789–1838.* <http://infoweb.newsbank.com>. February 24, 2006.

———. *Captures of American Vessels by the Belligerents. Communicated to Congress, April 23, 1812.* 12 Cong., 1st sess., 1812. In *American State Papers, 1789–1838.* <http://infoweb.newsbank.com>. April 12, 2006.

———. *Cherokees, Chickasaws, Choctaws, and Creeks. Communicated to the Senate, December 23, 1801.* 7th Cong., 1st sess., 1801. In *American State Papers, 1789–1838.* <http://infoweb.newsbank.com>. February 28, 2006.

———. *The Creeks, Communicated to the Senate, June 25, 1795.* 3rd Cong., 2nd sess., 1795. In *American State Papers, 1789–1838.* <http://infoweb.newsbank.com>. February 8, 2006.

———. *Cumberland Road. Communicated to the Senate, December 19, 1805.* 9th Cong., 1st sess., 1805. In *American State Papers, 1789–1838.* <http://infoweb.newsbank.com>. February 18, 2006.

———. *Georgia Cession. Communicated to Congress, April 26, 1802.* 7th Cong., 1st sess., 1802. In *American State Papers, 1789–1838.* <http://infoweb.newsbank.com>. February 28, 2006.

———. *Hostile Movements. Communicated to the Senate, June 24, 1812.* 12th Cong., 1st sess., 1812. In *American State Papers, 1789–1838.* <http://infoweb.newsbank.com>. April 13, 2006.

———. *Wyandots and Others. Communicated to the Senate, December 11, 1805.* 9th Cong., 1st sess., 1805. In *American State Papers, 1789–1838.* <http://infoweb.newsbank.com>. March 2, 2006.

———. Committee on the Yazoo Claims. *Report of the Committee to Whom Was Referred the Bill from the Senate, Entitled "An Act Providing for the Indemnification of Certain Claimants of Public Lands in the Mississippi Territory."* Washington, D.C.: A. and G. Way, Printers, 1814.

———. House. *Emigration of the Indians West of the Mississippi. Communicated to the House of Representatives, January 3, 1827.* 19th Cong., 2nd sess., 1827. In *American State Papers, 1789–1838.* <http://infoweb.newsbank.com>. July 17, 2006.

———. House. *Message from the President of the United States [James Monroe], Transmitting Pursuant to a Resolution of the House of Representatives of Ninth Dec. Last, Information of the Roads Made, or in Progress, under the Authority of the Executive of the United States; the States and Territories through Which They Pass, or Are Intended to Pass; the Periods When They Were Ordered to be Made, and How Far They Have Extended. January 23, 1818.* 15th Cong., 1st sess., 1818. In *U.S. Congressional Serial Set.* <http://infoweb.newsbank.com>. February 26, 2006.

———. House. *Proceedings of the Legislature of Georgia in Relation to the Treaty Made with the Creeks at the Indian Springs. Communicated to the House of Representatives, January 23, 1827.* 19th Cong., 2nd sess., 1827. In *American State Papers, 1789–1838.* <http://infoweb.newsbank.com>. July 17, 2006.

———. House. *Report from the Committee of Claims, on the Petition of Alexander Scott, of the State of South Carolina, on Behalf of Himself and Others, Referred on the Second Instant.* Washington, D.C.: William Duane and Son, 1805.

———. Senate. *Report of the Committee of the Senate of the United States, Appointed March 12, 1802, on the Subject of Transporting the Mail of the United States.* Washington, D.C.: Printed by order of the Senate of the United States, 1802.

U.S. Continental Congress. *An Ordinance for Ascertaining the Mode of Disposing of Lands in the Western Territory.* New York: s.n., 1785. Library of Congress, American Memory Site. <http://hdl.loc.gov/loc.rbc/bdsdcc.11201>. April 14, 2006.

U.S. Supreme Court. *Fletcher v. Peck,* 10 U.S. 87 (1810).

Usner, Daniel. "American Indians on the Cotton Frontier: Changing Economic Relations with Citizens and Slaves in the Mississippi Territory." *Journal of American History* 72:2 (1985): 297–317.

———. *Indians, Settlers, and Slaves in a Frontier Exchange Economy: The Lower South before 1783.* Chapel Hill: University of North Carolina Press, 1992.

Utley, Robert M., and Wilcomb E. Washburn. *Indian Wars.* 1977. Reprint, New York: First Mariner Books, 2002.

Vlach, John Michael. "Above Ground on the Underground Railroad." In *Passages to Freedom: The Underground Railroad in History and Memory,* ed. David W. Blight, 95–116. Washington, D.C.: Smithsonian Books, 2004.

Wallace, Anthony F. C. *The Long, Bitter Trail: Andrew Jackson and the Indians.* New York: Hill and Wang, 1993.

Warhus, Mark. *Another America: Native American Maps and the History of Our Land.* New York: St. Martin's, 1997.

Waselkov, Gregory A. *A Conquering Spirit: Fort Mims and the Redstick War of 1813–1814.* Tuscaloosa: University of Alabama Press, 2006.

———. "The Eighteenth-Century Anglo-Indian Trade in Southeastern North America." In *New Faces of the Fur Trade: Selected Papers of the Seventh North American Fur Trade Conference, Halifax, Nova Scotia, 1995,* ed. Jo-Anne Fiske, Susan Sleeper-Smith, and William Wicken, 193–222. East Lansing: Michigan State University Press, 1998.

Weisman, Brent R. "Archaeological Perspectives on Florida Seminole Ethnogenesis." In *Indians of the Greater Southeast: Historical Archaeology and Ethnohistory,* ed. Bonnie G. McEwan, 299–318. Gainesville: University Press of Florida, 2000.

White, Richard. *The Middle Ground: Indians, Empires, and Republics in the Great Lakes Region, 1650–1815.* New York: Cambridge University Press, 1991.

Wickham, Patricia. *The Tree That Bends: Discourse, Power, and the Survival of the Maskókî People.* Tuscaloosa: University of Alabama Press, 1999.

Williamson, Samuel H. "Six Ways to Compute the Relative Value of a U.S. Dollar Amount, 1790 to Present." Measuring Worth, 2008. <http://www.measuringworth.com/uscompare/>. January 9, 2009.

Wood, Peter. *Black Majority: Negroes in Colonial South Carolina from 1670 through the Stono Rebellion.* New York: Knopf, 1974.

Woodward, Thomas Simpson. *Woodward's Reminiscences of the Creek or Muscogee Indians, Contained in Letters to Friends in Georgia and Alabama.* Montgomery, Ala.: Barret & Wimbish, 1859.

Wright, J. Leitch. *Creeks & Seminoles: The Destruction and Regeneration of the Muscogulge People.* Lincoln: University of Nebraska Press, 1986.

Young, Mary Elizabeth. "Indian Removal and Land Allotment: The Civilized Tribes and Jacksonian Justice." *American Historical Review* 64:1 (1958): 31–45.

———. *Redskins, Ruffleshirts, and Rednecks: Indian Allotments in Alabama and Mississippi, 1830–1860.* Norman: University of Oklahoma Press, 1961.

Zolbrod, Paul G. *Diné Bahané: The Navajo Creation Story.* Albuquerque: University of New Mexico Press, 1984.

Index

Borders, 42; roads across, 5–6, 63; of
Creek Nation, 7, 17–18, 29, 33–34, 68,
74, 136, 138, 143; of Georgia, 18, 30, 45,
92, 102, 117, 123, 135, 154–55; and black
market trade, 26; marked on paper, 31;
and trespassers, 37–38, 50, 53, 85; surveying, 38–41; and intertribal diplomacy, 49–50, 119; slaves crossing, 53;
and westward expansion, 95; violence
along, 98, 102, 111, 118; of Tennessee,
104; roads as, 108. *See also* Boundaries
Boundaries, 17–22, 46, 180 (n. 40), 191
(n. 49); of Creek Nation, 1–2, 6, 17–
18, 21, 26, 29, 31, 39, 64–65, 134, 136–38,
165, 170, 185–86 (n. 110); travel across,
2, 25, 41, 159; indigenous concepts of,
19, 191 (n. 48); between Spanish Florida and United States, 28, 39–42; and
squatters, 29, 31, 43; natural vs. artificial, 30, 50–51; and surveying, 37–44,
120, 121, 156, 188 (n. 16); of Georgia, 43,
48, 129, 154–57; and intertribal diplomacy, 49–50, 62, 118–19, 195 (n. 121–
22); slaves crossing, 53; and Indian
Removal, 163, 165. *See also* Borders
Bridges: in Creek country, 15, 58, 139, 152,
168; building of, 64, 76, 80, 86, 89, 104,
111, 125, 128, 197 (n. 49); collection of
tolls, 83, 106–7, 125, 140, 165, 216
(n. 124); attacks on, 92, 106–7. *See
also* Internal improvement
Briggs, Isaac, 69–70
Brims, 12
British: presence in Carolinas, 1, 4, 23; and
Iroquois, 11; in deerskin trade, 17, 23,
25, 175 (n. 21), 185 (n. 105); boundaries
with Creeks, 18, 20, 25, 180 (n. 40);
and Revolutionary War (1776–83),
26–28; traders in Spanish Florida, 27–
29, 41, 105; support of Indian revitalization movements, 95–98, 101; support of Red Sticks during Creek War
(1813–14), 101, 105, 108, 111, 113, 118, 120,
209 (n. 158). *See also* War of 1812
(1812–15)

Calhoun, John C., 96, 211 (n. 44)
Canals, 145, 151–53. *See also* Internal
improvement
Captain Isaacs, 93, 106, 204 (n. 60)
Carolina, colony, 1, 4, 11–12, 21, 23, 48
Charleston, S.C., 4, 11, 17, 23, 197 (n. 33)
Chattahoochee River, 19, 46, 77–78, 125,
151, 160, 165, 167; Creek towns along, 4,
5, 13, 20–21, 56, 139, 143; travel on, 114,
167–68; as boundary, 135–36, 138, 150,
155, 157, 163–64
Cherokee Indians, 27, 29–30, 49, 79, 169–
71, 216 (n. 122); intertribal land disputes, 19, 50, 62–63, 80–81, 118–19, 185
(n. 105), 195 (n. 122); and roads, 21,
61–63, 75, 78–79, 129, 147, 179 (n. 26),
194 (n. 115); disrupting surveys, 44,
156–57, 159, 219 (n. 46); and smuggling, 81–82; Little Turkey's Town (or
Esenaca), 81–82, 84; and Creek War
(1813–14), 115, 117–19, 218 (n. 19); as
obstacles to southern development,
150–53, 155; and missionaries, 157, 163,
198 (n. 74); Supreme Court cases, 170
Chickasaw Indians, 5, 49, 60, 72, 175
(n. 18), 184 (n. 96); intertribal land
disputes, 19, 62–63, 80, 118–19, 191
(n. 53), 195 (n. 121); and roads, 21, 60–
64
Cho-chus Micco, 157
Choctaw Academy, 162–63. *See also*
Missionaries
Choctaw Indians, 175 (n. 18), 177 (n. 5),
189 (n. 19); intertribal land disputes,
19, 50, 63, 118–19, 191 (n. 53), 195
(n. 122); and roads, 21, 27, 60, 62–63,
195 (n. 118); and Creek War (1813–14),
115, 118–19
Civilization plan, 34–35, 50, 68, 86–87,
91–92, 94, 100, 109, 136, 204 (n. 61)
Claiborne, Ferdinand L., 108, 115
Clark, Elijah, 111–13
Clayton, Augustin S., 153–54, 157, 161
Cleanness, importance in Creek thought,
11–12, 93, 178 (n. 9)

Coffee, John, 115, 124, 128, 216 (n. 122)

Colbert, George, 61, 191 (n. 53), 215 (n. 109)

Columbus, Ga., 135, 167–68, 222 (n. 3)

Coosa River, 113, 139, 151, 165, 215 (n. 109); Creek towns along, 3–4, 8, 11; travel on, 81–84, 104, 114

Cornells, Alexander, 93, 98, 101–2, 109, 118, 139, 204 (n. 71)

Cornells, James, 106, 110, 205 (n. 92)

Cotton, 7, 34, 67–68, 92, 104, 129, 140; and southern commerce, 57, 72–73, 121–22, 145, 149, 159–60; expansion of cultivation, 87, 131, 134

Cowerther Mayit, 17–19, 21, 31, 175 (n. 21)

Coweta. See Towns, Lower Creek: Coweta

Cowetas, people known as, 20. See also Towns, Lower Creek

Crawford, William H., 122, 148

Creek Agency, 100, 122, 138, 163

Creek Indians, 8, 30, 70, 76, 83; hunting practices, 3, 20, 21; migration, 5, 15, 119, 134–35; and mental maps, 14, 43, 48; women as producers, 34, 158, 165, 187 (n. 128); attacks on travelers, 69, 87, 105–7, 135–36, 164–65, 167; mobility, 73, 80–81, 104–5, 73 (see also Paths, importance in Creek thought); as laborers on roads, 76, 92–93; as guides, 78, 93; attitudes toward American-owned ferries and stands, 79–80, 124; resistance to American travel, 83, 91–92; and tolls, 83, 140; and Shawnee revitalization movement, 89 (see also Creek War [1813–14]); destruction of property by, 163–64. See also Deerskin trade; Surveys: Creek participation in; Territoriality, importance in Creek thought

Creek Nation, 2–3, 8, 17, 48, 142; towns, 3, 4, 12, 175 (n. 13) (see also Towns, Lower Creek; Towns, Upper Creek); extent of territory, 3, 68; population estimates, 4, 222 (n. 4); hunting grounds, 18–20, 32, 42–43; land cessions, 31–32, 50–51, 56, 115, 117, 122, 136, 138, 141–43, 149–51, 154, 161–62, 185 (n. 105), 215 (n. 112) (see also Treaties); factory (or government trading house), 39, 48; boundaries, 50, 104, 119, 134; travel into, 54, 67; National Council, 65, 79, 83, 88–89, 92–93, 99, 142, 156, 165, 203 (n. 50); and famine, 87–88, 119, 137, 170; annuities, 101, 104, 204 (n. 61)

—internal political divisions, 98–99, 136–38, 141–43, 150, 195 (n. 126), 199 (n. 93), 215 (n. 99); related to roads, 86–87, 92–93, 99, 101, 108–9, 123

—intertribal diplomacy, 191 (nn. 52, 56); and land disputes, 50; with Choctaws, 63; with Cherokees, 80; with Chickasaws, 80

—roads, 7, 88–89, 119, 134–36, 139–40, 144, 165, 167; and Treaty of Washington (1805), 63–65; and wagon travel, 72, 80, 86, 91, 104; and smuggling, 82–83, 105; and surveys, 84–85; American travel on, 91–92, 103, 106, 122, 124–26, 138, 147; and Creek War (1813–14), 94, 97–108, 110–15, 117–18, 128; and travelers of African descent, 130–33. See also Creek Nation—internal political divisions, related to roads; Federal Road; Internal Improvement; Paths

Creek War (1813–14), 7, 62, 99, 101, 122; beginnings of, 98–100; travel during, 99, 102–3, 106–8, 112–15, 205 (n. 92), 207 (n. 132); attacks on roads during, 105–7; American involvement in, 111–12, 120; and commerce, 111–12, 205 (n. 81); roads built during, 113, 128; garrisons built during, 113–14; conclusion of, 117–18, 121; outcomes, 122–24, 134–35, 138. See also Red Sticks; Revitalization movements and prophecies

Crowell, John, 139, 157, 215 (n. 99), 218 (n. 23)